STAGING BRAZIL

STAGING BRAZIL

Choreographies of Capoeira

ANA PAULA HÖFLING

WESLEYAN UNIVERSITY PRESS

Middletown, Connecticut

Wesleyan University Press
Middletown CT 06459
www.wesleyan.edu/wespress
© 2019 Ana Paula Höfling

Manufactured in the United States of America
Typeset in Quadraat and Mostra by Tseng Information Systems, Inc.

Library of Congress Cataloging-in-Publication Data available upon request

Hardcover ISBN: 978-0-8195-7880-8
Paperback ISBN: 978-0-8195-7881-5
Ebook ISBN: 978-0-8195-7882-2
5 4 3 2 1

For my parents, Gilberto and Anna Maria

Mestre Moa do Katendê (Romualdo Rosário da Costa,
Oct 29, 1954 — Oct 8, 2018)
"Chamada de Angola" © Leandro Couri.
Printed with permission.
Mestre Moa, Presente!

CONTENTS

Acknowledgments ix

Palimpsests of Capoeira:
A Note on Sources xi

Introduction:
Staging Tradition, Inventing Modernity 1

1. Staging Brazil's National Sport:
Burlamaqui, Bimba, and Pastinha 19

2. Fighting and Dancing:
Capoeira Regional and Capoeira Angola 61

3. Capoeira for the Tourist Stage:
Bimba and Canjiquinha 100

4. Brazil's Folklore for the Global Stage:
Authorship, Innovation, and Spectacle 128

Conclusion 163

Notes 169

Bibliography 209

Index 217

ACKNOWLEDGMENTS

This book would not exist without the support I received throughout the various stages of research and writing. I am grateful to the two anonymous readers of my manuscript for their insightful and generous feedback, and to Suzanna Tamminen from Wesleyan University Press for choosing such knowledgeable colleagues as peer reviewers, as well as for her dedication and patience throughout the process. I was extremely fortunate to begin this research project under the rigorous guidance of my dissertation advisor Susan Leigh Foster, and I am grateful for the encouragement I received from her as well as from my dissertation committee members Janet O'Shea, Andrew Apter, and Sally Ann Ness.

I am grateful for the support of the Center for the Americas faculty at Wesleyan University, where I began to envision this book during my two-year Andrew W. Mellon postdoctoral fellowship. This book also benefited from the feedback I received during the Andrew W. Mellon Dance Studies in/and the Humanities Summer Seminar at Brown University, convened by Rebecca Schneider, Janice Ross, and Susan Manning. I thank Anne Parsons, Tara Green, and my colleagues in the College of Visual and Performing Arts, the School of Dance, and the Lloyd International Honors College at the University of North Carolina at Greensboro (UNCG) for their continual support.

My research and writing were supported by funding from various sources: at UCLA I received a Graduate Division Dissertation Year Fellowship, an International Institute Fieldwork Fellowship, and a Latin American Institute Research Grant; my postdoctoral fellowship at the Center for the Americas at Wesleyan University was funded by the Andrew W. Mellon Foundation; my fellowship at the Sacatar Institute in Itaparica, Bahia, supported the writing of chapter 3. I am grateful for the research support I received from UNCG's School of Dance and College of Visual and Performing Arts, as well as the International Programs Center and the Office of Research and Engagement at UNCG, which supported this book through research grants, travel grants, and publication grants.

The staff of the following archives generously and promptly facilitated obtaining the permissions for several of the images in this book: the Arquivo Histórico Municipal of Salvador, the Helinä Rautavaara Museum, the Fundação Pierre Verger, and ArenaPAL. Every effort has been made to identify the photographers, trace the copyright holders, and obtain permission to reproduce the photos in this book. I am especially grateful to Valerie Macon for her generosity and her expert assistance with my digital image files.

I am grateful to *contra-mestre* Danny Soares for lending me several items from the collection of photocopies held in the library of the Grupo Semente do Jogo de Angola so that I could make my own photocopies. I am indebted to colleagues who have shared rare sources with me over the years, in particular André Luiz Lacé Lopes and Frede Abreu (in memoriam). I thank the people who have taken time from their busy lives to share their capoeira stories with me: Mestre Itapoan, Mestre Acordeon, Mestre Brasília, Mestre Lua Rasta, Mestre Geni, Mestre João Grande, Mestre Pelé da Bomba, Mestre Suassuna, Mestre Cabello, Mestre Jogo de Dentro, Aricelma Borges, Neusa Saad, Lamartine Pereira da Costa, Guilherme Simões (in memoriam), and Carlos Moraes (in memoriam). I am deeply grateful to Emília Biancardi for her time, her generosity, and her trust. An earlier version of chapter 4, focused on Biancardi's Viva Bahia, appeared as "Staging Capoeira, Samba, *Maculelê* and *Candomblé*: *Viva Bahia's* Choreographies of Afro-Brazilian Folklore for the Global Stage," in *Performing Brazil: Essays on Culture, Identity, and the Performing Arts,* ed. Severino Albuquerque and Kathryn Bishop-Sanchez, © 2015 by the Board of Regents at the University of Wisconsin System.

I am grateful to Lu for her support, to my mother for taking me to countless ballet classes and dance recitals and constantly encouraging my dancing, and to my father for always taking a genuine interest in my life and, in recent years, always asking about this book.

PALIMPSESTS OF CAPOEIRA
A Note on Sources

In the summer of 2010 I attended Dancebatukeira, a capoeira retreat held on a cocoa farm–turned–cultural center in southern Bahia, where participants take classes in capoeira, dance, and percussion. This retreat honored both Mestre João Grande, the well-respected disciple of Mestre Pastinha who has taught capoeira angola in New York City for almost three decades, and Emília Biancardi, the founder of the folkloric ensemble Viva Bahia, active throughout the 1960s and 1970s. The presence of João Grande, a capoeira grand-master frequently invited to teach at capoeira workshops and retreats around the globe, was no surprise; the choice to invite Emília Biancardi, however, was an unexpected teaching moment for many of the capoeira students and teachers present at the retreat. While João Grande's presence established a connection to Pastinha and thus to capoeira's African heritage, Biancardi's presence was a reminder of capoeira's connection with staged folkloric shows — precisely the opposite of the pure, pristine capoeira thought to have been preserved by Pastinha and passed down to his disciples. When João Grande proudly acknowledged his past as a performer with Viva Bahia and publicly thanked Biancardi for being his own *mestra de palco* (master of the stage), he disrupted the narrative of purity that surrounds his own capoeira lineage, a narrative largely cultivated by his students rather than by João Grande himself. The organizers' choice to invite Biancardi and honor her alongside one of the oldest living *mestres* of capoeira angola destabilized the tradition/modernity binary, reclaiming and recognizing twentieth-century staged capoeira as part of capoeira's tradition.

Although my inquiry into the connections between capoeira and the stage was well underway when I witnessed this critical move by both the event organizers and João Grande himself, this moment strengthened my resolve to write about the formative connections between capoeira and the stage. At that time, I had already consulted the private archive of Biancardi, who graciously invited me into her home in 2008 so that I could look through her collection of newspaper clippings, photographs, and programs of the performances of Viva Bahia; this initial visit to Biancardi's home was the beginning of my research into the mutually constitutive relationship between capoeira and folkloric shows, an aspect of capoeira's history that has been downplayed and virtually ignored in the literature.

Many books and dissertations on capoeira rely primarily on interviews with living mestres and on the researcher's own intensive capoeira training as embodied research. During my early dissertation research, this was precisely my methodology: conducting interviews and trying to answer my research questions through my own practice and my own observations of present-day capoeira. My initial research probed the issue of what was considered traditional in capoeira; I was interested in identifying capoeira's much-discussed *fundamentos* (foundational principles). In my preliminary interviews, I noticed that a number of mestres gave me vague answers that felt rehearsed; they seemed to be answering someone else's questions from another interview. Tradition, the focus of capoeira research since the early twentieth century, had no doubt been a popular interview topic long before I turned on my own audio-recorder.

This initial interest in capoeira's tradition eventually led me to investigate its opposite, *descaracterização* (loss of character), often blamed on staged spectacles of capoeira. Interestingly, the minute I began asking my interviewees about capoeira onstage, they began earnestly answering my questions, sharing vivid memories with excitement and joy in their voices, bursting with pride in having toured and performed for thousands of spectators, both in Brazil and abroad. If this was such a memorable and pleasurable aspect of their capoeira histories, it had to be worth writing about. Of course interviews were only a small portion of my sources, and written primary sources would prove far more difficult to obtain than oral histories. I was embarking on a research project about a movement practice that does not have a centralized archive; key sources are scattered throughout Brazil in often-inaccessible private collections, and many historical newspapers are not available in digital form. But thanks to a few generous capoeira colleagues, I was able to get my hands on copies of rare primary sources not available through libraries. Many of the sources discussed here were consulted as paper photocopies or digital files.

As I began reading through these copies, I realized that the act of copying itself was in fact a theme connecting many of these texts. Sometimes the process of reproduction of a source was dizzying, as in the case of the first known capoeira manual: first published around 1906, this book was lost, but not before a capoeira practitioner and enthusiast (Anníbal Burlamaqui, discussed in chapter 1) sat at a typewriter and copied the entire manual, probably around the mid-1920s.[1] In the late 1990s her copy of the book was retyped again by a group of capoeiristas from the Associação de Capoeira Barravento, based in Niterói in the state of Rio de Janeiro; it was a photocopy of this copy that I was able to get my hands on. Unfortunately, since only the text was copied, any illustrations included in the original manual were lost. Burlamaqui wrote and self-published his own manual in 1928, which today circulates in photocopy form (or a scanned file of the photocopy) among capoeira scholars and enthusiasts.[2] In 1945, before photocopies were available, capoeira enthusiast and physical education scholar Inezil Penna Marinho decided to disseminate Burlamaqui's ideas through his own book, which he illustrated with drawings created by tracing the photographs that illustrate Burlamaqui's book.[3]

Mestre Pastinha also traced photographs, including photos of street capoeira by French photographer Pierre Verger, to create many of the drawings and prints used to illustrate a manuscript he hoped to publish (see comparison in chapter 2). Although his writings and illustrations were never published, they are available in scanned form through the website portalcapoeira.com, administered by a group of capoeiristas under the leadership of Luciano Milani. This digital version of Pastinha's manuscripts, scanned as individual pages labeled either "Drawings," "Thoughts," or "Pages," was the version I consulted for this book. For the section that focuses primarily on the history of Pastinha's capoeira center, I use the title written on the cover of the notebook, "Quando as pernas fazem miserêr," which can be loosely translated as "When legs do amazing things"; for the section written using both a fountain pen and a blue ballpoint pen, possibly written later, I cite the title of the digital files, "Pensamentos" (Thoughts). Some pages have two different series of numbers; I have decided to follow the numbers in pencil, which correspond to the digital pagination. The original manuscripts for these scanned pages were held in the private collection of Angelo Decânio, a disciple of Mestre Bimba who received the main notebook with Pastinha's writings from Bahian writer Wilson Lins, as well as a set of loose pages labeled "Pensamentos" from visual artist Caribé. In 1997 Decânio self-published an electronic book (widely available as a digital file) where he selected and reprinted short quotes from Pastinha's manuscript followed by an idiosyncratic style of analysis (short phrases and words connected by ellipses); this was the only published version of the contents of the manuscript before it was scanned and made available for download.

Copying also emerged as a theme connecting the repertory of the folkloric shows analyzed in chapters 3 and 4; Bahia's folkloric ensembles in the 1960s and 1970s often shared capoeira performers, and the fact that these performers were often co-choreographers and sometimes codirectors meant that movement patterns and repertory circulated freely between groups, resulting in shows that presented the same dances, often in the same order—all versions of each other and, simultaneously, all originals. Throughout my research, I realized that this layered circulation of ideas—palimpsests of capoeira, both on the page and on the stage— is not unlike the circulation of embodied knowledge in capoeira practice offstage. I hope this note prepares the reader to enter the *roda* and join me in a game of capoeira (through) history.

NOTES

1. The text was copied from the second edition of this book, published in 1907; the first edition must have been published one or two years earlier, around 1905 or 1906. O.D.C., *Guia do capoeira ou gymnastica brazileira*, 2nd ed. (Rio de Janeiro: Livraria Nacional, 1907).

2. Anníbal Burlamaqui, *Gymnastica nacional (capoeiragem) methodisada e regrada* (Rio de Janeiro: n.p., 1928). This manual is held in the private collection of capoeira scholar André Luiz Lacé Lopes in Rio de Janeiro; it is probably the last remaining copy from the original printing.

3. Inezil Penna Marinho, *Subsídios para o estudo da metodologia do treinamento da capoeiragem* (Rio de Janeiro: Imprensa Nacional, 1945).

STAGING TRADITION, INVENTING MODERNITY

hortly after I moved to the United States from Brazil to attend college, a bout of homesickness drew me into a capoeira school in my neighborhood in Berkeley, California. The *mestre* (master teacher)[1] at that school, Mestre Acordeon, happened to be a disciple of one of the great capoeira innovators of the twentieth century, Mestre Bimba (1900–1974), the architect of the style known as *capoeira regional*, a "modernization" of the practice that paved the way to its decriminalization in 1940. After college, I continued practicing capoeira regional intermittently, as a complement to my dance training. In 1998 I was introduced to the "traditional" capoeira style, *capoeira angola*, and moved to New York City to study with Mestre João Grande, a disciple of Mestre Pastinha (1889–1981), the mestre credited with safeguarding capoeira from the alleged losses brought about by Bimba's modernization. After about six months of capoeira classes at Mestre João Grande's Capoeira Angola Center, other priorities got in the way and I put my capoeira training on hold for about five years. But my curiosity about capoeira angola only grew during this hiatus, and in 2005 I resumed my practice, this time studying with Mestre Jogo de Dentro in my hometown, Campinas, in the state of São Paulo.[2] Having decided to immerse myself in capoeira angola, I attended classes and "jams" (*rodas*) five times per week, intent on becoming an *angoleira*.[3] I quickly discovered that my training in both the modern and the traditional capoeira styles, rather than an advantage, was in fact a handicap: if I were to become proficient in capoeira angola, I had to shed my embodied knowledge of capoeira regional.

As I continued learning this new movement style — moving with control and fluidity, slowly, close to the ground, my knees always bent, my arms aching from supporting the weight of my body as I repeatedly sank to the ground dodging imaginary kicks during these demanding training sessions—I began unlearning my previous capoeira training: fast, whipping circular kicks at the height of my opponent's chest, quick evasions to the side or to the back, and open, expansive cartwheels. The two styles were clearly incompatible, and it became clear that many *angoleiros* frowned upon influences from a style considered to have distanced itself from its African roots, a practice believed to have lost its "character."

My own embodied capoeira practice, in both the "traditional" and the "modern" styles, informed my decision to focus my research on the division of capoeira along the binaries tradition/modernity, Africa/Brazil, "folk"/erudite, and retention/loss. However, my experience as a capoeira practitioner for the past two decades is neither the object of my analysis nor my methodology. As I began my inquiry into the differences between these two styles, I realized that an ethnographic approach, based on my own participant-observation experiences in the present, would not provide answers to my questions. To trace the routes of the debate over the roots of capoeira, it became clear I had to look to the past. In the archive, I hoped to find out more about the two "great figures" of twentieth-century capoeira, Mestre Bimba and Mestre Pastinha, and understand, but also move beyond, the mythology that transformed these two black working-class men from the northeastern state of Bahia into symbols of Brazilian modernity and tradition, respectively.

My initial research questions pertained to the angola/regional split: Exactly when, how, and why did capoeira become divided? Was capoeira regional indeed a modernization of capoeira angola, or were both styles twentieth-century "invented traditions"? When did the capoeira historiography become almost obsessively focused on the contributions of the two "founding fathers" of these two styles, Bimba and Pastinha, and how did they come, respectively, to symbolize the modernity and tradition of capoeira? What were the markers of tradition and modernity at the movement level?

Instead of reproducing the binaries that have guided both capoeira scholarship and practice, I historicize these very binaries and propose a mutually constitutive relationship between them. I approach capoeira regional's sport-like modernity and its counterpart, capoeira angola's dance-like, nonviolent folkloric "tradition" with roots in Africa, as two sides of the same coin—both choreographed through the same nationalist and regionalist narratives that undergirded the imagining of a modern Brazil in the first half of the twentieth century. This book focuses on the foundational transformations brought about by Bimba and Pastinha, while moving beyond their personal histories and innovations to include the contributions of other capoeira practitioners such as Zuma, Canjiquinha, and Samuel Querido de Deus, as well as the influences of "erudite" capoeira advocates, folklorists, tourism bureaucrats, and directors of folkloric shows featuring capoeira.

Bimba and Pastinha have become synonymous with the opposing capoeira styles they developed in the mid-twentieth century: capoeira regional and capoeira angola, respectively. Today, more than thirty years after their deaths, their portraits decorate the walls of capoeira schools around the world, marking lineage and affiliation. A framed photograph of an elderly Pastinha, his own hands together in prayer, is often the centerpiece of altars, surrounded by flowers, candles, and incense. Pastinha today is remembered as the guardian of capoeira's "tradition" at a time when this tradition was believed to be threatened by Bimba's innovations and foreign borrowings. While for many years Bimba was blamed for going too far in codifying and sportifying (and therefore "whitening" capoeira),[4] today several practitioners and scholars have acknowledged Bimba's contributions to capoeira as a "black modernization" of the practice, shifting the blame for capoeira's "*descaracterização*" (loss of character) either to early twentieth-century national gymnastics or late twentieth-century capoeira shows for tourists.[5] This blame shifting, however, does nothing to take capoeira scholarship beyond the rescue/loss paradigm, for it perpetuates an analytic model where culture, either retained or lost, is considered a possession, a "thing," rather than a process. Throughout this book, I seek to disrupt the tradition/modernity, rescue/loss binaries symbolized by Pastinha and Bimba by foregrounding the interdependence rather than the opposition between these two modern "traditions."

In the early 1980s, Eric Hobsbawm and Terence Ranger examined the processes through which traditions are established; they proposed the term "invented tradition" to refer to new rituals and practices that establish legitimacy through an imagined continuity with the past. I propose that while capoeira angola is a classic Hobsbawmian "invented tradition," capoeira regional is an "invented modernity": the old recycled and repackaged as new; past practices staged in the present as symbolic of modernity and progress. Throughout this book, I identify recurring instances in twentieth-century capoeira where old embodied "customs" are reconfigured as innovation, renewed through a process I am calling "invention of modernity."[6] I propose that it was precisely through this "invented modernity"—the old "disguised" as new and improved—that capoeira was able to attain legitimacy after more than half a century of criminalization and persecution.

Disguise, in addition to being a key tactical element in the game of capoeira (in the form of feints and deception), provides the foundation for the widely circulated myth of origin of capoeira as a "fight disguised as dance." It also recurs in the writings of Pastinha, who used the idea of disguise to explain the relationship between a "real" capoeira, which he proposed was hidden in "the self" of the practitioner, and a capoeira for the stage (discussed in chapter 2). In his 1951 *O Jogo da capoeira*, visual artist Carybé (Hector Julio Páride Bernabó) explains that capoeira was able to survive repression during slavery through disguise: "In the same way that they camouflaged their religion with that of their masters, they camouflaged the fight of capoeira with pantomime, miming and dancing, accompanied by music."[7]

Although the term "syncretism" has recently been used as a synonym for cultural mixing and hybridity, in early African diaspora research syncretism refers to specific processes of acculturation based on correspondences, fusion, and disguise. Afro-American studies pioneer Melville J. Herskovits examined syncretism in the context of slavery in Brazil (among other places in the African diaspora), where recently arrived Africans were baptized against their will but continued to worship their African deities in secret. He explained syncretism as "the tendency to identify those elements in the new culture with similar elements in the old one, enabling the persons experiencing the contact to move from one to the other, and back again, with psychological ease."[8] Afro-Brazilian studies scholar Arthur Ramos theorized syncretism as a fusion (and confusion) between two religions, where the "weaker" or "inferior" culture was assimilated by the "stronger" one.[9] French sociologist Roger Bastide proposed that "syncretism, which was originally merely a mask, a means of distracting the white man's attention and evading his watchful eye, is transformed into the system of equivalences, of correspondences between saints and *orixás*."[10] Rejecting Ramos's idea of fusion and assimilation, Bastide emphasized that saints and *orixás* (candomblé deities) are not confused with each other—they are linked, but not merged. While

Ramos's syncretism consisted of a passive model of cultural contact that relied on a determinist and hierarchical understanding of cultures as "stronger" or "weaker," for both Herskovits and Bastide the syncretic process, although still based on the conservative idea of retention or loss of culture, allowed for purposeful, tactical, and creative correspondences between two cultures.

Anthropologist Andrew Apter has proposed that we rethink "syncretism in the African diaspora as a critical and revisionary practice." Apter recasts what Herskovits identified as correspondences that allowed movement back and forth between cultures as "a much more powerful process of discursive appropriation."[11] He proposes that rather than understanding the adoption of Catholicism as a screen to allow the African deities to continue being worshipped in secret, the concept of syncretism can be redeployed to account for agency; in the classic example, the hegemonic religion is appropriated, and its power and resources are harnessed for the benefit of Africans and Afro-descendants in the diaspora. Following Apter, I consider several instances of "discursive appropriation" in the process of legitimization and modernization of capoeira in the twentieth century. In a syncretic relationship, the discourses of modernity (such as improvement, order, and progress) were appropriated to fashion a counterhegemonic modernity choreographed through Afro-diasporic embodied knowledge—one where Africanity is not an obstacle to progress but one of its foundational building blocks. From the "classic" model of syncretism as a cloak, I have borrowed the concepts of deception and simultaneity as analytic tools in my inquiry of a practice reconfigured simultaneously as folklore and sport, dance and fight, simultaneously African and Brazilian, simultaneously traditional and modern.

I argue that twentieth-century capoeira was developed through a doubleness similar to the concept of double consciousness articulated by W. E. B. Du Bois in 1903 in *The Souls of Black Folk*.[12] Seen "through the eyes of others"—through published manuals, public matches, demonstrations, and full-fledged folkloric shows for tourists—both capoeira styles, regional and angola, were shaped with and against prevailing notions derived from scientific racism. According to early twentieth-century pseudoscientific racist theories, *mulatos* possessed superior agility while blacks possessed strength. But in addition to being considered agile and strong, brown and black bodies were also associated with "degeneration," violence and criminality, and capoeira practitioners were sharply aware of the need to "rebrand" capoeira as wholesome folklore and salubrious physical culture if decriminalization was to be achieved. Dance scholar Thomas DeFrantz, extending the notion of double consciousness and drawing on Roger Abrahams and Robert Hinton's ideas of black performance as capable of addressing insiders ("dances of celebration") and outsiders ("dances of performance") simultaneously, has proposed that black social dances "contain dual transcripts of 'public' and 'private' meaning."[13] DeFrantz's ideas inform my analysis of Mestre Pastinha's writings, where he expresses his preoccupation with presenting a capoeira suitable for outsiders in public demonstrations while maintaining elements of the practice available only to insiders.

Dance scholar Jacqueline Shea Murphy has argued that rather than a site of containment, disempowerment, or loss of authenticity, the stage can be seen as a site of resilience and cultural continuity of cultural practices persecuted offstage.[14] Extending Shea Murphy's idea of the stage as a space that allows for continuity, I regard mid-twentieth-century stage adaptations of capoeira's violence (the very aspect of capoeira that was criminalized) as tactical ways of rehearsing this violence in public. While capoeira angola choreographed a dance-like, understated, suggested violence, capoeira regional amplified and magnified contact and violence as *capoeiristas* performed increasingly virtuosic and acrobatic choreographed sequences, staging violence without carrying it out. In chapter 3, I show that capoeira performances for tourists in the mid-twentieth century, in particular the folkloric shows directed by Mestre Canjiquinha, simultaneously functioned as tourist spectacle and as training ground for the performers to practice their capoeira fighting skills.

Throughout this book, I use the word "choreography" in two ways: to mean preestablished movement sequences set in space and time, usually for performance in front of an audience, and in Susan Leigh Foster's expanded use of the term, where choreography refers to "a structuring of deep and enduring cultural values that replicates similar sets of values elaborated in other cultural practices."[15] Parallel to Foster's use of the term "choreography" as a term with analytic capabilities that go beyond the stage, I introduce the concept of "staging" as a rubric for analyzing not only the theatrical interventions necessary to present "vernacular" movement onstage, but also the purposeful and tactical modifications of movement practices offstage. In my analysis of capoeira manuals in chapter 1, I apply this broader understanding of staging to shed light on the efforts toward legitimization that reshaped capoeira as "national gymnastics" and physical culture. I argue that a new, respectable capoeira was "staged" and disseminated through print, and later adapted for the stage. My use of the term "staging" differs from dance scholar Rebekah Kowal's use of the term in her analysis of the Greensboro lunch counter sit-ins in 1960, where Kowal analyzes these protests through analogies with theatrical conventions.[16] However, in my use of the term, I do share with Kowal an attention to agency: in the same way the Greensboro protesters purposefully and carefully presented themselves as respectable and responsible citizens, capoeiristas in mid-twentieth-century Brazil purposefully reframed capoeira as a respectable activity practiced by law-abiding citizens.

My use of the term "staging" also draws from critical tourism studies. Sociologist Erving Goffman's[17] concept of "regions" was influential in the development of early theories of tourism studies: his idea that social behavior could be divided into a front region, where people "keep up appearances" and follow standards of decorum, and a back region, where people are able to drop this "front" — even when complicated as a continuum of staged authenticity, as proposed by Dean MacCannell[18] — seems exceedingly simplistic from a post-structuralist perspective. However, this "real"/"fake" dichotomy speaks directly to the pressing concerns with authenticity expressed by capoeira innovators and directors of folkloric shows analyzed throughout this book. My proposed use of staging as an analytic rubric gestures toward Goffman's regions through an acknowledgment of intent, that is, when cultural practices with an offstage corollary are *purposefully* modified for public performance. In the same way that Apter reconsiders syncretism as a process of discursive appropriation that acknowledges agency, I consider processes of staging a contrived version of one's own offstage embodied practices as a creative endeavor that has been devalued and deserves further inquiry.

In *Staging Tourism: Bodies on Display from Waikiki to Sea World*, dance scholar Jane Desmond analyzes bodily display, both animal and human, in live performances in tourist contexts. Desmond addresses the confusion and conflation between performer and performance in these settings: "The performers become signs of what the tourist audience believes them to be."[19] Desmond's discussion of the illusion of unmediated performances by racialized bodies has been influential in my analysis of capoeira onstage, where black, working-class "folklore bearers" (*portadores de folclore*), framed as rural and primitive people, lent an aura of authenticity to folk-loric shows in the 1960s and 1970s (discussed in chapters 3 and 4). "Primitive" black and brown bodies performing "themselves" met a "destination image" of Brazil on European and North American stages. Desmond has defined destination image as "a set of visuals and ideas associated in the tourist's mind with a particular locale."[20] I extend Desmond's concept of destination image and suggest that the same "set of visuals and ideas" can also apply to expectations about moving bodies perceived as racially and culturally "other"—a kinesthetic destination image. In touring folk-loric shows that included capoeira, while other performers fulfilled various desirable destination images of Afro-Brazilian bodies (happy, convivial, exotic, sensual), capoeiristas in particular fulfilled a destination image of violent, wild, and primitive Afro-diasporic bodies, barely contained by the fourth wall of the proscenium stage. While these barely contained "wild" capoeiristas staged an acrobatic violence, the safety of these choreographed sequences allowed players to engage in creativity and innovation.

Dance scholar Anthea Kraut's groundbreaking study of Zora Neal Hurston's "stagings" recovers an overlooked aspect of the creative work of this well-known African American anthropologist and novelist. Kraut recognizes Hurston's labor of arranging, staging, and directing concerts based on "folk" dances, and considers the implications of labeling Hurston a choreographer, a term Hurston never claimed for herself.[21] My inquiry parallels Kraut's in that few of the innovators discussed in this book ever considered themselves artists, and none thought of their work for the stage as choreography. Yet I propose that the stage offered performing capoeiristas—in their majority, black, working-class men—the opportunity to experience capoeira as artists, focusing on the "beauty" of choreographed capoeira games in a setting where they were able to drop their guard. Like Kraut's research on Hurston's stagings, my work "revisibilizes" unacknowledged capoeira innovators such as Mestre Canjiquinha, discussed in chapter 3, whose significant work for the stage and the screen has been overshadowed by the codification projects of his older colleagues, Mestre Bimba and Mestre Pastinha. My work also acknowledges the work of the only female director of folkloric shows in the 1960s and 1970s, Emília Biancardi, who much like Hurston struggled with the paradox of maintaining folk "authenticity" while at the same time claiming authorship.

For the past two decades, academia has closely reflected the growing interest in capoeira practice worldwide, resulting in dozens of theses, dissertations, articles, and books on capoeira, primarily in Portuguese and English. These range from historical research based on nineteenth-century police records[22] to books based primarily on ethnographic research.[23] While synchronic analyses based on ethnographic participant-observation often offer ample movement description and analysis, diachronic research on capoeira has largely overlooked the embodiment of the practice. My research combines archival research with movement analysis in an effort to trace the roots and routes of capoeira's "traditions." While I acknowledge the Africanity of capoeira—the fact that capoeira is an Afro-diasporic practice is not in question—I am not interested in identifying, quantifying, classifying, or analyzing capoeira's Africanity based on allegedly universal "Africanist" aesthetic principles.[24] "Africanist" principles, an analytic rubric widely used in dance studies, hark back to scholarship in art history from the 1970s that we must carefully reconsider, as I will discuss in more detail below.

Capoeira regional has been largely associated with "loss"—loss of capoeira's rituals, traditions, and loss of its very Africanity—while capoeira angola, either implicitly or explicitly, has been understood as a retention of these traditions. In this binary approach to capoeira, upright movement, faster games, and contact between players (correlated with increased violence) characterize a de-Africanized or "whitened" capoeira regional; capoeira angola's slow-paced, close-to-the-ground movement, lack of contact between players, and its nonviolent games have been interpreted as more "traditional," that is more "African."

In the early 1990s, capoeira research began shifting the debate away from the retention-and-loss model, focusing instead on the practice as a whole rather than analyzing the two styles separately.[25] For these authors, capoeira stood in a symbolic and metaphoric relationship to social and cultural processes. John Lowell Lewis's influential *Ring of Liberation: Deceptive Discourse in Brazilian Capoeira* presents capoeira as a metaphoric "liberation from slavery, from class domination, from the poverty of ordinary life, and ultimately even from the constraints of the human body."[26] Physical inversion, he argues, is "a sign corresponding to the desired inversion of the social hierarchy," a sign that he sees as acting as a "kind of sympathetic (iconic) magic, like causing like, or as a kind of Freudian wish fulfillment, a play in fantasy for what could never be the case in reality."[27] While symbolic of social change, the embodied actions of capoeiristas according to this model are incapable of effecting change in the world. Other publications on capoeira from the 1990s, similarly influenced by Mikhail Bakhtin's theories of carnivalesque inversions, analyze capoeira's movement as symbolic of social inversion. In her essay "Headspin: Capoeira's Ironic Inversions" in *Samba: Resistance in Motion*, Barbara Browning reproduces this model when she reads a cartwheel (*aú*) in capoeira as a symbolic inversion: "The aú literally inverts the sign of the cross, demonstrating the ambivalence of 'the above' and 'the below.'"[28] Reading capoeira's upside-down-ness or any of its other features as merely symbolic overlooks capoeiristas' ability to perform what DeFrantz calls "actionable assertions" — movement as performative utterance.[29]

Influenced by the revival of capoeira angola in the late 1980s, a few doctoral dissertations in the mid-to-late 1990s began focusing exclusively on capoeira angola.[30] Greg Downey's phenomenological analysis of capoeira angola focused on the embodied experience of learning capoeira and its ability to repattern one's habitus. Downey's work shifts the analytic paradigm, considering the transformative potential of capoeira practice rather than focusing on capoeira as a symbol or metaphor for impossible inversions of social order.[31] Since then, several books and dissertations have focused exclusively on capoeira angola — a choice that implicitly dismisses capoeira regional as an unworthy object of study, a style easily discarded as "outside the scope" of such analyses.[32] Even though such texts problematize the term "traditional" by adding quotation marks when referring to capoeira angola as "more traditional," they implicitly reinforce the equation tradition = past (and past = Africa) by relying on ethnographic research on the "more traditional" and "more African" capoeira to make assumptions about capoeira's past. I challenge the persistent conflation of tradition with "Africa" (an Africa nostalgically located in the past, imagined as modernity's Other), and raise the possibility of an Afro-diasporic "tradition" capable of being articulated both through and as modernity.

The idea of capoeira as "more" or "less" African harks back to the tenacious notion of Africanisms as measurable, proposed by Melville J. Herskovits. In his 1945 essay "Problem, Method and Theory in Afroamerican Studies," in *The New World Negro*, Herskovits proposed his methods for mapping, measuring, and analyzing "New World African-isms." Herskovits established an "African base-line,"[33] which allowed him to trace degrees of retention or loss of "Africanisms" in the New World through a "scale of intensity."[34] Although Herskovits's work was significant for shifting the focus of the discourse on race from biological determinism to cultural contact, his research was "rushed and shoddy"[35] and his African baseline "remains a myth of African origins, not a documented or even documentable point of empirical departure."[36]

The enduring pursuit of African/Afro-diasporic universals, particularly when it comes to movement analysis, is a testament to Herskovits's foundational and lasting impact on the field of African diaspora studies. Art historian Robert Farris Thompson, in his 1974 book *African Art in Motion*, proposes a pan-Africanist aesthetic through a comparison of dances from selected African regions with exemplars of African art from the Katherine Coryton White collection. Although his conclusions are implicitly extended to all of Africa, Thompson's data come from the "West and Central African civilizations" he visited, "together with Bantu societies for which the literature yields pertinent material on art and dance.[37] Islamic North Africa, Ethiopia, and the Horn and most of East and South Africa are lamentably omitted from the scope of this study."[38] Thompson's conclusions are based on reactions of "existential experts" (his term for "native" dance experts) to film viewings of dances from African regions *other than their own*. Thompson's "most exciting finding," one that proved his hypothesis of the existence of universal traits in African dance, was that "village after village evaluated dance from hundreds of miles away precisely as if the dances stemmed from their own traditions."[39] In addition to his unconventional methods of selection and analysis of his dance data — dances from areas he happened to have visited analyzed by "experts" who were nevertheless unfamiliar with the dances they were asked to analyze — Thompson was selective in his choice of objects from the White collection: "Most felicitously, it was agreed, when I undertook to write this book, that I would be free to omit those objects in the collection which were not germane."[40]

In 1996 dance scholar Brenda Dixon Gottschild applied some of Thompson's theories to her analysis of Afro-diasporic influences in Euro-American concert dance (her much-cited "five Africanist characteristics"), aspects that she noted had been "invisibilized" in George Balanchine's ballets.[41] Dixon Gottschild, however, adapts some of Thompson's ideas to her analysis of an Africanist presence in American ballet, making no claim to universal "Africanisms" to be applied to all of the African diaspora. Although Thompson's work, through Dixon Gottschild, has given dance scholars important analytic tools to discuss Afro-diasporic dance practices (his "aesthetic of the cool" has become almost obligatory when writing about dances of the African diaspora),[42] I believe his "canons of fine form" should be approached with caution, taking into account how Thompson arrived at his theories on African dance.[43] Sifting through data to find evidence of his own "destination image" of African dance,[44] Thompson seems to have selected only the examples that were "germane," that is those which corroborated his theories.[45] Furthermore, Thompson reinforces not only the fiction of "African culture" as authorless, created and practiced by homogeneous groups as a whole (the Dahomean, the Akan, the Ashanti), but also the fiction of a timeless culture that has changed little "for at least four hundred years."[46] Thompson may be knowledgeable about African textiles and sculpture; his dance theories, however, deny the modernity and the creativity of his informants (who were interviewed in the 1960s), reinforcing the equation *Africa = tradition = past.*

PLAYING CAPOEIRA THROUGH THE ARCHIVE

Rather than trying to identify capoeira's Africanisms, my analysis focuses on claims of continuities and discontinuities with Africa. Tracing the development of the competing capoeira styles fashioned through narratives of loss and retention of Africanity, I consider the values ascribed to these African (dis)continuities. I do analyze continuities with the past, but I rely on a documented and documentable past instead of on continuities with Africa that both reproduce Herskovits's analytic model and reinforce ideas of a homogeneous Africa located in the past.

Early in my research process I understood why so much of capoeira scholarship is based on ethnographic research, drawing primarily on the researchers' observations in the field and on their own capoeira practice: the absence of a centralized capoeira archive makes historical research on capoeira an extremely challenging and at times frustrating undertaking. The capoeira archive is woefully incomplete and scattered, and no museum or library holds a significant capoeira collection. Not only is there no capoeira archive, but many primary sources—photographs, film recordings, unpublished manuscripts, and newspaper articles—either are inaccessible in the private archives of older capoeira mestres, or have been destroyed in Bahia's humid, archaic, and understaffed archives.[47] Digitalization efforts have often worsened the problem: paper records are transferred (and subsequently destroyed) to restricted and unwieldy databases not available online, such as Édison Carneiro's personal collection of newspaper clippings about capoeira digitalized by the Édison Carneiro Folklore Museum in Rio de Janeiro. Although a few Bahian newspapers are available in digital form, most newspapers relevant to my research were not, so I spent many hours at the public library of Salvador consulting their historical newspaper collection. Patiently, for the past decade I have been able to compile my own capoeira archive: capoeira manuals, photographs, drawings, interviews, and newspaper articles obtained through various libraries, personal collections, and databases.[48]

As I pored over descriptions, drawings, and photographs of capoeira going back to the late nineteenth century, I found that the movement qualities today considered "more traditional" do not necessarily correspond to a capoeira practiced farther back in the past. Until the mid-1930s, the historical record points to a capoeira comprising jumping, hopping, kicking, ducking, and headbutting—suggesting a directness and quickness markedly different from what is considered traditional today.[49] Changes in capoeira's movement vocabulary throughout the twentieth century make it difficult to identify movement features of capoeira that have "remained" constant (movement qualities, patterns, pathways, and levels), much less reach conclusions about what kinds of movement may be "more" or "less" African. The historical record points to a practice that has decidedly not remained unchanged for the past four hundred years, as Thompson's principles might suggest.

In her seminal essay "Choreographing History," Susan Leigh Foster reflects on the relationship between the historian's body and the historical bodies she studies, and proposes that these historical "dead bodies" are anything but static; in fact, paying attention to past corporealities creates "a kind of stirring that connects past and present bodies."[50] As I engage with this incomplete archive, I am guided by Foster's notion of "choreographing" history, keeping in mind that history is made by bodies; my task as a capoeira historian is to move with and learn from the historical bodies whose traces are present in the archive. In her research about early twentieth-century dancer Loïe Fuller, Ann Cooper Albright proposes that through embodying fragments of the past, dance historians are able to transform traces into tracing, going "beyond the image into the motion."[51] In this book, I trace the lived experiences and embodied practices of capoeiristas, both on- and offstage, a process that connects my own embodied knowledge of capoeira in the present with the capoeira practice of my historical capoeira colleagues in the past.

To set in motion the seemingly static traces present in the archive, I often stand up and step away from my desk to try a movement as it was described or illustrated. Moving from one still image to the next, my body bridges the historical gaps. I am able to partially recreate the corporeality of these traces, which allows me to access a history of capoeira that goes far beyond the binaries through which capoeira was shaped in the mid-twentieth century and through which capoeira has been analyzed. Through a close analysis of this movement evidence, framed by contemporaneous literature from the emerging fields of Afro-Brazilian studies and folklore studies, changes in movement patterns and preferences begin to emerge. How did certain ways of moving, such as capoeira angola's slowness and groundedness, become associated with tradition? Which traditions became associated with Africa? When did grappling emerge as part of capoeira practice and why was it associated with "loss" of tradition? Most important, who were the people responsible for these changes and what was at stake for them?

In identifying, historicizing, and analyzing changes and continuities in capoeira practice throughout the twentieth century, I seek to restore authorship to capoeira practitioners who took (and still take) great pride in their innovations. It would be unthinkable to write a book about ballet "in general" without discussing specific innovations and innovators in specific locations and exact time periods; similarly, I believe that writing about capoeira "in general" perpetuates the myth of an authorless practice. This book recognizes the authorship of capoeira's innovators and the particularities of their experiences. I purposefully and consciously avoid general descriptive statements about capoeira ("capoeira is . . .") that would mask the rich diversity of the practice and occlude the agency of capoeiristas who have done more than passively give continuity to traditions from the past.[52] My work challenges the persistent practice in capoeira research of uncritically conflating a "traditional" present with an authorless past.

I propose innovation and adaptability as capoeira's primary tactics, and the reason for its longevity and global popularity.[53] Riffing on Eric Hobsbawm's invention of tradition, I propose that capoeira's only indisputable tradition is its "tradition of invention." Of course capoeira innovators do not reinvent the form anew with every modification. Innovation accompanies continuity; past practices are renewed and made relevant in the present through modification and addition of new material, but also through subtraction of practices deemed antiquated, obsolete, or seen as antithetical to new trends. In this book I trace the contentious presence of the practice of grabbing and throwing, known as *balões*,[54] which until recently had been considered one of Bimba's modernizations, a borrowing from foreign martial arts responsible for capoeira's "loss of character." Through my analysis of grabbing and throwing, I counter claims of loss regarding "national gymnastics" proposals of the 1920s; I identify the invented modernity of capoeira regional; and I analyze the choreographed sequences that were later developed into the signature acrobatic spectacle of capoeira in folkloric shows.

A preoccupation with capoeira's roots has prevented capoeira scholarship from moving beyond a constant search for continuities in capoeira, resulting in the dismissal of innovation as undesirable "loss." Throughout this book, I focus on capoeira's routes instead, proposing an embodied practice capable of staging Brazil as both modern and Afro-diasporic.

STAGING THIS BOOK

In the following chapters, I analyze the development of capoeira during the mid-twentieth century, defined here as the period between the years of 1928 and 1974—the four decades that reshaped a loosely defined and criminalized street-fighting practice into the "Afro-Brazilian art" we recognize as capoeira today.[55] Although the book covers these four decades, it is not strictly chronological; throughout the book, I revisit the same decades from different perspectives, informed by different sources. My research focuses primarily on the state of Bahia and its capital, Salvador, where much of the labor of staging capoeira as/in Brazil took place. I also analyze writings by capoeira innovators based in Rio de Janeiro in order to establish them as influences in later developments in Bahia.

In chapter 1, I compare three capoeira manuals: one published in 1928 by Anníbal Burlamaqui, a white, middle-class practitioner who called for the transformation of capoeira into Brazil's national gymnastics, and two manuals published in the 1960s by working-class Afro-Brazilians, Bimba and Pastinha.[56] Although written more than thirty years before the other two, Burlamaqui's manual reveals more similarities than differences from the ideas put forth in these later manuals. Through a comparative analysis of both the words on the page and the illustrations and photographs that accompany these texts, I challenge previous studies that have framed both Burlamaqui's national gymnastics and Bimba's capoeira regional as loss and co-optation. Instead, I propose that all three authors, including Pastinha, the "guardian" of capoeira's traditions, shared the same goals in publishing their manuals: attaining legitimacy and respect for capoeira. I argue that through similar processes of discursive appropriation, all three innovators employed nationalist rhetoric in staging a "respectable" capoeira while making few actual changes to capoeira's core practices.

In chapter 2, I return to the innovations of Bimba and Pastinha, bringing into my analysis two important "players" in the process of shaping attitudes toward these two styles: folklorist Édison Carneiro and novelist Jorge Amado. I examine the relationships between intellectuals, artists, and capoeira practitioners, and the intersecting and mutually constitutive discourses that gave rise to the two dominant styles of capoeira we know today. I propose that 1936 marks the beginning of a clear division between capoeira regional and capoeira angola, spurred both by Bimba's much-publicized participation in public matches and by Carneiro's publication of an article titled "Capoeira de Angola" in the same year. Although Carneiro did not invent the term "Capoeira de Angola" (Capoeira from Angola), he was instrumental in establishing the binaries pure/impure, traditional/modern, and more African/less African, and in asserting Angola as both an origin and a distinct capoeira style. Through close readings of descriptions and images of capoeira from the 1940s through the 1960s — photographs, drawings, and film — I trace the alliances between intellectuals and practitioners who choreographed capoeira's "tradition."

Chapter 3 locates the debates over capoeira's tradition within Bahia's growing tourism industry. I trace the influences of tourism bureaucrats such as Waldeloir Rego and analyze the strategies used for staging Bahia as a successful national and international tourist destination throughout the 1950s and early 1960s. I draw attention to the overlooked innovations of Mestre Canjiquinha, the capoeira mestre who directed folkloric shows sponsored by Salvador's Tourism Department for over a decade. Canjiquinha's refusal to align himself with either capoeira "camp" as well as his active participation in the tourism industry have relegated him to the footnotes of capoeira scholarship. This chapter draws much overdue attention to the contributions of this prolific and creative capoeira innovator who participated in several films in addition to directing and performing in his nightly folkloric shows, attended by hundreds of tourists every week. I investigate Bimba's equally overlooked participation in the tourism industry in the 1960s, focusing on his choreographed sequences for the stage, where the practice of grabbing and throwing was transformed into acrobatic assisted flips and flying kicks — spectacular and thrilling movements well suited for the entertainment of tourist audiences.

In chapter 4, I focus on Salvador's folkloric ensembles that were able to rise from informal tourist stages to "high art" stages and sponsored participation in national and international folk festivals. While most of these ensembles were directed by men and featured capoeira as their most spectacular number, Viva Bahia, created by music teacher Emília Biancardi, was the only ensemble directed by a woman. In this chapter, I analyze Viva Bahia's repertory from 1962 until 1974 and propose that the ensemble fulfilled destination images and helped establish capoeira as iconic of Brazil. With an acrobatic, virtuosic capoeira as its featured "number," Viva Bahia fulfilled European and North American fantasies of a vigorous, wild, barely-under-control Afro-diasporic corporeality. I argue that while capoeira's violence was magnified and staged for foreign audiences, the lack of actual violence onstage allowed capoeiristas to experiment with capoeira's aesthetics rather than its function, resulting in a wide vocabulary of *floreios* (flourishes), including headspins, backflips, and other acrobatic maneuvers that have since become part of capoeira vocabulary, both on- and offstage.

Thinking about capoeira in its temporal and kinesthetic specificities rather than considering the practice as a mythic "tradition" borne by equally mythic capoeira practitioners has allowed me to consider innovation in capoeira beyond a loss-and-rescue prism. By reframing the "great figures" of capoeira as living, breathing people contending with practical concerns such as gaining notoriety and respectability for themselves or for a particular style of capoeira, I have been able to acknowledge their modernity without equating this modernity with loss. Untangling the triad tradition/past/Africa has opened up the possibility of a modernity choreographed through Afro-diasporic corporeality.

A NOTE ABOUT CAPITALIZATION

I have maintained the original capitalization of the two capoeira styles discussed throughout this book. While *capoeira de Angola* was written with a lowercase "c" and capital "A"—when Angola was understood as a geographical origin rather than a distinct "style"—the practice begins to be referred to as *Capoeira Angola* (both words capitalized) after its codification. Pastinha consistently capitalizes the term, so I have chosen to follow this capitalization when referring to his style of capoeira.[57] Occasionally the term appears as *capoeira Angola* (without the preposition) or *capoeira d'angola* (with the preposition abbreviated by an apostrophe). The style developed by Bimba, *Capoeira Regional*, is often capitalized in writings that date from Bimba's period of activity. I have chosen to maintain the capitalization of each source. When writing about *capoeira angola* and *capoeira regional* as "umbrella" terms, as they are often used today, I use lowercase letters.

CHAPTER I

STAGING BRAZIL'S NATIONAL SPORT

Burlamaqui, Bimba, and Pastinha

While today capoeira is best known as a cooperative and nonviolent game, nineteenth-century descriptions of capoeira often portray it as a violent practice that not infrequently ended in bloodshed. Johann Moritz Rugendas, a German painter who first traveled to Brazil in 1821, described a capoeira match in *Malerische Reise in Brasilien* (Picturesque travels in Brazil), first published in 1835. After briefly mentioning a martial dance that included the manipulation of wooden clubs, he adds: "Negroes have yet another war pastime, much more violent, the "capoeira": two champions advance against each other, trying to hit with their heads the chest of the adversary they want to knock down. Attacks are avoided with jumps to the side and parrying equally as dexterous; but, throwing themselves against each other like rams, they hit head against head, not infrequently causing the game to degenerate into a fight and knives are brought in making it bloody."[1] Rugendas describes a combative, violent, and potentially bloody "pastime," very different from the acrobatic, dance-like martial art we have come to know as capoeira. Nineteenth-century *capoeiragem*, as the practice was known until the 1930s, was practiced by *capoeiras*, who organized in *maltas* ("gangs" or brotherhoods) and were known to carry straight razors, knives, and clubs.[2] Plácido de Abreu, author of the 1886 novel titled *Os capoeiras*, highlights the violence of capoeiragem. Abreu describes training that consisted of strikes with the head and the feet, as well as use of straight razors and knives: "At first strikes were rehearsed, using only the hands; when the disciple put his lessons in to practice, wooden weapons were used and finally they would use their own metal [weapons], sometimes resulting in the practice space becoming bloody."[3] Like the game described by Rugendas fifty years earlier, this practice session of capoeiragem also included weapons and ended in bloodshed. It seems unlikely that a typical practice session or friendly game would end in bloodshed—it would certainly be impractical not to mention painful and even life-threatening to be wounded during practice on a regular basis. Emphasizing the violence of capoeiragem, however, made for exciting and spectacular denouements for written descriptions of this still mysterious Afro-Brazilian practice. It is difficult to know the extent to which everyday capoeiragem was violent. Although nineteenth-century police records show numerous arrests for capoeiragem, often including injuries and even death, it is difficult to know whether or not those arrested were in fact capoeiras; as anthropologist Katya Wesolowski has noted, capoeiragem had become synonymous with "any act of social vagrancy—disorderly conduct, drunkenness, public fighting, or curfew violation."[4]

Even though capoeiragem was not included in Brazil's first criminal code of 1831, practitioners were persecuted throughout the nineteenth century, their punishment left at the discretion of the local authorities.[5] However, the persecution of capoeiras during the monarchy pales in comparison to the systematic attempts to completely eradicate capoeiragem that began after the military coup of 1889, which deposed the monarchy and gave rise to the Brazilian Republic.[6] As one late-nineteenth-century observer stated, "the repression of capoeiragem . . . was an admirable fact, since in less than one year the work had been consummated, that is, there were no more capoeiras infesting the city and its many neighborhoods."[7]

According to capoeira historian Carlos Eugênio Líbano Soares, the first targets of republican repression were capoeiras living in the capital, then Rio de Janeiro, especially those involved with the Black Guard (Guarda Negra), a monarchist black political militia.[8] João Baptista Sampaio Ferraz, the first republican police chief, arrested and sent into exile hundreds of known capoeiras, who along with other supporters of the monarchy were shipped to a penal colony on the island of Fernando de Noronha. These arrests were lauded by the media, who praised Sampaio Ferraz for ridding the country of "the worst plague" inherited from the monarchy.[9] Criminalized alongside vagrancy and idleness, the practice of capoeiragem was punishable by imprisonment, forced labor, and deportation.[10] Decree 847, Chapter 13, Article 402 of the Penal Code of the United States of Brazil officially criminalized capoeira on October 11, 1890: "Art. 402. To practice on the streets and public squares any exercise of agility and corporal dexterity known by the name of *capoeiragem*: to run, with weapons or instruments able to cause bodily harm, to cause tumult or disorder, threatening a person directly or indirectly, or inciting fear of any harm."[11] Equating capoeiragem with causing "tumult or disorder" or "threatening a person directly or indirectly," Article 402 provided police with a vague and ample enough definition of the crime of capoeiragem that it could be invoked to arrest anyone perceived to threaten public "order." The 1890 penal code also criminalized other elements of Afro-Brazilian culture such as divination as well as the prescription of herbal remedies, which were integral to Afro-Brazilian religious practice.[12] Enacted only two years after the abolition of slavery, several aspects of this criminal code focused on controlling Afro-Brazilian citizens, thus replacing the private control exerted through the system of slavery.

At the turn of the twentieth century, the influential ideas of psychiatrist Raymundo Nina Rodrigues, based on cranial measurements and social Darwinism, dominated the discourse on race in Brazil. He believed that Afro-Brazilians were responsible for Brazil's "inferiority as a nation."[13] Through eugenicist and social hygienist arguments, specifically the associations between black men and violence, capoeiragem was deemed a "moral disease" and subsequently criminalized, as Brazil strived toward "progress."[14]

It is against this backdrop of capoeiragem defined as a violent crime, and capoeiras (the majority of whom were black and brown men) defined as criminals, that I propose we understand the efforts to "stage" capoeira as a respectable national sport. Despite the systematic persecution of capoeiragem in Rio de Janeiro, the practice was not eradicated; rather, it was reformulated in nationalist terms. Since the turn of the century, Brazilian intellectuals had voiced their disapproval of the criminalization of capoeiragem, proposing instead that it should be valued as a uniquely Brazilian tradition. In 1893, only three years after its criminalization, folklorist Alexandre Mello Moraes Filho proposed that capoeiragem be considered "Brazil's own fighting style."[15] During the first two decades of the twentieth century, capoeira enthusiasts who had access to the press—including writer Henrique Coelho Netto, who was a member of the Brazilian Academy of Letters—published essays, articles, and manuals calling for the decriminalization of capoeira. They argued that all the elements for a perfect "physical culture" could be found in this homegrown Brazilian practice, and proposed the adoption of capoeira as Brazil's national gymnastics.

A testament to the growing interest in capoeiragem despite its criminalization, the first known manual of capoeiragem was published circa 1906, with a second edition published in 1907. Understandably, given the illegality of capoeiragem, its author did not dare identify himself, using as a pseudonym the initials O.D.C.[16] Capoeira scholar Antônio Liberac Cardoso Simões Pires raises the possibility that O.D.C. may have been Coelho Netto himself, but concludes that the author was a navy officer named Garcez Palha.[17] Several other manuals of capoeiragem followed this anonymous publication, as the interest in capoeira steadily increased throughout the twentieth century.[18] In this chapter I compare the three most influential capoeira manuals published in the twentieth century, paying close attention to the movement descriptions as well as the illustrations included in each manual. I compare the only surviving illustrated manual from the early twentieth century, Anníbal Burlamaqui's *National Gymnastics (Capoeiragem) Methodized and Regulated*, with two manuals/booklets published in the second half of the twentieth century by the iconic innovators Mestre Bimba and Mestre Pastinha.

Mestre Bimba, born Manuel dos Reis Machado, and Mestre Pastinha, born Vicente Ferreira Pastinha, have become the two most famous capoeira mestres of the twentieth century. Although other capoeira practitioners and mestres, such as Aberrê or Samuel Querido de Deus,[19] might have matched or exceeded their skill, influence, and fame at the time, Bimba and Pastinha were the ones who left the most enduring legacies.[20] By formalizing the teaching of capoeira, bringing the practice from streets and backyards into "academies" and sports centers,[21] the two mestres transformed *capoeiragem*, the informal "doing" of it, into *capoeira*, a self-contained practice with well-defined styles and movement repertories. Bimba's and Pastinha's enduring legacies as the founders of Capoeira Regional and Capoeira Angola can be attributed not only to the many disciples who have given continuity to these mestres' ideas, but also to their illustrated manuals, both published in the early 1960s, through which Bimba and Pastinha recorded and disseminated their pedagogical approaches, rules of conduct, and movement vocabularies.

By placing Bimba's and Pastinha's manuals side by side with the manual published in 1928 by national gymnastics proponent Anníbal Burlamaqui, I show the continuities between these three capoeira projects. Burlamaqui, framed as a "white intellectual," has become the target of accusations of loss, whitening, and excessive modernization of capoeira—accusations previously directed at Bimba. Through a careful analysis of these manuals (close readings informed by my own embodied tracing of the movement present in their illustrations and photographs), I counter the narratives of loss that continue to obscure the mutually constitutive, productive relationship between tradition and modernity. Although Burlamaqui proposed innovations congruent with eugenicist ideas of "improvement," I show that all three innovators engaged in similar processes of discursive appropriation while choreographing an Afro-diasporic Brazilian modernity.

This chapter is divided into three sections, each focused on a manual published by these capoeira innovators: Burlamaqui's *National Gymnastics (Capoeiragem) Methodized and Regulated* (1928), Bimba's *Capoeira Regional Course* (c. 1963), and Pastinha's *Capoeira Angola* (1964). I also bring in the ideas found in Pastinha's unpublished manuscripts, written in the mid-to-late 1950s, which include drawings, prints, and song lyrics. Although written more than thirty years before the other two, Burlamaqui's book reveals more similarities than differences with the ideas put forth in these later manuals. Through a comparative analysis of both the words on the page and the illustrations and photographs that accompany the texts, I place these three innovators' ideas in conversation in an effort to understand the tactics of legitimization that successfully "elevated" twentieth-century capoeira from criminal activity to "national gymnastics"—from social "carcinoma"[22] to a form of physical culture capable of "improving the Brazilian race,"[23] ushering Brazil into the future through Afro-Brazilian modernity.

There has been debate about a national, Brazilian art, about
Brazilian music, etc. [. . .] But does anyone talk about a national sport?
Unfortunately not. And under these circumstances, Zuma's book is
equivalent to a shout of Brazilianness.
— Mario Santos, Preface to *Gymnastica nacional*
(capoeiragem) metodisada e regrada

Much has been written about Bimba and Pastinha, but less biographical information is available about Anníbal Burlamaqui, also known as
Zuma.[24] Burlamaqui, who was familiar with o.d.c.'s manual, self-
published *National Gymnastics (Capoeiragem) Methodized and Regulated* in
1928.[25] The manual—Burlamaqui's attempt to legitimize the practice of
capoeiragem—contains illustrated descriptions of attacks and defenses
as well as proposed rules and regulations aimed at "improving" the practice. Anthropologist Letícia Reis has analyzed Burlamaqui's work as part
of what she calls a "white erudite" rethinking of capoeira, while framing
the emergence of Mestre Bimba's and Mestre Pastinha's styles as "black
working class"[26] innovations aimed at legitimizing capoeira and sym-
bolically bringing blacks closer to full Brazilian citizenship and social
inclusion. Reis's analysis is groundbreaking in that it questions previous
analyses of Bimba's capoeira regional as simply co-optation and "whitening" by foregrounding the fact that Bimba himself was black. Reis recasts
Bimba's innovations as dynamic Africanist appropriations of hegemonic
rituals and symbols such as formal graduation ceremonies and the conferral of medals—tactical reformulations of capoeira as sport which allowed this marginalized Afro-diasporic practice to play a key role in the
construction of Brazilian national identity. Furthermore, Reis positions
both capoeira regional and capoeira angola as coeval, albeit distinct,
"black working class" rearticulations of capoeira as sport, which she sees
as diametrically opposed to the "white erudite" nationalist project which
sought to "hygienize, that is, to minimize or strip of its African origins
that which was a Brazilian gymnastics par excellence."[27]

Other authors have similarly reclaimed and valorized Bimba's innovations while blaming Burlamaqui for a process of "loss of character"
and "whitening" of capoeira. Matthias Röhrig Assunção asserts that
Burlamaqui's "kinesthesics overall seem more inspired by Europe than

Africa," and that the price to pay for his methodization was the complete erasure of "the Afro-Brazilian roots of the art and the cultural context of its practice."[28] Tracing an argument similar to Reis's, Assunção concludes that Bimba's innovations should be considered a form of "black modernization, which differed in many fundamental aspects from the 'whitening' or 'westernized' model proposed by Burlamaqui."[29] Assunção continues: "Without [Bimba] only a Burlamaqui model of a completely de-Africanized capoeira might have survived, parallel to entirely folklorized shows for tourists without any martial efficiency. . . . Mestre Bimba created an alternative model of black modernization for an African derived combat tradition, which seemed to be the only one capable of avoiding both total Westernization and folklorization for capoeira."[30] Rather than seeing continuity between Burlamaqui and Bimba's innovations, Assunção supports a narrative where Bimba breaks with this de-Africanized model and rescues capoeira's Africanity. It is interesting that Assunção draws a parallel between the "losses" brought about by Burlamaqui and those allegedly caused by folkloric shows for tourists, a topic I explore further in the next three chapters.

Burlamaqui is often blamed for capoeira's de-Africanization and "loss of character" (*descaracterização*) in much of the contemporary capoeira literature. Jair Moura blames this loss on Burlamaqui's borrowings from foreign forms: "[Burlamaqui] inserted a series of movements and blows from alien fighting techniques, while maintaining others belonging to the mestizo's original and traditional fight. The adoptions of these influences and forms damaged contemporary capoeira, which consequently lost its genuine character."[31] Moura is unequivocal about the damage and loss brought about by Burlamaqui's foreign borrowings, even though Bimba, Moura's own mestre, proudly claimed to have engaged freely in borrowing elements from foreign fighting techniques. Greg Downey also equates foreign borrowings with loss in his analysis of *National Gymnastics* and concludes that Burlamaqui creates "an amalgamation of distinct violent fighting techniques" which "necessarily reduces capoeira to its most effective attacks and defenses." Downey further claims that Burlamaqui "makes no mention of the *roda*, the capoeira ring with musicians that so dominates and is a hallmark of Bahian forms of the art. His regulations only stipulate a circular area for competitions, without mention of musical instruments, rituals, or stylistic elements of play."[32]

Burlamaqui's critics seem to agree that the addition of foreign movement material coupled with the lack of attention to music and ritual result in a "reduction" or loss of capoeira's traditions. Antônio Liberac Cardoso Simões Pires writes that Burlamaqui "removes almost all play (ludicidade) from capoeira: its songs, its drumming, clapping and improvisation disappear to make room for a capoeira that has lost its most sensational side."[33] Both Pires and Downey implicitly equate musical and ritual elements with a "retained" Africanity, lost in Burlamaqui's manual. This view is also shared by critics of Bimba such as Frigerio, who, writing in the 1980s, concludes that Capoeira Regional "eliminates or reduces the emphasis on the ceremonial, ritual and ludic elements of Capoeira Angola and incorporates new elements from fighting [techniques], which, up to that time, were foreign to it: grabbing, defenses against [grabbing] and some new movements."[34]

In this chapter, I question the assumption that a capoeira prior to nationalist efforts of legitimization was necessarily more imbued with "ritual"—a term that, unless carefully defined, tells us more about the writer's nostalgic ideas about rituals than about the ritual itself. Similarly, I question analyses that have equated innovation and modernization with loss and with a reduction of both the complexity and the Africanity of capoeira. Tropes of loss and rescue of a capoeira perceived to be in decline recur as narrativizing devices not only in academic analyses of capoeira but also in the development of the practice throughout the twentieth century. I argue that it is in fact through these narratives of loss and recuperation that innovation is legitimized and permitted.

Burlamaqui, Bimba, and Pastinha each engaged in his own process of rescue: Burlamaqui's goal was to rescue and reform the "still ill-defined" practice of capoeiragem through methodization and regulation. Bimba claimed a need to rescue capoeira from a loss of efficiency, while Pastinha hoped to rescue the form from the losses brought about by Bimba's codifications. All three innovators, however, had a common underlying goal: to remove the stigma associated with the practice and to distance capoeira(gem) from marginalization. All three were born within a few years of the official criminalization of capoeiragem through the criminal code of 1890; they learned and practiced the form clandestinely and knew firsthand the importance, indeed the urgency, of decriminalization.

In National Gymnastics, Burlamaqui clearly draws on the social prestige ascribed to his own "white" phenotype in early twentieth-century Brazil. However, I question previous dismissals of Burlamaqui's practice on the grounds that he was a white intellectual engaging in a project of de-Africanization of capoeira. I recast, instead, Burlamaqui as a practitioner—in the language of his time, a "sportsman"—whose embodied knowledge of capoeira often contradicts the eugenicist rhetoric present in his text; in a move to acknowledge Burlamaqui as a practitioner rather than an outsider, I refer to him throughout my analysis by his capoeira nickname, Zuma.[35] Both his rich movement descriptions and the photographs that illustrate the book point to an in-depth knowledge of the practice. While the text socially "improves" capoeira by associating it with foreign sports, Burlamaqui's movement descriptions and prescriptions assert national superiority through Afro-diasporic corporeality. I propose that we consider his methodization instead as a discursive appropriation, similar to Bimba's and Pastinha's innovations, aimed at modernizing and "improving" capoeira while bringing Afro-diasporic embodied epistemology from the margins to the center of Brazilian national identity.

From the photo of a dapper young Zuma printed in *National Gymnastics*—in his late twenties or early thirties—it is safe to assume that he was born around the turn of the twentieth century, only a few years apart from his two better-known capoeira colleagues.[36] Arms crossed, Zuma looks out at the camera dressed in a suit and bow tie, his hair immaculately slicked back with pomade in a photo labeled simply "The author." In the book's brief introduction, Zuma positions himself as a practitioner, stating that it was not his intention to create literature; rather than literary value, the reader should hope to find utility in the book. The book's utility is also emphasized by Dr. Mario Santos in the preface: the work is "modern, it's practical: it doesn't meander, it goes straight to the point. . . . In short, it is a useful book."[37]

Santos, whom Zuma identifies as a "talented lawyer," lends legitimacy to Zuma's book not only through his written endorsement and praise in the preface but also through photographic evidence of his own embodied practice: it is Santos himself we see posing as Zuma's opponent in the twenty photographs that illustrate the attacks and defenses listed in the book. Zuma deems Santos's acceptance of his invitation to pose for the photos a "patriotic gesture" aimed at the "destruction of the archaic and silly prejudice that 'BRAZILIAN GYMNASTICS'—*capoeiragem*—tarnishes those who practice it."[38] Santos deploys the social evolutionary rhetoric of his time to predict that the decriminalization and acceptance of capoeira was only a matter of time. Pointing out that English boxing, French *savate*, and Japanese *jiu-jitsu* all went through a period of marginalization before reaching social acceptance and national recognition, Santos asks, "Why, if the law of evolution is the same in the entire Universe, would capoeiragem, in Brazil, escape the evolutionary march of its sister forms? . . . Why should we not create rules and regenerate capoeiragem?"[39]

Throughout *Gymnastica nacional*, Zuma does just that. Bringing in elements from boxing and "foot-ball,"[40] Zuma prescribes the diameter of the circular playing "field," the starting position of the contenders, the duration for each "round" (three minutes, with a rest of two minutes), and the criteria for establishing a winner for each match: either a fighter would win by incapacitating the opponent or, if so agreed beforehand, points would be counted by a referee who would proclaim as the winner the fighter causing the most falls.[41] Creating (new) rules and "regenerating" capoeiragem, "turning it into a weapon, [a form of] self-defense, a sport like any other" is presented, in fact, as Zuma's patriotic duty.[42]

While many of Zuma's rules—the presence of a referee, a point system, a match divided into rounds of a certain duration of time—clearly constitute borrowings from "legitimate" foreign sports, Zuma rearticulates street capoeiragem in hegemonic terms through these very foreign borrowings. For example, Downey has pointed out that Zuma "makes no mention of the roda, the capoeira ring with musicians that . . . is a hallmark of Bahian forms of the art," and that he "only stipulate[s] a circular area for competitions."[43] Indeed Zuma does not mention the roda, with its musical instruments and "rituals" as we know it today; however, he does stipulate a circular area for matches of capoeiragem, when many popular sports at the time were practiced on rectangular spaces.[44] The circularity of the playing area is not a mere geometrical coincidence with the present-day roda; rather, it rearticulates the circular formation intrinsic to many Afro-diasporic forms within twentieth-century transnational notions of sport.[45] A careful analysis of Zuma's regulations, movement descriptions, illustrations, and photographs reveals recurring movement tropes I have identified as central to capoeiragem, rearticulated by Zuma as "improvements" to the practice.

Movement descriptions that precede *National Gymnastics* point to continuities rather than discontinuities between Zuma's "purely Brazilian game" and nineteenth-century street capoeiragem.[46] In one of the earli-

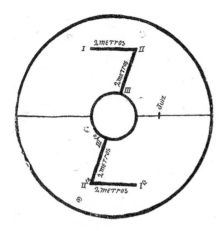

Figure 1.1 Circular "field" for matches of "Brazilian Gymnastics" proposed by Zuma in Gymnastica nacional (capoeiragem) methodisada e regrada, 1928. Here the contenders enter by jumping from points I to II to III, drawing the letter Z as they begin the match. The author notes the "happy coincidence" that the letter Z is also his initial.

est detailed movement descriptions of capoeiragem, included in Brazilian folklorist Mello Moraes Filho's 1893 collection of Brazilian folk celebrations and traditions entitled *Festas e tradições populares do Brasil*,[47] we find accounts of several attacks and defenses almost identical to the ones included in Zuma's *National Gymnastics*. In a vivid description of the movement possibilities of the game of capoeiragem, the author states that "the capoeira, placing himself in front of his contender, dives in, jumps, stretches out, spins, deceives, lies down, stands up and, in one instant, employs his feet, his head, his hands, the knife, the straight razor."[48] Making ample use of the present tense, Mello Moraes's accounts clearly speak of a capoeiragem very much present in his day, still organized in *maltas* and persecuted by police. This is likely the same capoeiragem that Zuma learned and later sought to "improve" and legitimize. When Mello Moraes describes the attacks and defenses by name, more than half of the movements he lists are also found in Zuma's book: the *rabo de arraia* (lit. stingray's tail), *cabeçada* (headbutt), *rasteira* (leg sweep), *escorão* (straight kick to the adversary's stomach), *tombo da ladeira* (tripping a jumping adversary, in midair).[49] The list of movements included in Plácido de Abreu's novel *Os Capoeiras* (1886) shares the *bahiana* and the *rabo de arraia* with Zuma's list, and here the headbutt is called *chifrada* (a strike with the horns).[50]

In a short article in an eclectic collection of essays entitled *Bazar* (1928), Coelho Netto, a journalist, novelist, sports enthusiast, and practitioner of capoeiragem, lists many of the same attacks and defenses mentioned by Abreu, Mello Moraes, and Zuma: the headbutt, here called a *cocada*,[51] the *rabo de arraia*, the *rasteira*, and also the *bahiana*,[52] a move where one player quickly lowers down and, using his hands, pulls the adversary's legs from under him, making him fall—an attack also present in Zuma's *National Gymnastics*. Rather than an idiosyncratic "amalgamation" of foreign martial or pugilistic traditions, as has been claimed, Zuma's techniques, at the movement level, seem closely connected to street capoeiragem.

With headbutting, tripping, jumping, and kicking while bearing weight on the hands, Zuma gives continuity to several movement tropes found in nineteenth-century capoeiragem, but he also engages in its "tradition of invention": Zuma takes credit for inventing the *queixada* (kick to the chin), the *passo da cegonha* (lit. stork's step, where the defending player grabs the attacker's raised leg while sweeping his standing leg),[53] and the *espada* (lit. sword, a kick aimed at disarming the opponent).[54] Claiming authorship, he adds the words *do autor* (of the author) next to these three strikes.[55]

While much attention has been paid to Zuma's rules and point system, his manual is invaluable for its detailed movement descriptions. Zuma begins with the starting position, the *guarda*, the "bellicose attitude" from which one begins to learn capoeiragem: "One brings the body upright, in a natural alignment, in a noble and erect attitude, twisting to the right or the left."[56] However, in more than half of the photos that illustrate the attacks and counterattacks, the author appears bearing either partial or full weight on his hands. Although the practice of national gymnastics should begin with an upright, "noble and erect" stance, the photographs and descriptions in Zuma's book point to a practice that demanded players constantly move away from this "noble and erect" starting position, crouching down and bearing weight on their hands for attacks, defenses, and counterattacks.

In preparation for a headbutt, the player or fighter,[57] "approaching the adversary and suddenly crouching low, strikes with his head the [adversary's] lower jaw or chest, belly or even [his] face."[58] To defend from a *rabo de arraia*, one should "get down as low as possible and take advantage of this defense" by preparing a subsequent attack. Some attacks and defenses should be performed "having fallen over (almost lying down)."[59] These and other examples point to a technique that demanded movement close to the ground, either by ducking under a kick or initiating a kick or headbutt from below. The erect stance that Zuma further describes as "the first position, noble and loyal, of the queen of national gymnastics" remains almost entirely rhetorical, invoking nobility and royalty as part of his effort to remove the stigma that marred the practice of capoeira in the early twentieth century.[60]

Other than the three-minute rounds and the presence of a referee, Zuma's national gymnastics seems to have little in common with boxing. The bulk of Zuma's attacks and defenses are based on leg sweeps and kicks rather than punches or strikes with the hands, precisely because the hands are instead used for supporting the weight of the body. In describing a kick he considers one of the most dangerous, Zuma explains: "The capoeira will perform the rabo de arraia by placing the palms of his hands on the floor and, appearing to go into a back flip, he will place the soles of his feet on the [adversary's] chest or face . . . and this results always in the adversary falling backwards."[61] Freeing the feet to attack by placing the palms of the hands on the floor,[62] Zuma's capoeiragem demands that players constantly shift weight from feet to hands and from hands to feet. Excessive verticality, often equated with loss of Africanity, seems only to be present in theory in Zuma's national gymnastics.

Zuma's technique has been interpreted as a stiff, upright version of capoeiragem where movements do not flow from one another. Downey claims that Zuma "only hints at how sustained interaction might actually continue throughout the three-minute rounds."[63] However, a reader following Zuma's descriptions and instructions, as I did, would constantly rise, fall, dive, duck, and jump. The text provides ample evidence of sustained interaction, and in fact Zuma instructs his readers to initiate an attack from a defensive move, in much the same way strikes and evasive maneuvers flow from each other in present-day capoeira. A move Zuma calls *pentear* (to comb) or *peneirar* (to sift) not only gives further evidence of the game's flow but also embodies *tapeação* (trickery), the epistemology of deception central to capoeiragem. Zuma instructs, "One throws the arms and the body in every direction in a swinging motion [*ginga*], in order to disturb the attention of the adversary and better prepare for the decisive attack."[64] Contrary to today's understanding of the ginga within capoeira practice as a foundational back-and-forth connecting step, Zuma's "sifting" has the express intention to confuse and deceive, a tactical maneuver in preparation for an attack.[65]

The description of the rabo de arraia above offers another example of capoeiragem's epistemology of deception: *appearing* to go into a backflip, the player "places his feet" on the adversary's chest or face. Deception, trickery, and unpredictability, the same tactics considered central to ca-poeira today, run through Zuma's *National Gymnastics*.[66] However, Zuma downplays trickery in his manual: the description of sifting is found at the end of the list of attacks, without an illustration, almost as an after-thought. Trickery, not surprisingly, was not foregrounded in a book that aimed at the legitimization and decriminalization of capoeira. Similarly tucked away at the end of the book are Zuma's "deceptive moves" (*golpes de tapeação*): stepping on the adversary's foot, deceiving him by looking in the direction of one body part but attacking another, pretending to pick up something from the floor, or even pretending to prepare to spit in the adversary's face, prompting him to close his eyes and rendering him vulnerable to an attack.[67] These are listed as additional attacks, and Zuma provides no in-depth descriptions or illustrations for these trickery moves. However, trickery and deception also permeate Zuma's descrip-tions of more "legitimate" attacks and counterattacks: in the *banda for-çada* (forced sweep), the player "advances towards his adversary, deceiv-ing him as much as possible (sifting) and pretending to slip, he places his hands on the floor and extends his leg, stiff (right or left) beside the ad-versary's legs ... pushing the adversary to one side or backwards, making him fall."[68] Deceiving the adversary by pretending to slip or looking in the opposite direction of the attack would, by twenty-first-century stan-dards, not only be considered effective feints; they would also certainly provoke laughter and embody the ludic aspect of capoeira—an aspect often interpreted as Afro-diasporic and "traditional."

Despite his hyperbolic claims to the nobility, purity, perfection, and even holiness of Brazil's newfound national gymnastics,[69] trickery is still at the core of Zuma's capoeiragem, as are numerous other aspects that have been theorized as Afro-diasporic, such as the circular formation, bearing weight on the hands and kicking with the feet, and using head-butts.[70] Analyses that focus solely on Zuma's text, filled with nationalist rhetoric, miss the ample evidence of Zuma's Afro-diasporic embodied knowledge present in *National Gymnastics*, and thus dismiss Zuma's work as a "complete de-Africanization" of capoeiragem.

The nationalist rhetoric of valorization of the national over the for-eign permeates early twentieth-century publications that argued for the adoption of capoeiragem as national sport. In the preface to Zuma's book, Mario Santos writes: "It's time that we freed ourselves from for-eign sports and gave a little [more] attention to what is ours, what is from home. And in the end it's all worth it, because Brazilian Gymnastics is worth more than all foreign sports. It even exceeds them."[71] Coelho Netto, in his aptly named 1928 essay "Nosso jogo" (Our game), similarly calls for the recognition of the superiority of capoeiragem, which offered "a means of self-defense superior to all those extolled by foreigners and that we, for this reason alone, are ashamed of practicing."[72] Both Mario Santos and Coelho Netto call for an end to the shame associated with all things homegrown, recognizing the value and indeed superiority of capoeiragem. Coelho Netto proposes that rather than continuing to get punched by "bulky thugs" (a reference to boxing), Brazilians would prevail in the ring by using techniques from capoeiragem, such as bending the body at the waist and attacking from below.[73] Expressing his frustration with the valorization of the foreign, Coelho Netto ends his essay in a sarcastic tone: "Let's learn to throw punches—[boxing is] an elegant sport, because people practice it with gloves, its profits come in dollars and it's called box, an English name."[74] Elegance, precisely what boxing lacked, could be found in abundance in capoeiragem, "one of the most agile and elegant [forms of] exercise."[75]

Journalist A. Gomes Cartusc, appealing to the good taste and patriotism of Brazilian youth, called for the cultivation of "our" elegant and invincible "game of noble dexterity": "Our game, wherever it is placed against another [form] . . . has always won, and still this game without equal is always hidden and only with fear is practiced among people of low social strata as if it were a crime knowing how to headbutt, to apply a leg sweep and to stretch [into] a rabo de arraia!"[76] The superiority, efficiency, and invincibility of capoeiragem are repeatedly invoked as justification for the form to be brought out of hiding and illegality. Cartusc brings the readers' attention to the absurdity of criminalizing headbutts and leg sweeps and regarding this "game without equal" as a crime.

Zuma's text similarly foregrounds the superiority and elegance of capoeiragem in order to strengthen the argument for its social acceptance. While Zuma undoubtedly sought to "improve" capoeiragem through codification, he also championed its intrinsic value: capoeiragem "encompasses, albeit still a little confused and ill-defined, all the elements for a perfect physical culture."[77] Zuma in fact proposed capoeiragem as a tool of self-improvement: young "family" men, he argued, could improve themselves through this "strange game of arms, legs, head and torso, with such agility and such violence, capable of providing stupendous superiority."[78] "Cultivating" the body through capoeiragem, Brazilian men would become "strong, feared, brave and daring."[79] If all young men learned capoeiragem, Zuma predicted, the Brazilian citizen of the future would be "respected, feared [and] strong."[80] Although he proposes to "improve" capoeiragem, Zuma imagines a Brazilian "citizen of the future" improved through an Afro-diasporic practice that already encompassed all the elements "for a perfect physical culture."

Appropriating the hegemonic discourses of his time, Zuma invokes the eugenicist proposition that sports and physical fitness should be used as a means of improvement of the "citizen of the future": "Today parents should raise their children outdoors, on the beaches, on a sports field, in a center where athleticism is cultivated with love and vanity, so that in the future, [our] youth may shine in sports fields, showing courage and dexterity."[81] Echoing the emerging belief that physical activity and fresh air were beneficial rather than harmful to one's health,[82] but at the same time cautioning against foreign sports that caused the body to "atrophy," Zuma calls for including capoeiragem in the roster of salubrious and edifying sports: "Oh! How beautiful would it be if all true Brazilians took the initiative to learn [capoeiragem], studying the smallest secrets of this purely Brazilian game. . . . Oh! If everyone followed this idea, the Brazilians of the future would be respected, feared, strong, and would pride themselves in knowing the secrets of the wisest game known to this day."[83] Zuma cleverly frames his appeal as patriotic dare aimed clearly at the upper classes where parents would "quiver, shout, become desperate with sons who have the fortunate idea of learning this amazing game."[84] Cultivating both body and body politic through an Afro-diasporic game turned eugenicist thought on its head, allowing Africanity to be viewed as a source of "regeneration" rather than degeneration, and as a source of strength and national pride.

Zuma described capoeiragem as "the most beautiful game, the most intelligent sport."[85] His emphasis on intelligence and beauty is also significant in his labor toward legitimization through the appropriation of eugenicist discourse; while invoking beauty and intelligence indeed "whitened" capoeira for readers who equated these two attributes with whiteness, this choice of words simultaneously allowed intelligence and beauty to describe an Afro-diasporic movement practice. Zuma's valorization of Afro-diasporic knowledge, lauding its beauty and intelligence, is consonant with emerging ideas among social scientists, who since the mid-1920s had begun reconsidering earlier pessimistic views about Brazil's future.[86] Through the prism of scientific racism, the country's considerable Afro-diasporic population represented an obstacle to progress. African heritage and racial mixing were seen as the cause of "problems as diverse as criminality, sterility and degeneracy."[87] Zuma rejects this model of "degeneration," proposing instead the regeneration of the Brazilian citizen through a beautiful and intelligent Afro-diasporic practice.

Zuma's impassioned defense of Brazil's "national gymnastics" had a lasting impact on the development of capoeira(gem). Despite the initial limited circulation of Zuma's self-published *National Gymnastics*, it was likely duplicated through available technologies such as the mimeograph or simply by retyping the text, as Zuma himself did with O.D.C.'s manual. A book published almost two decades later reproduced most of the contents of Zuma's manual, including its illustrations and movement descriptions: Inezil Penna Marinho, a navy officer and physical education bureaucrat who briefly studied capoeiragem with Mestre Sinhôzinho,[88] published *Subsidies for the Study of the Methodology for the Training of Capoeira-gem* through the physical education division of the ministry of education and health in 1945. The drawings used in this book are exact reproductions of the photographs of Zuma and Mario Santos included in *National Gymnastics* (see figures 1.2 and 1.3). The most significant difference between Zuma's and Penna Marinho's movement descriptions can be found in the paragraph on "sifting" (*peneirar*).[89] Reflecting or perhaps setting a new trend in the practice of capoeiragem, Penna Marinho uses the word *ginga* as a synonym for sifting rather than meaning simply "to sway," as does Zuma. He writes, "The *ginga* of the body, a *bamboleio* in which the arms throw themselves in every direction and the body dances over the semi-bent legs, is called combing or sifting."[90] Using the word *bamboleio*, which can be loosely translated as "swinging motion," Penna Marinho emphasizes this move's dance-like qualities and its efficiency rather than its trickery. He clarifies that although the aim of sifting was to distract the opponent, this was necessary for "applying one's strike with greater efficiency and unexpectedly."[91] It is significant that in Penna Marinho's adaptation of *Gymnastica nacional*, sifting is listed as the first movement. Penna Marinho foregrounds the importance of sifting and foreshadows both the change in nomenclature and the importance of the move now considered the "foundational step" in capoeira training, the ginga, which Bimba goes on to further codify in his own booklet *Capoeira Regional Course*, published in the early 1960s.[92]

CAPOEIRA AS PHYSICAL CULTURE:
BIMBA'S *CAPOEIRA REGIONAL COURSE* (C. 1963)

Bimba's method is considered, by the experts, as the most practical and perfect, capable of crossing borders and becoming known globally.
—Wilson Ribeiro, Bimba's biography in *Curso de Capoeira Regional*

Although Penna Marinho may have given *National Gymnastics* a second life through his adaptation/reinterpretation, perhaps giving more readers access to Zuma's proposed regulations, it is clear that *National Gymnastics* had made its impact well before *Subsidies* went to press in 1945. By the mid-1940s, both Bimba and Pastinha had undoubtedly come into contact with Zuma's ideas: Cisnando Lima, a medical student and first-generation graduate of Bimba's school who was known to "walk with Zuma Burlamaqui's book under his arm," was likely responsible for introducing his teacher to Zuma's manual.[93] Bimba was undoubtedly also influenced by the ideas articulated by Gomes Cartusc, Coelho Netto, and other early twentieth-century proponents of capoeiragem as national sport.[94] Jair Moura, a former student of Bimba, proposes a direct link between Zuma's ideas and Bimba's Capoeira Regional project: "In Salvador, in the 1930s, following in the footsteps of Anibal [sic] Burlamaqui, Bimba . . . opened a school, where capoeira, disciplined, regulated, methodized, attracted individuals from several segments of the population."[95] Zuma's manual and his call for improving a "still ill-defined" capoeiragem through regulation and methodization clearly provided a foundation, or at least a precedent, for Bimba's own codification. Capoeira reseacher Frederico Abreu, discussing the capoeira matches held in the Bahian capital throughout the 1930s that propelled Bimba into the limelight, finds evidence of Zuma's influence in a note published in the newspaper *Diário da Bahia* in 1936: "The police will regulate these capoeira demonstrations according to the work of Anníbal Burlamaqui (Zumma) [sic] published in 1928, in Rio de Janeiro."[96] Despite the attention Zuma's regulations have received in contemporary capoeira scholarship—the alleged cause for the near loss of capoeira's "tradition"—his regulations were not very

Figures 1.2a and 1.2b Zuma, on the left, delivers a queixada to the chin of his opponent, Mario Santos. This strike is listed in National Gymnastics as Zuma's own innovation. The drawing on the right illustrates the same strike in Inezil Penna Marinho's Subsidies for the Study of the Methodology for the Training of Capoeiragem.

Figures 1.3a and 1.3b Zuma trips his opponent with the banda amarrada, one of the many examples in National Gymnastics of leg strikes delivered from a position supported by the player's arms. The drawing on the right illustrates the same strike in Inezil Penna Marinho's Subsidies for the Study of the Methodology for the Training of Capoeiragem.

detailed and left much room for individual interpretation. It is likely that the rules followed in these matches pertained to the dimensions of the space where the contest was to take place, the presence of a referee, and the practice of determining the winner through a point system.[97]

Bimba drew attention to himself and to his new capoeira technique through his participation in public matches against other capoeira players as well as fighters of other martial arts. During the 1930s and 1940s, the sports pages of all major Bahian newspapers reported on boxing and jiu-jitsu matches almost as much as they reported on soccer. Bimba cleverly joined this pugilistic craze and with his typical bravado issued challenges to other fighters through newspapers: "Here I leave my challenge to those who practice or know capoeiragem as well as to any other fighter (jiu-jitsu, etc). Whatever they want. I will face them with my capoeira."[98] Through his "invincibility" in public matches, many of them against fighters of other combat forms such as boxing or jiu-jitsu, Bimba offered living proof of the superiority of capoeiragem over imported forms of self-defense (a recurring argument used by Zuma as well as other early twentieth-century apologists of the practice).[99]

Reminiscing over these matches in an interview in 1973, Bimba boasted: "I, Mestre Bimba, challenged all the tough guys and I won: the match that lasted the longest, lasted one minute and two seconds."[100] Bimba's emphasis on efficiency and superiority—defeating the adversary in the shortest possible time—appropriated prevailing nationalist discourses of his time while at the same time disrupting lingering notions of racial hierarchies and Afro-Brazilian inferiority. Bimba, a dark-skinned black man, with his carefully cultivated image of invincibility—the embodiment of Zuma's idealized "strong, feared, brave and daring" fighter—changed the physiognomy of the Brazilian citizen of the future.[101] A black man from a poor socioeconomic background, Bimba nevertheless embodied the elegance, efficiency, and superiority of the "noble game" lauded by proponents of capoeiragem as national sport.

Bimba began elaborating and teaching his new capoeira around 1918. In an interview in his later years, Bimba stated that by 1928 he had already "created [capoeira] Regional in its entirety."[102] Dating the completion of his capoeira technique to the same year as the publication of Zuma's *National Gymnastics* was no coincidence; this protected Bimba against claims that his technique might be derivative of Zuma's. Unfortunately, this early twentieth-century codification of Capoeira Regional was not recorded through writing or illustrations, and there is little to no record of his pedagogical approach at this time. Bimba's *Capoeira Regional Course*, an LP and a twenty-page illustrated booklet published in the early 1960s, is the culmination of forty years of "improvement" and codification.[103] In this process, Bimba transformed capoeiragem—the *doing* of it—into capoeira, a rigidly codified system, with attacks and defenses prearranged in "sequences" and a clear pedagogical method divided into fourteen lessons. Combining the technologies of vinyl audio recording and print media, this publication offers an easily reproducible way of disseminating Capoeira Regional beyond the master-disciple, face-to-face relationship. *Capoeira Regional Course* goes beyond Zuma's unpretentious illustrated list of attacks and defenses and a few proposed rules for competition; it offers a carefully regulated teaching method where knowledge is imparted through set movement sequences.

Bimba's publication is in fact intended *as* instruction. The text, almost entirely in the imperative (e.g., "raise your right leg," "repeat the exercise with the left leg"[104]), takes the capoeira student through Bimba's fourteen lessons, aided only by the music supplied by the accompanying LP. The presence of a flesh-and-blood teacher is rendered unnecessary and even redundant. Any anxieties over the integrity of this "teacherless" learning system are allayed in the preface, where the reader is reassured that the "regionalist essence" that characterizes Bimba's capoeira was maintained and "all the authenticity of the inventions of this famous capoeirista" were transferred to paper and vinyl.[105]

Capoeira Regional Course expanded the reach of Bimba's system beyond the region, "contributing in an efficient and practical way in disseminating this magnificent and original folkloric sport—Capoeira Regional."[106] As a "folkloric sport," capoeira regional offered the best of both worlds: the modernity of sport legitimized by the authenticity of folklore.[107] Efficient and practical, capoeira regional was capable of ushering both capoeira and its practitioners, now called capoeiristas, into modernity. Appropriating the nationalist rhetoric of proponents of national gymnastics but reframing it as "regional," Bimba cleverly co-opts the momentum generated during the previous decade and definitively codifies the still-marginalized game of capoeiragem into a respectable form of physical education he called "regional" capoeira.[108]

In the process of transforming capoeiragem into capoeira, Bimba focuses on shaping the student's body in and out of exact reproducible positions rather than on the student's movement. While Zuma's sifting embodied improvisation and deception—the player should throw his arms and his body "in every direction in a *ginga*"—with the intent of distracting the opponent, Bimba's ginga becomes the "capoeirista's 'fundamental' position." The torso should be slightly inclined forward, and the arms should be placed at the height of the forehead.[109] After shaping the body of the student, Bimba maps his path in space: "In order to execute this movement, draw a square with chalk on the floor and place both feet in [positions] A [and] B. Take the right foot behind the left (D) and return to the initial position (A). Next, take the left foot from position D to C and return to B. This is the cycle that will be repeated indefinitely. . . . Ask your colleague to take you by the hands, and practice the ginga as many times as you can. Repeat the movements alone."[110] Far from an unpredictable, deceptive "sifting" motion, with limbs thrown in "every direction," Bimba's ginga is disciplined as a regulated action of moving in and out of symmetrical, mapped positions, which should be "repeated indefinitely." Bimba transforms a preparatory, deceptive tactic into a kind of callisthenic exercise, to be repeated as many times as possible: an innovation that has shaped capoeira pedagogy, in both angola and regional styles, to this day.[111]

Bimba is unequivocal about the importance of the ginga: "Every lesson should be initiated with the ginga motion [*gingado*]. It is important to stress the importance of the 'ginga' in all phases of capoeira. It is indispensable for the student to learn the ginga motion [*gingado*] well. Use all the tracks of side A of the LP."[112] In these instructions, the newness of the ginga as a position or step—a "thing" to be learned and practiced in isolation, "indefinitely" or until the end of side A—is signaled by Bimba's quotes around the word "ginga" and its alternation with the word "gingado," a verbal noun that insists on the *movement* of the ginga, which I have translated here as "ginga motion," still resisting its fixity as a thing. In fact, "ginga" appears infrequently throughout *Capoeira Regional Course*, being instead referred to as "gingado," the gerund "gingando," and the verb "gingar." Nevertheless, Bimba shifts the focus from process to product, which is a technique that could be learned in as little as six months, transposed to paper and vinyl, and disseminated throughout the nation.[113]

Capoeira Regional's efficiency relied on the easy reproducibility of standardized sequences (*seqüências*), described and illustrated in each of the fourteen lessons of *Capoeira Regional Course*. In these sequences, players rehearse attacks and defenses in set numbers of repetitions, symmetrically alternating right and left sides. The illustrations, labeled with letters and numbers, include broken lines with arrows indicating the path of each motion. Zuma's *National Gymnastics* simply lists and illustrates attacks and counterattacks without proposing any kind of order for these movements. Using Zuma's trickery moves, assessing the needs of each game, and taking advantage of opportunities, the player/reader, "armed with and defended by perfect and good intelligence," was responsible for ordering his own attacks and counterattacks.[114]

Bimba's pedagogical innovation of teaching attacks and defenses in preestablished sequences did maximize the efficiency of the learning process by eliminating the experimentation necessary to arrive at such sequences through improvisation. However, Bimba did not remove improvisation altogether from his Capoeira Regional; during unstructured games that took place after training sessions, playfully known as *esquenta banho* (shower warm-up), students were allowed to engage in improvised (and often rough) games while waiting for their turn in the shower.[115] Similarly, Bimba's own pedagogy at his school was anything but teacherless; several of his disciples report learning the ginga from Bimba through touch, as he famously would take each beginning student by the hand to teach this movement.[116] While Bimba disseminated his modern, multimedia capoeira technique throughout the nation (disembodied and transposed to paper and vinyl), his own pedagogy at home valued embodied transmission of knowledge and improvisation.

Bimba not only emphasized the efficiency of his new capoeira method—improving his students' technique in the "shortest possible time"—he also championed its efficacy as self-defense.[117] In fact, one of Bimba's justifications for his need to create Capoeira Regional was that in his opinion capoeira angola had lost its efficacy, "leaving much to be desired."[118] In his 1968 *Capoeira Angola: Socio-ethnographic Essay*, Waldeloir Rego reports asking Bimba why he invented Capoeira Regional, to which Bimba answered that he "found capoeira Angola very weak, as a pastime, physical education [and as a form of] attack and self-defense."[119] Inefficient and useless as self-defense, according to Bimba, capoeira Angola found itself in need of "improvement."

A journalist from *A Tarde*, writing in 1946, praised Bimba for improving "capoeira d'angola" and creating the "'Bahian regional fight,' whose efficacy is known to all who are acquainted with it." This efficacy, he continues, "has been conclusively demonstrated when we are forced to put movements into practice, in order to save our skin."[120] Bimba had demonstrated the superior strength of his new capoeira technique in the ring during the capoeira matches that made him famous in the 1930s. The capoeira technique he consolidated and formalized in the following three decades was organized around principles of self-defense and efficacy in real-life confrontations.[121] The modernist ethos of practicality and utility, also present throughout *National Gymnastics*, not only guided but also justified and authorized Bimba's innovations.

Bimba took pride in his innovations and borrowings, practices he often boasted about in interviews throughout his life. In conversation with Waldeloir Rego, Bimba stated that he chose movements for his Capoeira Regional that he considered "capable of fulfilling the needs that capoeira angola does not fulfill. He answered that he used strikes from *batuque*, such as *banda armada, banda fechada, encruzilhada, rapa, cruze de carreira* and *baú*, as well as details from *maculelê* choreography, from other folk celebrations and many other things he didn't remember, as well as strikes from Greco-Roman wrestling, jiu-jitsu, judo and savate, adding up to a total of 52 moves."[122]

This list of sources is significant for its breadth as well as for its unapologetic acknowledgment of foreign sources in the creation of this "regional" folkloric sport. Bimba's borrowings came from the folk as well as the foreign, and from "many other things he didn't remember."[123] Comtian ideals of progress as well as neo-Lamarckian notions of evolution and improvement not only allowed but invited Bimba's innovations. Ironically, Bimba incorporated the foreign to create this regional and national "folkloric sport," going as far as incorporating the very foreign punches from boxing criticized by Coelho Netto into a capoeira where efficiency was the basic organizing principle.[124]

Bimba's claim of having incorporated elements from *batuque* reflects his desire to portray himself as an innovator, claiming as his own elements which may have already been part of the overlapping practices of batuque and capoeiragem.[125] In *National Gymnastics*, Zuma describes some of the same batuque steps mentioned by Bimba above, such as the *rapa* (a type of leg sweep) and the *baú* (described by Zuma as a strike with the belly),[126] which he acknowledges as elements from "smooth batuques and sambas."[127] The fact that Bimba's father was a known practitioner of batuque allowed Bimba to assert himself as an innovator while simultaneously drawing national "character" from a movement tradition practiced within his family—a move that undoubtedly helped in allaying criticism regarding the foreign sources of his other innovations. Despite his claims to innovation, Bimba's Capoeira Regional, like Zuma's national gymnastics, included many elements from nineteenth-century street capoeiragem, such as headbutts (arpão de cabeça), leg sweeps (banda or rasteira), and using the arms for support while kicking, as in the rabo de arraia mentioned by Mello Moraes and Plácido de Abreu, renamed meia-lua-de-compasso by Bimba.[128]

The technique of partnered throws that Bimba called cintura desprezada— often used as an example of his borrowings from foreign sources—sheds lights on Bimba's complex approach to innovation. (I have translated cintura desprezada as "abandoned waist"; this practice is also loosely referred to as balão [sing.] or balões [pl.], lit. balloon[s].[129]) The tenth lesson in Capoeira Regional Course introduces students to Bimba's abandoned waist techniques, where students learn attacks and defenses that involve grabbing and throwing the adversary. In the first sequence, Bimba instructs: "Begin with the ginga motion. Deliver a cartwheel [aú]. Your adversary seizes this opportunity and crouches down; placing his shoulder on your waist, he tries to lift and throw you in the air. As you fall, apply the scissor move [tesoura]."[130] As one of the players begins a cartwheel-like maneuver called the aú, the opponent approaches and lifts him momentarily into the air (see figure 1.4). The balões that follow increase in complexity, danger, and amount of contact between players; gripping the opponent across the chest, by the neck, or by the upper arm, players grab and propel each other into the air and onto the ground. Several of the descriptions of the balões in Capoeira Regional Course end with a warning. The final warning for the balão-de-lado (side throw) reads, "This move, after the initial grip, has no defense, resulting in the dangerous fall of the adversary"; the instructions for the gravata cinturada (lit. waisted necktie) caution the reader, "Dangerous move"[131] (see figure 1.5). Bimba's innovations allegedly increased the effectiveness of capoeira as self-defense, and balões were exemplary of the danger and possible lethal consequences of these powerful innovations.

Luiz Renato Vieira has argued that balões were one of the "great innovations introduced by Mestre Bimba in the context of capoeira of the 1930s," and points out that this innovation has been the source of much

Figure 1.4 *Illustrations for the tenth lesson of Bimba's Capoeira Regional Course: "Cintura desprezada, tesoura, saída-de-aú."*

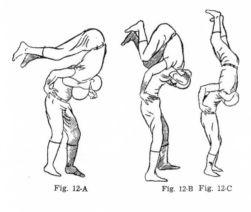

Figure 1.5 *Illustrations for the twelfth lesson of Bimba's Capoeira Regional Course: "Gravata cinturada."*

Fig. 12-A   Fig. 12-B   Fig. 12-C

controversy as it is considered to be the result of borrowings from judo, jiu-jitsu, and savate.[132] Despite similarities between Bimba's balões and judo's and jiu-jitsu's throws, as well as Bimba's own admission that he did indeed borrow from every source available to him—regional, national, and foreign—Mello Moraes's nineteenth-century description of a game of capoeiragem points to the possibility, in fact the likelihood, that aerial throws had been used in capoeira since before Bimba was born:

> Let us picture an arena. The contenders approach, their eyes shining, their lips whispering scorns, threats. Undulating in a snake-like motion, their arms swing, maintaining their heads and neck

immobile. One of them, wrapping the other's upper body and thorax with his right arm, with the speed of lightning, with the quickness of thunder, brings him close, flank against flank, and thus caught, he anchors [the contender's] lower limbs against his leg, [and] tossing him high, [the contender] fall[s] behind him, as cold as a cadaver, as inert as death.[133]

Acknowledging his own melodramatic ending to this description, Mello Moraes clarifies that "this move is not always fatal, since the art offers even in this case admirable resources."[134] Although this description has been dismissed as the author's inability to understand or accurately describe what he saw, I believe that Mello Moraes did indeed describe a practice of grabbing and throwing commonly practiced in capoeiragem, which was later claimed and codified by Bimba.[135]

Bimba's mission of "improving" and modernizing capoeira in fact required innovation — drawn from a variety of sources, including capoeira's past. Capoeira scholar Muniz Sodré proposes that balões should be considered Bimba's "invention" only as a systematized practice, since some of Bimba's contemporaries who practiced capoeira de Angola, such as Cobrinha Verde, also included balões in their capoeira.[136] Writing in 1937, folklorist Édison Carneiro lists balões as part of the movement repertory of capoeira de Angola: "The hands almost never work in attacks, except in the neck strike [golpe de pescoço] and the finger in the eyes [dêdo nos olhos], not to mention several balões, where the hands support the body of the adversary so as to throw him, over the head, backwards."[137] Bimba himself acknowledged that balões were also present in capoeira de Angola when he listed its attacks and defenses during an interview in 1936. He adds that from capoeira de Angola's thirteen moves, he had removed two and added another fifteen to create his Capoeira Regional. However, Bimba clarifies that these lists of attacks and defenses should not be considered exclusive; in fact, "with the intent of making these contests of capoeiragem more interesting and more violent[,] all the moves (and tricks) of capoeiragem will be part of the game."[138] Maximizing the violence and efficiency of his new capoeira indeed required Bimba to deploy all its moves and tricks, including balões. Ironically, the very "innovations" that allowed Bimba to increase the violence and efficiency of capoeira, often assumed to be foreign borrowings, may have been borrowed from capoeira's not-so-distant past.

Bimba portrayed himself as an innovator while simultaneously grounding his own training in an unbroken African "tradition." According to Bimba, his early training was in the form "called capoeira de Angola, practiced by my mestre, the African Bentinho."[139] Establishing capoeira de Angola as his previous training, Bimba creates a narrative of evolution and progress for his Capoeira Regional. Bimba's short biography printed on the last page of *Capoeira Regional Course* confirms that Bimba began studying capoeira with an African mestre who taught him the "capoeira de Angola method." At the end of his studies, the biographer continues, Bimba taught the same style of capoeira as his mestre for ten years.[140] Having established a direct connection with Africa through his studies with Mestre Bentinho, Bimba was firmly grounded in the "method" of capoeira de Angola, which he could then proceed to "improve" and "civilize." As a reporter from *A Tarde* stated in 1946, "Mestre Bimba[,] knowing the 'angola,' civilized it, corrected its rustic manners, increased the number of strikes, composed its new physiognomy, which allowed it to enter the salons and to be accepted, with the name 'regional.'"[141] Bimba was praised for civilizing, correcting, and expanding capoeira. Situating Capoeira Regional firmly within an Afro-Brazilian "tradition" allowed Bimba to innovate while simultaneously allaying criticism (although never completely) over his ample borrowings. Claiming that capoeira angola was "in [a process of] decay," Bimba aimed at bringing respectability to capoeira and capoeiristas, even if this meant composing a new "physiognomy" for the practice. The reporter quoted above, using the language of racial determinism, lauds Bimba's improvements to the physiognomy—the outward appearance from which one can judge inner character—of capoeira. Capoeira Regional's outward appearance now included increased violence (efficacy) and codification (efficiency), which, combined, ushered capoeira's upward mobility and recognition as national sport.

Although several of Bimba's students were white and came from privileged socioeconomic backgrounds, many of the players embodying capoeira's new "physiognomy" were black, as was Bimba himself. Countering prevailing notions of "passive" and "brutish" blacks, Bimba's capoeira embodied strength, agility, and at least a mythical if not factual invincibility. Bimba's capoeira, like Zuma's capoeiragem, also embodied intelligence—not merely a "raw" intelligence in need of regulation, but a highly codified intelligence that resulted from purposeful invention.

Whether Bimba invented, remembered, recycled, or borrowed the new elements in his capoeira technique, it is clear that he took credit for (and pride in) these innovations.

While Bimba approximated capoeira to hegemonic notions of sport, organizing his training into reproducible sequences, using a point system for matches, and incorporating rituals such as the conferral of medals and formal graduation ceremonies into his training, I argue that Bimba's innovations and borrowings were part of a series of discursive appropriations rather than simply a process of co-optation.[142] Bimba's innovations did "improve" the outward appearance of capoeira in a syncretic relationship with a capoeira(gem) that preceded codification. Bimba took advantage of opportunities to invent a modernity for capoeira that recycled current and past movement patterns such as sifting (codified as ginga), balões (codified as abandoned waist), as well as strikes borrowed from batuque and strikes deriving directly from street capoeiragem.

Codified and claimed as his own innovation, abandoned waist techniques (cintura desprezada) reframed tradition as modernity so successfully that it became the most criticized aspect of Capoeira Regional, symbolizing a "loss of character" brought about by excessive foreign borrowing; his transformation of Zuma's deceptive and unpredictable sifting (peneirar) into a uniform, "foundational" callisthenic exercise, today known as ginga, inflected preexisting movement patterns in hegemonic terms. Despite the codification and homogenization of certain aspects of the practice, however, Bimba's capoeira, like Zuma's capoeiragem, gave continuity to several core aspects of nineteenth-century capoeiragem, such as the use of headbutts and kicking while bearing weight on the hands.

Through his adaptability and inventiveness, as well as his multiple syncretic discursive appropriations, Bimba inflected Brazilian modernity in Afro-diasporic terms. A semi-literate black man born only twelve years after the abolition of slavery, Bimba was undoubtedly aware of his status as a "second class" citizen, despite Brazil's global reputation for having "conquered" racism.[143] Conscious of being seen through the eyes of others as "brutish" and potentially violent, Bimba appropriated the very discourses of positivism and eugenics used to oppress him to create an efficient and respectable capoeira style located at the "evolved" end of a narrative of progress.

PASTINHA'S *CAPOEIRA ANGOLA* (1964)

Mestre Pastinha has kept . . . Capoeira Angola in its original purity,
as he received it from the African mestres, not allowing . . . it to be deformed
through the introduction of practices from other fighting traditions.
—J. B. Colmenero, Preface to *Capoeira Angola*

Located at the opposite end of the evolutionary continuum from Bimba's Capoeira Regional, capoeira de Angola (*of* Angola, with the preposition, as it was known in the 1930s and 1940s) was said to be in a state of decay, leaving "much to be desired." The eugenicist language of "degeneration" continued to be used even by mulatto intellectuals, such as Édison Carneiro, who advocated for the valorization of Afro-Brazilian culture; in the chapter titled "Capoeira de Angola" in *Negros bantus,* Carneiro warns that despite capoeira's increasing appeal to the middle class, despite the fact that capoeira matches had begun attracting large audiences, and that in fact "capoeira de Angola reveal[ed] an enormous vitality," the "process of decomposition" of capoeira was accelerating. "Progress," Carneiro continues, "sooner or later, will deal the final blow [to capoeira]."[144] With capoeira de Angola so firmly positioned at the "primitive" end of the racial/social evolutionary scale, even ample evidence to the contrary—its growing appeal, popularity, and vitality—was not enough to convince Carneiro that capoeira was indeed compatible with progress.

One of the goals of Pastinha's *Capoeira Angola,* published in 1964 immediately after Bimba's manual, was to establish Capoeira Angola as a respectable sport and an efficient form of self-defense and physical culture. Pastinha's nationalist, even patriotic language echoes Zuma's "shout of Brazilianness" in *National Gymnastics.* In a section titled "Capoeira Today," Pastinha states that "the tendency nowadays is to consider Capoeira Angola as the national fighting style which, honorably, places it in a privileged position, serving as a definitive consecration of this style of sport."[145] Rather than being in the final stages of a "process of decomposition," destined to recede into disappearance as predicted by Carneiro, Pastinha's Capoeira Angola had achieved the honorable and privileged position of "national fighting style." Nationalism and progress, rather than announcing capoeira's demise, were in fact two foundational pillars in the ideology that fueled its growth and expansion. Looking to the future, Pastinha makes an uncannily accurate prediction about the global expansion of Capoeira Angola: "The day is not far when Capoeira Angola academies will be sought by an immense legion of people, not exclusively as a means of self-defense, but also as a magnificent means of maintaining perfect physical shape and prolonging youth."[146] Drawing on early twentieth-century proposals of capoeiragem as the key to a healthy physical development, Pastinha similarly frames his Capoeira Angola as a means of shaping youthful and physically fit "citizens of the future" (a recurring theme both in *Capoeira Angola* and in his manuscripts). Pastinha reiterated Zuma's assertion that capoeiragem offered "all the elements for a perfect physical culture";[147] Capoeira Angola fostered physical development and overall health, including "psycho-physical balance."[148] This neo-Lamarckian physical "evolution," however, was to be achieved through rather than in spite of Afro-diasporic corporeality. As Capoeira Regional's success depended in part on the narrative of decline and imminent demise of Capoeira Angola, it comes as no surprise that Pastinha's *Capoeira Angola* countered this narrative by proposing a capoeira that fostered health and physical development, as well as a capoeira in a process of expansion, soon to be sought by a "legion of people."

Although Pastinha's approach to the dissemination of capoeira shared Bimba's expansionist goals, Pastinha did not subscribe to expanding capoeira's movement vocabulary to include what was perceived to be foreign movement material. Rather than taking pride in increasing the number of possible kicks, as Bimba had done, Pastinha acknowledges that indeed Capoeira Angola "has a small number of moves in comparison with some fighting techniques such as Judo, Jiu-jitsu, American freestyle fighting, etc." Condemning borrowing from other fighting techniques, which he warned could result in an eclectic form of self-defense, Pastinha called for "improving [capoeira's] technique without losing its characteristics."[149] In the same way that Bimba built his success in part on Capoeira Angola's alleged decline, Pastinha valorized his capoeira style by cautioning against the losses that could result from unrestrained borrowing.

Although Pastinha's and Bimba's capoeira styles both certainly derived from the informal street practice of capoeiragem—both conceived in and through modernity—Pastinha drew legitimacy from the very position of anteriority used by Bimba to justify the need to improve on an "old" capoeira in decline. Pastinha, along with early Capoeira Angola advocates, appropriated scientific racism's rhetoric of purity to secure Capoeira Angola's status as the "original" capoeira. Writing in 1937, Édison Carneiro declared capoeira de Angola to be the purest form of capoeira.[150] In the preface to *Capoeira Angola*, J. B. Colmenero, a former student, claims that Pastinha had maintained the teachings of Capoeira Angola in their "original purity, such as he had received it from the African masters, without allowing it to be deformed by the introduction of practices belonging to other fighting methods."[151] A nationalist rhetoric of purity intersected perfectly with narratives of untainted African origins, lending Capoeira Angola a legitimacy that, by comparison, Bimba's capoeira seemed to lack.

Pastinha, like Bimba, began studying capoeira with an "old African" from Angola. The story, repeated by Pastinha in several interviews, can be summarized as follows: Pastinha, a frail and skinny ten-year-old, was often bullied by a larger, stronger boy in his neighborhood. They often got into fights but Pastinha always lost. One day, an old African named Benedito watched the fight and invited Pastinha to come to his home to learn "a very valuable thing." After some time learning capoeira, Pastinha was able to defeat the bully "with one blow."[152] The fact that both Pastinha and Bimba report having learned directly from Africans is significant in that it dissociates both these innovators' capoeira techniques from the marginal and criminal status of nineteenth-century straight-razor-wielding *valentões*.

Pastinha further detached both himself and his Capoeira Angola from a capoeira practiced by rough, dangerous men known as valentões by creating a mysterious twenty-nine-year gap in his personal history of capoeira practice.[153] This gap helped establish a direct link between Pastinha's initial contact with capoeira, learned from "an old African," and his position as the guardian of the "original" capoeira. According to Pastinha's unpublished manuscripts, written throughout the 1950s and 1960s, on February 23, 1941, at the urging of his former student Aberrê (Antônio Raymundo Argolo 1895–1942), Pastinha went to watch a roda led by a mestre named Amorzinho, who shook his hand and said, "I have been waiting for a long time to hand over this capoeira to you; so you can teach it." Pastinha then tried to decline the invitation, but another mestre, Antônio Maré, insisted, "There is no other way, Pastinha, you're the one who is going to teach this."[154] Reluctantly, and only with the support of these mestres, Pastinha accepted the invitation to "take care" of Capoeira Angola, and in the same year he founded the Centro Esportivo de Capoeira Angola, or CECA (Capoeira Angola Sports Center). This narrative provides Pastinha with a clean slate, allowing him to start over as a much-awaited "prodigal son" who returns to protect Capoeira Angola.[155]

Mestre Noronha (Daniel Coutinho, 1909–77) offers a slightly different account in his own manuscripts.[156] According to Noronha, the first center of capoeira angola was founded by himself and twenty other capoeira players, and it was only after the death of its director, Amorzinho, that the group handed over the leadership to Pastinha.[157] Noronha's writings portray Pastinha not as a trailblazer, single-handedly defending a "dying" tradition, but rather as one capoeira player among many, chosen to be in a position of leadership in a thriving capoeira angola collective of over twenty members. A different entry in Pastinha's manuscripts offers a less heroic account of the founding of CECA, one that actually corroborates Noronha's memory of a capoeira collective: outraged that Paulo Santos Silva claimed to be the founder of CECA in the center's statute published in 1952,[158] Pastinha takes back the credit for having the initial idea of creating the center in 1941, but also gives credit to several other capoeiras, many of whom Noronha also lists as founders.[159] Pastinha writes: "Excuse my expression, Mr. Paulo, the legitimate founders are: Amosinho, Aberrêr, Antonio Maré, Zeir, Daniel Noronha, Livino Diogo, Vitor H.U., Olampio, Onça preta, alemão, Pompílio dos Santos, Domingo de Magalhães, Athalydio Caldeira President, Aurelydio Caldeira V. President, and Vicente Ferreira Pastinha the conceptualizer who named the Capoeira Angola Sports Center, I chose the colors of the shirts and [they were] made by me."[160] Pastinha sets the record straight in this passage but also contradicts the narrative where he is ceremoniously chosen as the long-awaited steward of capoeira angola. Elsewhere in Noronha's manuscript, he mentions Pastinha's name in a long list of known early twentieth-century valentões. Pastinha's twenty-nine-year absence, then, whether total or partial, actual or fabricated, was instrumental in legitimizing his position of leadership: not only did it provide a direct link to capoeira's African "tradition"; it also allowed Pastinha to distance himself from the image of the valentão and reinvent himself as a respectable citizen who could continue the ongoing efforts to remove the social stigma against capoeira.

Pastinha was in many ways the ideal candidate for this leadership role. Having had a solid primary education at the Navy Apprentice School, not only was he literate and able to express himself well through writing, but he was also familiar with the positivist thought that undergirded the Brazilian Republic.[161] In addition, Pastinha was well connected with the intellectual elite of Bahia, most famously with Brazilian novelist Jorge Amado, writer and politician Wilson Lins, sculptor Mario Cravo, visual artist Carybé, and photographer Pierre Verger. Pastinha's profile would allow him to serve as a bridge between the members of the Capoeira Angola Sports Center, many of them semiliterate, and the intellectual, artistic, and administrative elites of Bahia—opening doors and providing opportunities for visibility and financial support.[162]

Pastinha's success can also be attributed to his opportune physical characteristics: his "frail" frame and light brown skin—the son of a Spanish father and an Afro-Brazilian mother—coincided with the "ideal type" understood as being suited for the practice of capoeira at the time.[163] Capoeira de Angola, from or of Angola (as it was called before Pastinha omitted the preposition), was not only a capoeira that might have come from the region of Angola through Pastinha's first teacher; it was also the capoeira of the "Angola type," a racial type that was described as crafty and imaginative but not suited for heavy labor. According to historian Braz do Amaral, "the Angolas," as a racial type, were "taller, slenderer than other Africans, physically weaker ... [and] were known to be loquacious, imaginative, indolent, insolent, with no persistence for work, fertile in resources and craftiness."[164] Associations between a crafty and resourceful racial type and the stereotype of the nineteenth-century capoeira practitioner followed the logic of racial determinism. This crafty but "physically weaker" Angola type is often conflated with "the mulatto" and "the capoeira," perceived to lack blacks' "athletic complexion."[165] For Penna Marinho, "the mulatto" shared many characteristics with "the Angola" and exhibited the desired physical traits for the practice of capoeiragem: "The mulatto, generally less bulky than blacks, less burdened by strong muscles developed by heavy labor, more agile, more flexible, more elastic, more nerves and fewer muscles, represented the ideal type of capoeira."[166] Whitened through miscegenation, "the mulatto" becomes the ideal type for capoeiragem, blacks being "too muscular." For Penna Marinho, the brown (not black) body of the mulatto transcends the "burden" of blacks' strength and is able to cultivate embodied intelligence in the form of agility and flexibility. In his 1945 *Subsidies*, we learn that mulattos possess the ideal mixture of black and white traits: they are "more intelligent than blacks and more dexterous than whites" and miscegenation has freed them "from the spirit of submission rooted in the black race."[167] Both Pastinha's small frame and hybrid ancestry (African and European) perfectly matched still lingering models of racial types, folding "the mulatto," "the Angola," and "the capoeira" into one.

While Bimba countered notions of capoeiras as weak, crafty "types" through the rigid codification of Capoeira Regional paired with a personal image of invincibility, Pastinha embraced the intelligence, agility, and flexibility ascribed to him through his skin color while simultaneously rejecting the craftiness and "no persistence for work" associated with "the mulatto" stereotype. Pastinha insisted that his students be model citizens, always appearing in public wearing the school's uniform.[168] His Capoeira Angola Sports Center was ruled by a statute and was hierarchically organized, with a president, vice president, three secretaries, two treasurers, and one librarian.[169] His advanced disciples were assigned specific functions: field master, song master, percussion master, training master, archivist, supervising master, and *contra-mestre*.[170] In his manuscripts, Pastinha stated proudly, "We are registered, we have a building [for our school], we have identification, legal documents signed by the country's parliamentary leaders."[171] Although Pastinha did not codify capoeira to the same extent as did Bimba, he certainly institutionalized the practice and successfully redeemed the reputation of its practitioners.

Pastinha expressed a preoccupation to educate, civilize, and improve not only the practitioner of capoeira but the form itself.[172] Almost thirty years later, Pastinha's goal seems remarkably similar to Zuma's: to legitimize capoeira and facilitate its acceptance into "society." Writing in the early 1960s, aware of a growing interest in capoeira both in Brazil and abroad, Pastinha asks: "Does it or does it not have a name in history[?] It is well-regarded by hundreds of thousands of Brazilians, and foreigners.... And capoeira is trying to enter and live in society, the capoeirista of today [and] of the future is respectful and decent."[173] Determined to carve a place in history and society for capoeira, Pastinha often refers to capoeiristas as respectful and decent citizens. The introduction to the statute of Pastinha's school reflects this recurring preoccupation with improving the image of both capoeira and capoeirista: "My brothers ... the fundamental base of our center is good behavior. Social behavior, human solidarity and above all doing good, not using the powerful weapon that Capoeira is unless in legitimate defense or in the name of the Nation."[174] A "well-behaved" citizen, the new capoeirista was authorized to use violence only in self-defense or in the "name of the Nation." A valentão turned prodigal son, Pastinha applied a similar strategy of rebranding to the legitimization of capoeira, whose violence was carefully downplayed—a "powerful weapon" to be used only in self-defense.

Pastinha tamed capoeira's violence by emphasizing control in capoeira games. Like Bimba, Pastinha acknowledged that some of capoeira's blows could be dangerous and even fatal. Such violence, however, could not actually be applied in "sports demonstrations" and should be controlled: "Capoeira is either 'played' for keeps, with serious consequences, exceeding the limits of sport, or in demonstrations where the blows, in more or less slow movements, come close, grazing, or are stopped just before the chosen target."[175] Stopping a kick "just before the chosen target" or grazing the opponent (still a valued skill in present-day capoeira angola) *demonstrates* violence without carrying it out. The demonstration of a safe and nonviolent capoeira was in fact at the core of Pastinha's project of legitimization. He reassures the readers of *Capoeira Angola* that capoeira's moves can be safely controlled in friendly contests and that, in fact, Capoeira Angola disciples can dedicate themselves to its practice "without any fear."[176]

The safety and control emphasized by Pastinha reawakened comparisons between capoeira and dance, which date back to descriptions by nineteenth-century travelers and foreign observers, such as Johann Moritz Rugendas (1835) and Charles Ribeyrolles (1859).[177] Pastinha explains that when movements graze the opponent, "Capoeira Angola is similar to a gracious dance where the deceptive 'ginga' shows the capoeiristas' extraordinary flexibility. But Capoeira Angola is, above all, a fight [technique], and it's a violent one."[178] Pastinha reconfigures the comparison between Capoeira Angola and dance, the same used in the argument of capoeira's decline and inefficiency, establishing a syncretic relationship between capoeira's violence and its dance-like qualities.[179] Veiled behind a deceptive façade of dance, Capoeira Angola "retained" its violent potential: "One understands better by watching the fight. It looks like a dance, but it isn't. Capoeira is a fight [technique], and a violent one. It can kill, and it has killed. Beautiful! In its beauty, its violence is contained. The boys are only showing [the kicks], [they] graze or are contained before reaching the adversary. And even then it's beautiful."[180] Capoeira Angola's violence is contained but not lost. Although this "dance" might look harmless, it remains potentially lethal. Pastinha's statement that the "boys" (a new generation of players) "are only showing the kicks" (only *recently* showing) points to the newness of the idea that kicks should be held back and only graze rather than strike the opponent—a practice that Pastinha transformed into a guiding, even defining principle of Capoeira Angola. It is important to note that the idea of containment, "showing" the kicks, is absent in both Bimba's and Zuma's methods. However, although Pastinha may have "trademarked" a nonviolent, dance-like capoeira, he did not innovate in a vacuum; other players, such as Samuel Querido de Deus and Onça Preta, observed by Ruth Landes in the late 1930s, also subscribed to a more controlled playing style.[181]

Embracing the "fight disguised as dance" story of origins, Pastinha dissociates capoeira from its violent past and brings it into modernity as both sport and dance, where violence is safely controlled and staged rather than enacted. Pastinha defines Capoeira Angola as an art form, and its practitioners as dancers and artists: "We are dancers, men who live the art of capoeira as sincere artists."[182] The ginga, for Pastinha, embodied deception while simultaneously "lending [the body] the smoothness and grace of a dancer."[183] Defining capoeira as dance and art, Pastinha approximates capoeira to "high culture" and inserts the practice into hegemonic discourses of legitimacy. The smoothness and grace of the dancer/capoeirista replaced, at least on the surface, the violence of nineteenth- and early twentieth-century capoeira.

Like Bimba, Pastinha foregrounds the ginga in *Capoeira Angola*. Pastinha's ginga is his capoeira's core principle, its "fundamental characteristic," not unlike Bimba's *gingado* (capoeira's "fundamental position").[184] However, Pastinha emphasizes the ginga's aim to distract, deceive, and confuse the opponent rather than the uniform callisthenic repetitions emphasized by Bimba. In one of the seventeen photos that illustrate Pastinha's *Capoeira Angola*, two slender young men dressed in the uniform of Pastinha's school face each other and demonstrate the ginga for the camera, their bodies and faces relaxed, knees bent in wide stances, and torsos inclined forward. One player's incomplete weight shift from one leg to another signals that this photo was not posed. Their movement is neither symmetrical nor in unison. Like Zuma's sifting and trickery moves, the objective of Pastinha's ginga was to "distract the attention of the adversary in order to render him vulnerable to the application of your blows."[185] Pastinha emphasizes the importance of *malícia* (craftiness or cunning) and its connection with the ginga: "Capoeira . . . possesses a quality that renders it more dangerous—it is extremely crafty [*maliciosa*]. The capoeirista employs several artifices to fool and distract the adversary. He pretends to leave and comes back quickly. He jumps from side to side. He lies down and stands up. He advances and retreats. He pretends he doesn't see the adversary to lure him. He spins every which way and contorts himself in a deceptive and disconcerting 'ginga.'"[186] The rigid paths and positions delineated by Bimba are clearly of no concern here. Far from uniform repetitions following a path mapped on the floor with chalk, Pastinha's ginga involves pretending, spinning, and contorting. Pastinha's ginga requires the on-the-spot decision-making that could not be achieved through Bimba's predetermined repetitions. Rendering capoeira simultaneously dangerous and dance-like, the ginga embodied the syncretic relationship between violence and dance galvanized by Pastinha.

Malícia or *maldade*—the same craftiness ascribed to "the mulatto," "the Angola," and "the capoeira" racial types—is one of the core principles of Pastinha's capoeira philosophy.[187] In the illustrations that accompany his manuscripts, some drawn with pencil and blue ball-point pen, some made using a kind of printing or stamping technique, Pastinha labels attacks and defenses by number (1 for attacks, and 2 for defenses) and adds a few notes on the margins that are more like tips on execution than descriptions of these paired movements. *Maldade*, as well as the word "*dibre*,"[188] label both attacks and defenses, indicating moments of premeditated, deceptive attacks or skillful evasions. Similar to Bimba's sequences, these drawings constitute Pastinha's recommendations for effective attack and defense combinations, providing a glimpse into his teaching methodology.

The material published in the book *Capoeira Angola*, a few years later, differs remarkably from the manuscripts; rather than tips on paired uses of trickery to knowledgeable players, the overall tone of the book is that of a general introduction to Capoeira Angola—including its origins, its health benefits, its music, and finally an illustrated list of eleven movements.[189] The ginga, featured prominently among these eleven movements as capoeira's "fundamental characteristic," is curiously absent from Pastinha's earlier drawings, suggesting that the concept of ginga as a "move," separable from the rest of capoeira practice, may have been introduced and disseminated by Bimba's *Capoeira Regional Course*, published shortly before Pastinha's book.

Figures 1.6a and 1.6b Two illustrations from Pastinha's manuscripts. The drawing in pen and pencil on the left is labeled "The first exercises for an excellent development." In the print to the right, Pastinha writes, "The headbutt done sideways after a turn is dangerous," and "excellent defense/ dodge of the body." Note the numbers 1 and 2 labeling the players in this image.

Not always labeled as such, Pastinha's idea of maldade nevertheless weaves its way through *Capoeira Angola*. Several attacks and defenses rely on deception: in the *chapa de costas* (back kick), "the victim is hit, violently, when he thinks that the attacker is leaving"; the *cabeçada* (headbutt) "is a deceptive move, which could be applied against the thoracic region or the face, in a quick twist of the torso when the victim thinks that the attacker is leaving."[190] Pretending to leave and coming back with an attack is a recurring tactic in Pastinha's capoeira technique. However, Pastinha explains that "the capoeirista is 'suspicious' and doesn't let himself be fooled by the apparent retreat of the would-be attacker."[191] Rather than eliminating trickery in *Capoeira Angola*, Pastinha socially "improves" it through the dance-like beauty of the ginga, while simultaneously emphasizing its utility as self-defense. In an interview in his later years, Pastinha stated that capoeiristas should be "really deceptive, sly and crafty [malicioso]. Against strength, only this [can be effective]."[192] By dissociating maldade from the days when "troublemaker" capoeiristas were responsible for shameful incidents of public disorder, Pastinha revalues trickery as a powerful resource in Capoeira Angola, now practiced by sportsmen who were to employ it only in self-defense.[193]

Appropriating the discourse of eugenics, Pastinha called for a capoeira "perfect and free of errors, of a healthy and strong race."[194] However, Pastinha's search for perfection did not deny or seek to eradicate capoeira's Africanity; on the contrary, it was precisely through its Afro-diasporic corporeality that capoeira was to evolve into the "perfect" capoeira of the future: "Friends[,] the body is a great system of reason. Behind our thoughts there is a powerful lord, a wise stranger. I correct the realities, through the natural inversion of the logical order transforming the past into future."[195] Embodied knowledge, as an alternative epistemology that lies "behind our thoughts," is linked here (albeit tenuously, as adjacent thoughts) with Pastinha's goal of ushering capoeira into the future as an "art form" practiced by respectable citizens.

Like the idea of capoeira as a "fight disguised as dance," embodied knowledge that lies "behind our thoughts" establishes yet another syncretic relationship in the development of Pastinha's Capoeira Angola. Appropriating the ideas of doubleness and simultaneity inherent in the concept of syncretism—a widely disseminated model for understanding Afro-diasporic cultural continuities and "survivals" at the time—Pastinha constructs a capoeira capable of being simultaneously safe and violent, dance-like and potentially lethal, sport and high art, deceptive and "well-behaved." Through embodied knowledge, Pastinha imagined a capoeira able to dance-fight with and through these apparent contradictions, inverting and subverting a "logical order," and transforming a capoeira "doomed" by progress (as predicted by Carneiro) into the capoeira of the future.

CONCLUSION

Reconsidered through the framework of discursive appropriation, the grandiose positivist, eugenicist, and nationalist language that permeates Zuma's, Bimba's, and Pastinha's writings takes on new meaning. A comparison of the movement descriptions and photographs that illustrate these manuals with the nationalist ideas expressed through the text revealed numerous productive contradictions and dissonances. By enlisting my own body in the process of reading these manuals as instruction, I was able to challenge previous readings of these codifications projects as either rescue or loss of capoeira's traditions. I have shown how these three innovators appropriated the dominant discourses of their time—chiefly the notion of progress from Comte's positivism and the related idea(l)s of racial, physical, and national "improvement"—in order to stage capoeira in and as Afro-Brazilian modernity and legitimize this marginalized practice.

Zuma's intent to cultivate the "ill-defined" game of capoeiragem articulated notions of eugenic "improvement"; however, his use of numerous elements from street capoeiragem, as well as the rearticulation of the Africanist circle as a ring for matches of capoeiragem, point to a process of "cultivation" that did not deny, but instead reconfigured Afro-diasporic embodied epistemologies in hegemonic terms. Zuma's insistence on using terms such as nobility, elegance, beauty, and intelligence to describe capoeiragem— "the most beautiful game, the most intelligent sport"—when juxtaposed with the game's Afro-diasporic movement, reassigns these adjectives (associated at the time with European and Euro-Brazilian people and culture) to describe an Afro-diasporic movement practice.[196]

Bimba's codification of capoeira into sequences, his innovations allegedly borrowed from foreign martial traditions, and his multimedia teacherless training method embodied progress and modernity. Bimba countered racist notions of "brutish" blacks through an intelligent, highly codified "sport"; Bimba "improved" capoeira but did so through Afro-diasporic corporeality. Although Bimba's codification did indeed approximate capoeira to definitions of sport, as exemplified by his redefinition of the ginga as a callisthenic exercise, his systematized and codified Capoeira Regional staged elements from nineteenth-century capoeiragem, such as balões, as his own innovation. Developing a capoeira "for the weak to defend against the strong,"[197] Bimba presented his no-nonsense, streetwise, powerful fighting style through the language of efficiency, thus rearticulating in hegemonic terms the violence that was at the core of street capoeiragem practiced by valentões—the same violence used as justification for the criminalization of capoeira.

While Pastinha's "capoeira of the future" was institutionalized, it was never codified to the same extent as Capoeira Regional. Although Pastinha demanded obedience and "good behavior" from his students, Capoeira Angola continued to rely on improvisation and embody malícia, an element downplayed by both Bimba and Zuma in their efforts to legitimize capoeira(gem). Even though he choreographed a capoeira based on nonviolence, where players "showed" strikes rather than fully delivering them, Pastinha continued to insist on capoeira angola's violent, even lethal potential. Pastinha embraced these contradictions through a syncretic simultaneity that allowed him to appropriate positivist discourse while at the same time redefining progress, modernity, and even the future—when capoeira would be sought by legions of people—through Afro-diasporic corporeality.

Although these three innovators have been analyzed as having engaged in diametrically opposed projects, a comparative analysis of their respective approaches to the modernization and legitimization of capoeira has yielded more similarities than differences. These three practitioners of capoeira(gem) struggled with the same social stigmas against the practice and deployed similar tactics of legitimization. Through a series of discursive appropriations, they staged capoeira(gem) as both sport and folklore, both national and Afro-Brazilian, both modern and traditional.

CHAPTER 2

FIGHTING AND DANCING

Capoeira Regional and Capoeira Angola

At the same time as capoeiragem was being codified as capoeira, taught through preestablished sequences and institutionalized in private learning spaces, in public spaces — precisely where the practice of capoeira(gem) was explicitly prohibited by law — capoeira was being staged as both modern fighting style (*luta*) and folklore. In this chapter I consider how public matches and folkloric demonstrations shaped capoeira in mid-twentieth-century Salvador; former public "disorder" now reframed as staged spectacle. I examine the relationships between intellectuals, artists, and capoeira practitioners, and the intersecting and mutually constitutive discourses that gave rise to the two dominant styles of capoeira we know today.

I argue that the 1936 public capoeira matches that took place in Salvador, coupled with folklorist Édison Carneiro's writings about Bantu culture published in the same year, mark the beginning of a clear division between Capoeira Angola and Capoeira Regional. I identify the model of decline and rescue of culture, which guided early folklore studies in Brazil, as the intellectual environment that enabled the valorization of a "Pastinian" lineage of Capoeira Angola and the dismissal of Capoeira Regional as inauthentic in mid-twentieth-century Bahia. While I focus on the two innovators, Mestre Bimba and Mestre Pastinha, who have become synonymous with these two opposing styles of capoeira, I also consider the influences of other capoeiristas who although well known and respected at the time have been overshadowed by the codification and institutionalization projects spearheaded by Bimba and Pastinha.

MESTRE BIMBA'S CAPOEIRA REGIONAL:
STAGING A NEW CAPOEIRA

If I got up on the ring eleven years ago it was only so that the difference between
capoeiragem per se and the fighting technique that I teach would be established.
—Mestre Bimba[1]

Although the criminal code of 1890 officially prohibited the practice of capoeira "on the streets and public squares," capoeira continued to be tolerated as long as games were supervised by police.[2] Testimony from capoeira practitioners active in the early 1920s attests to a capoeira in public spaces restricted and supervised through a kind of permit system. Bimba remembers that "there were rodas of capoeira on the street corners, in front of dry goods stores, in the woods. The police prohibited [capoeira], and I, on one occasion, even paid 100 *contos* to play for two hours."[3] In his manuscripts Noronha recounts several instances of capoeira gatherings (*rodas*) that were broken up by police in the 1920s, often violently, for taking place without the required permits.[4]

It is in this context of violent repression of capoeira in public spaces that Bimba began teaching capoeira in private spaces in 1918.[5] By the mid-1920s Bimba's capoeira lessons had already attracted the attention of young white men from Bahia's elite: several medical and law students, including the sons of influential political families, went on to become the first formal Capoeira Regional graduates. The social prestige of his new students often allowed Bimba to circumvent police repression. In 1924, through the influence of one of its members, Joaquim de Araújo Lima, Bimba's group was able to stage a public exhibition of capoeira without police interference.[6] By 1927 Bimba and his students began receiving invitations to perform the "regional" Bahian fighting style for state officials, and by the early 1930s his group was performing in Salvador's soccer stadiums.[7] Bimba's claims of regeneration and improvement of a criminalized Afro-diasporic practice were made visible through disciplined white, male, middle/upper-class bodies engaging in wholesome physical culture, a display that undoubtedly played an important role in removing capoeira from under the "claws of police."[8] It is significant that Bimba's unsupervised capoeira in public spaces were *exhibitions* rather than informal rodas like the ones described by Noronha, where players from different capoeira groups tested their skills, more or less amicably, against each other. In fact, Bimba's students were forbidden to attend informal capoeira rodas.[9]

In 1936 Bimba's group was invited to participate in the July 2 Independence Day festivities in Salvador.[10] However, the struggle toward legitimization was far from over, and capoeira in public spaces was still met with skepticism. A short note accompanied by a photograph published in the newspaper A Tarde on July 1 exposes the lingering prejudices against the practice; the caption, printed below a photograph of Bimba in mid-handstand evading a headbutt, claims that capoeira had been "ill-placed" among the commemorations and "regrettably" would be part of the civic program of the following day.[11] Despite being criticized by the mainstream media, the invitation to take part in the official program of the July 2 commemoration reflects a changing public image of capoeira and foreshadows the de facto decriminalization of capoeira in the following year, 1937, marked by Bimba's successful attempt to register his school with the Department of Education, Health and Public Assistance.[12]

Although Bimba has been credited with single-handedly bringing capoeira out of illegality, a closer look at the increased interest in capoeira in the late 1930s suggests that although Bimba was an astute, intelligent man capable of recognizing opportunities and building valuable alliances, he must share the credit for the decriminalization of capoeira not only with the rest of the capoeira community—including those who were by then beginning to identify as practitioners of capoeira de Angola—but also with Bahian intellectuals who advocated for the elimination of the permit system and police supervision, not only for the practice of capoeira but also for the activities of Afro-Brazilian religious temples (candomblé houses).[13]

The second half of the 1930s saw an increased presence of capoeira in public spaces, in part as a result of an easing in police persecution. Capoeira practitioners willingly displayed their skills in public matches, while scholars and journalists eagerly observed and recorded these performances. By the mid-1930s, Bimba had cleverly begun taking advantage of the national infatuation with boxing matches in order to propel capoeira into the limelight; Bimba and his students began participating in public matches not only against other capoeira practitioners but occasionally also against boxers and jiu-jitsu fighters.

The 1936 pugilistic season (February–July) took place in a stadium located at Odeon Park in Salvador.[14] Bimba participated as both fighter and referee in several matches, offering capoeira unprecedented media visibility. The controlled visibility of the ring/stage provided practitioners with the opportunity to stage a "reformed" capoeira, transforming "tough guys" into respectable athletes, and later into dancers, entertainers, and artists. Although no photos of the stadium are available, it is likely that this was a rustic, temporary structure, a raised boxing ring (referred to as *tablado*, which can also mean "stage") surrounded by bleacher-type seating.[15] Although centrally located, Odeon Park, where the stadium was erected, was not exactly prime real estate. Novelist Jorge Amado described the area in his nonfiction "guide" to the city of Salvador, *Bahia de todos os santos*, first published in 1945: "Next to the [Sé] church there was a kind of Park used for everything. For meetings of suspicious couples, for scandalous fornications, for beggars to rest after a hard day at work, a strategic spot where cheap whores invited sailors for love, for poor variety theater, fairs, various celebrations. Sometimes a ring would be set up in the center of the park for boxing fights.... There were public toilets at the park and their regrettable odor permeated almost the entire Square."[16] The stadium, described as a "modern center for entertainment and sports matches," was likely part of an effort to improve the conditions of the area.[17] Despite being a modest structure, with a capacity for at most two hundred patrons, the stadium held the grandiose title of Odeon Center and Stadium for Physical Culture, sharing the term "physical culture" with the name of Bimba's school, the Center for Regional Physical Culture.[18]

Newspaper reports describe sold-out matches attended by enthusiastic audiences who favored games marked by agility, violence, and efficiency.[19] Bimba and his students were prominently featured in this season; while his students always confronted each other in preliminary matches and were listed as "amateurs," Bimba himself was paired with other established practitioners of capoeiragem, his matches listed in the "professional" category.

Reporters praised players' "agility and feline contortions," and audiences enthusiastically cheered decisive kicks that projected the loser to the ground "in great style."[20] In the inaugural fight between Bimba and Henrique Bahia, Bimba won after applying a "decisive kick to the chest," causing his adversary to fall. "Projections" seemed to be a crowd-pleaser: news reports highlight violent kicks that projected the opponent to the ground;[21] also of note was the use of throws (*balões*), the practice of grabbing and throwing that was present in capoeira since at least the nineteenth century, which Bimba expanded into his "abandoned waist" techniques and claimed as his own innovation.

With his new, efficient capoeira style, Bimba was declared the winner of all matches in which he participated. However, his invincibility was not without controversy. Reporters challenged the point system used in the fight between Bimba and Zey, suggesting that the referee favored Bimba unfairly.[22] In the fight between Bimba and Victor H.U., Bimba's use of a hand blow to the ear (*galopante*) prompted an indignant H.U. to storm out of the ring in midcontest, claiming that the strike was forbidden in capoeira. Samuel de Souza (likely the same capoeirista known as Samuel Querido de Deus) wrote a letter to a local newspaper protesting the results of Bimba versus Zey, claiming that "the capoeira introduced by Bimba at Odeon Park is not the legitimate from Angola," and adding that he would gladly accept a challenge if one was issued.[23] These veterans of capoeiragem—Zey, Victor H.U., Samuel de Souza, among others—did not take Bimba's glorification lying down.

Throughout this controversy, it is telling that there are no reported objections to kicks and throws, no matter how forceful, effective, or violent. The protests, instead, address unfair practices such as referee favoritism or use of prohibited strikes. Although it is clear from Samuel's letter that practitioners of capoeiragem were beginning to embrace ideas of authenticity, the range of movement accepted by both "camps" during these matches indicates that the dance-like Capoeira Angola taught by Pastinha, where violence is shunned and kicks are suggested, barely grazing the opponent, had not yet been developed as a separate style.

Indeed, Bimba's agenda seemed to be to distinguish his new capoeira from capoeiragem. During this season, Bimba issued challenges to specific players through local newspapers, a practice common at the time in boxing and jiu-jitsu;[24] significantly, these were players of the "old style" of capoeira.[25] Through these challenges, Bimba sought to publicly question the efficiency of the "old" capoeira style and assert his own "improved" and modern capoeira training technique as the solution. His undefeated status, achieved fairly or otherwise, offered proof of the superiority of his "Bahian regional fighting style" (*luta regional Bahiana*).

Despite the controversy over legitimacy and fairness, however, both the public and the press seemed enamored with Bimba's "modern" fighting style. A contest between two players of the style "from Angola,"

Henrique Bahia and Américo Sciência, was loudly jeered by a packed stadium. Bimba, not coincidentally the referee of this match, did not miss the opportunity to declare the players' style "too antiquated."[26] To repair the damage done by this fiasco and show the public that capoeira was indeed a "real" fighting technique, Bimba and Aberrê[27] immediately stepped in and delighted the audience with an "excellent demonstration not in the program, being enthusiastically applauded."[28] As noted by Abreu, these two fighters "turned the ring into a stage."[29] Ironically, Bimba chose Aberrê, a player of the "antiquated" capoeira style, rather than one of his own students to stage a demonstration of capoeira's efficiency.

Aberrê, immortalized through Pastinha's accounts as the catalyst for the founding of the first Capoeira Angola center, and consecrated as part of the "old guard" of capoeiragem, understood what the audience wanted just as much as the politically savvy innovator Bimba. The fact that the two players knew each other's styles well enough for a successful impromptu demonstration of capoeira provides further evidence of more similarities than differences between Bimba's new Regional style and the "antiquated" style from which Bimba hoped to distance himself. It is likely that Aberrê and Bimba shared the same movement vocabulary of attacks and defenses, including knowledge of the partnered throws Bimba went on to codify as "abandoned waist"; a few well-performed "projections" and "feline contortions" may have offered the crowd the thrill they sought, drawing cheers and applause.[30]

The compatibility of Bimba's and Aberrê's styles signals a capoeira not yet fully divided into the angola/regional binary, despite Bimba's claims to the contrary. The capoeira matches at Odeon Park, however, mark the beginning of this division. The season included matches by Bimba against "Angola" players as well as intrastyle games; these games, as one reporter wrote for the newspaper *Diário da Bahia*, would help answer the question of which capoeira style would be "more accepted by our audiences — Capoeira Angola or Bahian Regional?"[31] Although there are no subsequent reports of a "winning" style, this question continued to guide the development of the two styles throughout the twentieth century.

Despite Bimba's success at Odeon Park, by the mid-1940s he had begun to distance his capoeira from the ring, possibly as a result of jiu-jitsu star George Gracie's confession of his own participation in rigged matches, which he claimed to be a common practice.[32] In an attempt to assert capoeira's integrity as a legitimate fighting style, Bimba issued a lengthy declaration in the newspaper *A Tarde*: "Regional is not a fighting style for the 'ring.' It doesn't obey the conventional rules for pugilistic encounters, it is a fight for decisive situations and [in its practice] anything goes. . . . Recognizing that Regional is not a fighting style for the 'ring' I never presented it as such. If I got up on it eleven years ago it was only so that the difference between capoeiragem per se and the fighting technique that I teach would be established."[33] Here Bimba stresses that capoeira is intended for "decisive situations," that is, actual confrontations where "anything goes" (and hence not suited for public matches on rings), and clarifies his purpose in having participated in public matches: to distinguish his Capoeira Regional from street capoeiragem associated with "tough guys" and criminality. By staging his capoeira at Odeon Park as an efficient and respectable fighting style, Bimba brought unprecedented interest and visibility for a new, modern capoeira that simultaneously established its other: an old, traditional capoeira "from Angola."

ÉDISON CARNEIRO: RESCUING CAPOEIRA DE ANGOLA

The [capoeira] fight is a demonstration of the prodigious agility of the angola [type],
who executes the most difficult corporeal movements without any effort, smiling.
—Édison Carneiro, *Negros bantus*

The 1936 matches at Odeon Park, as Bimba had hoped, indeed established the difference between his new and "improved" capoeira and street capoeiragem. However, these matches also mark the beginning of the transformation of capoeiragem into another emerging capoeira style: capoeira de Angola, legitimized through claims of authenticity and purity.

Some of the first mentions of "Angola" as a style of capoeira date from 1936; in addition to the use of the term in the newspaper reportage of the games at Odeon Park, Édison Carneiro published an article in the newspaper *O Estado da Bahia* titled "Capoeira de Angola."[34] In this article Carneiro briefly mentions Bimba's recent success in the ring, but declares capoeira de Angola "the purest" capoeira and therefore best suited for his analysis. While it is unclear whether Carneiro actually coined the term "capoeira de Angola," his endorsement of both the term and the style greatly influenced the consolidation of this new "old" style of capoeira.[35] Carneiro, who went on to become one of the leaders of Brazil's folkloric movement and one of the most influential scholars of Afro-Brazilian culture of his generation, collaborated with leading capoeira practitioners in the process of "rescue" and "re-Africanization" of capoeira, and its reformulation as the "Angola" style.

In 1936 Carneiro was a twenty-four-year-old recent law school graduate, described by anthropologist Ruth Landes as "a mulatto, of the tan-skinned color called 'pardo' in Brazil" from a poor but respected "Negro" family.[36] The son of Antônio Joaquim de Souza Carneiro, a local expert in Afro-Brazilian folklore, Carneiro learned early on to valorize Afro-diasporic popular culture, and such values went on to shape his research, his writings, and his political activism. Carneiro began his career as a journalist. Writing for the Salvador newspaper O Estado da Bahia, he published a series of articles aimed at changing public opinion about candomblé, hoping to end the police repression of Afro-Brazilian houses of worship in Bahia.[37] For Carneiro, his scholarship was inseparable from the lived experiences in the black community.

In 1936 Carneiro was no doubt a regular audience member at the capoeira matches at Odeon Park. In his article "Capoeira de Angola" he reports that "lately, in the space at Odeon Park at Sé Square, some capoeiristas have measured forces, attaining great box office success."[38] Carneiro notes Bimba's appeal to middle-class students and clarifies that "this black man, of rare agility, reassured me that his capoeira was no longer the one from Angola, but an extension of it, since it uses many blows from other fighting styles, from Roman wrestling to boxing and jiu-jitsu. So much so that Bimba has dubbed his special capoeira Bahian regional fight [technique]."[39] As I have shown, despite the possible incorporation of foreign borrowings, Bimba's style at this time shared more similarities than differences with capoeiragem and the emerging style "from Angola." However, Bimba insisted on having invented a new style of capoeira, reassuring Carneiro that "his capoeira was no longer the one from Angola." Consciously presented as modern and eclectic, Capoeira Regional did not interest Carneiro, whose focus was on studying and valorizing Brazil's African heritage. In his 1936 article, after acknowledging Bimba's success among the middle class, Carneiro goes on to praise the "real" representatives of capoeira in Bahia: "The blacks tell me that the greatest capoeirista of Bahia is Samuel 'Querido de Deus,' a fisherman of noteworthy quickness of the body. Much talked about are the capoeiristas Maré (stevedore), Siri do Mangue, from Santo Amaro, and a man named Oséas, who opened a school in Rio."[40] Significantly, these were black capoeiristas elected by "blacks" themselves as among the greatest, listed here as authentic representatives of the Angola style.[41] That Bimba was also black seems to be overshadowed by the fact that his acclaim came from white middle-class university students and the mainstream media rather than from the black community.

Carneiro further Africanizes the "Angola" style by connecting it with "the Angola" racial type: "The [capoeira] fight is a demonstration of the prodigious agility of the angola [type], who executes the most difficult corporeal movements without any effort, smiling."[42] Even though in this passage Carneiro revisits previous theories of racial types, his research departed from the biological determinism of his predecessors by focusing on cultural rather than biological "traits." Carneiro's ideas also differed from those of his colleagues writing on Afro-Brazilian culture; while the superiority, purity, and complexity of Yoruba culture[43] are taken for granted by Arthur Ramos and Gilberto Freyre,[44] Carneiro draws attention to the Bantu legacy in Brazil, considered to be impoverished and almost lost.[45] In *The Brazilian Negro*, published in 1934, Ramos explains that the Bantu legacy was at that time "an unpublished page in our religious ethnography. And this is due to many reasons. First is the bantu mythic poverty, in relationship to the Sudanese, a fact recognized by all ethnographers, which resulted in its almost complete absorption, in Brazil, by *gegê-nagô* fetishism."[46] Inherently "poor," Bantu cultures barely survived contact with their "stronger" Ewe-Yoruba (*gegê-nagô*) counterparts, widely accepted as the most significant "Sudanese" cultural strain in Brazil. For Ramos, what was left of Bantu culture was now "disfigured and transformed" and "almost unrecognizable."[47]

These allegedly impure, vanishing Bantu cultures—the "Angola" heritage in particular—intrigued Carneiro, leading him to publish *Negros bantus* in 1937.[48] In this book, Carneiro proposes that some of Bahia's most significant embodied cultural practices—samba and capoeira—were in fact of Bantu origins. In the chapter devoted to capoeira de Angola,[49] Carneiro disrupts the Yoruba purity and superiority paradigm by declaring capoeira de Angola "the purest" form of capoeira.[50] However, Carneiro does not explain how capoeira de Angola relates to an overall "Bantu legacy"; the evidence he presents is restricted to language, such as the use of the word *Aloanguê* in song lyrics, which he associates with Luanda, the capital of Angola. Carneiro does, however, offer a detailed list of capoeira attacks and defenses, including references to forbidden strikes and the use of a point system.[51] Carneiro's interest in embodied culture, which went on to become the focus of Brazilian folklore studies under his leadership, distinguished his work from the work of his contemporaries.

Carneiro was the main organizer of the Second Afro-Brazilian Congress. Held in Salvador in January 1937, this congress marked a turning point in the way scholars from various disciplines converged to discuss the Afro-diasporic presence in Brazil. With the support of his friend Aydano do Couto Ferraz and the guidance of Arthur Ramos, Carneiro organized a congress that sought to distance itself even further from biological and racial determinism than did the First Afro-Brazilian Congress, held in the city of Recife in 1934. Carneiro was openly criticized by U.S.-trained sociologist Gilberto Freyre, the organizer of the first congress, who claimed that Carneiro's conference would not only be too political but would also lack academic rigor: "The organizers of the present congress are only interested in the most picturesque and most artistic side of the topic: the 'rodas' of capoeira and samba, the drum beats of 'Candomblé,' etc. This side is very interesting, and in Bahia it will have a unique color. But the program followed by the first congress was a more extensive program, including the elements of scientific research and work—dry elements, but equally important to social studies."[52] Indeed, Carneiro's work was "too political"; one of the overt aims of the congress was to end police interference in both capoeira and candomblé gatherings. Freyre sought to discredit the second congress for its interest in the "picturesque" and the "artistic"—his euphemisms for Afro-diasporic embodied practices such as capoeira, samba, and candomblé, which he deemed suitable for adding "local color" to the congress, but not appropriate as the main focus of a "scientific" congress.

In a bold move, Carneiro invited Afro-Brazilian practitioners of candomblé, samba, batuque, and capoeira to participate in the congress, not as objects of study but as experts on Afro-Brazilian culture, participating in debates on equal standing with their "academic" counterparts. Although demonstrations were included in the program, where practitioners performed their "traditions" to scholars, Carneiro took the scholars to visit these cultural producers in their communities and places of worship rather than asking them to stage performances at the conference site. As for the capoeira performance, despite Bimba's popularity at the time, or indeed because of it, Carneiro invited Samuel Querido de Deus, considered "the greatest capoeirista of Bahia," to lead the capoeira demonstration at the second congress.[53]

While the first congress made modest advances toward breaking away from racial determinism, it still included papers based on cranial measurements and color indices that equated blackness with social degeneration. By placing Afro-Brazilian candomblé, capoeira, and samba practitioners side by side with scholars writing about them, the second congress invited scholars to appreciate the intellect of these cultural producers and rethink previous "scientific" approaches that associated blackness with "degeneration." In addition, this format also disrupted the binary categorization of knowledge as "folk" and "erudite." By focusing on embodied knowledge, Carneiro gave voice and authority to Afro-Brazilian cultural producers, acknowledging them as experts in their fields. Carneiro spearheaded the creation of the "Union of Afro-Brazilian Sects"; in collaboration with candomblé leaders, he drafted a petition demanding religious freedom, which argued the unconstitutionality of subjecting black religions to police control while leaving other religious gatherings undisturbed.[54] Carneiro also intended to create a "Union of Capoeiras of Bahia," a project that unfortunately was never carried through.[55]

Carneiro's activism and his valorization of Afro-diasporic practices differed vastly from the nationalist approach to culture sponsored by the Getúlio Vargas dictatorship, which regarded "folk culture" as an ingredient for crafting a unified national identity rather than something with intrinsic value. Folk "traditions" were to be collected, improved, and transformed into a modern "national culture." Musicologist and ethnographer Mario de Andrade (1893–1945) and composer Heitor Villa-Lobos (1887–1959) played leading roles in fashioning national culture during the Vargas regime, Andrade as an advocate for the continued collection and mapping of music and dance traditions from "the interior," and Villa-Lobos as the promoter of mass choir spectacles and leader of the national choir and musical education program known as Canto Orfeônico (Orpheonic Song).

Andrade served as director of the Municipal Department of Culture of São Paulo (1935–38); he authored the preliminary study for the creation of the National Artistic and Historical Patrimony Service (an agency responsible for overseeing the classification and preservation of "national patrimony") and founded the Society of Ethnography and Folklore, both in 1936.[56] Andrade was influential in the process of imagining Brazil-ian modernity—to be found in the urban centers of Rio de Janeiro and São Paulo—in contrast to Brazil's "primitive roots," preserved in the "in-terior" of the country.[57]

Villa-Lobos was appointed director of the Superintendence of Musi-cal and Artistic Education of schools in the capital, then Rio de Janeiro, making Canto Orfeônico an obligatory part of the school curriculum. Although Villa-Lobos did not coin this term or invent this choir style— which had already been in use in Normal Schools in the state of São Paulo during the early twentieth century—he turned this practice into a na-tional musical education program.[58] Canto Orfeônico instilled discipline and collectivity in school children through a repertory of songs drawn primarily from "national folklore."[59] Villa-Lobos also "improved" the folk through his compositions, which drew from folk melodies in creating a uniquely Brazilian "erudite" culture.

The "folk" material collected in the 1930s and 1940s was "improved" through a European "erudite" music aesthetic and deployed to fashion national cohesion. Although Carneiro did not align himself with Var-gas's nationalism, his theories of cultural production were guided by notions of decline and loss—the flip side of the rhetoric of regeneration and progress of Vargas's New State. In *Negros bantus*, Carneiro himself re-produced this narrative when he stated that "despite everything—despite the Negro's better adaptation to Brazil's social milieu, despite the police reaction, despite the advanced process of decomposition and symbiosis of capoeira against other fighting styles—capoeira, especially capoeira de Angola, reveals an enormous vitality. Progress, however, sooner or later, will deal the final blow [on capoeira]. And capoeira, along with other elements of black folk-lore, will recede to small coastal villages."[60] Despite its "enormous vitality," capoeira was doomed to recede to small coastal villages. The model of folklore as always already endangered was so powerful that Carneiro failed to consider the possibility that capoeira de Angola's "enormous vitality" would in fact lead to its expansion rather than its decline. And as a scholar and activist, Carneiro saw it as his mis-sion to protect and preserve the folklore of a community in which he was both personally and professionally invested.

Carneiro was an active member of the National Folklore Commission (Comissão Nacional de Folclore), a committee organized in 1947 by the Brazilian Institute of Education, Science and Culture and the Ministry of

STAGING BRAZIL

Foreign Relations to represent Brazil at UNESCO (United Nations Educational, Scientific and Cultural Organization). The goals of the commission, according to its first director, Renato Almeida, were to research and collect data, protect folklore from "regression," and assure folklore's continuity through its dissemination in the national school curriculum.[61]

The commission's mission of collection, preservation, and protection was guided by the ideology of progress and decline. By 1950, however, Carneiro had begun questioning the notion of folklore as inherently endangered. In his essay "Folklore's Dynamics" (Dinâmica do folclore), Caneiro begins with a quote by folklorist Richard Dorson that summarizes his revised approach: "The idea that folklore is dying out is itself a kind of folklore."[62] Carneiro posited that folklore was not made up of static survivals from the past, but was rather a result of creative, dynamic processes that reflected not only the present but also the future of the population. He rejected the prevailing idea that cultures were divided into "primitive," "folk," and "erudite" stages of evolution, and insisted that folklore should not be understood as produced only by the "folk"; instead, he proposed that folklore was a result of a dialectic process "where the whole society participates, either actively or passively."[63]

The idea that folklore was produced by everyone (rather than just "the folk") disrupted the very hierarchies on which Brazilian folklore studies were based. Proposing folklore as dynamic and dialectic, Carneiro struggled with the issues of collection, protection, and preservation. He nonetheless justified folklore studies' mandate to collect, map, and record, arguing that records of "folk" traditions could be used for a possible reinstatement and reconstruction of lost folk traditions in the future. However, Carneiro cautioned that such collecting and archiving should be carried out without "denying or removing [folklore's] spontaneity or its prospects of progress."[64]

In 1958 the National Folklore Commission was transformed into a full-fledged government agency, the Campaign for the Defense of Brazilian Folklore (Campanha de Defesa do Folclore Brasileiro). Under Carneiro's leadership, the mission of the campaign was summarized as follows: "(a) to promote recording, research and assessment, training and specialization courses, exhibits, publications, and festivals; (b) to protect folkloric patrimony, the arts and popular celebrations; (c) to organize museums and libraries, film and audio archives and centers for documentation; (d) to maintain an exchange with similar organizations; (e) to disseminate Brazilian folklore."[65] A mission based on recording, assessing, exhibiting, and protecting raises questions about folklore's "spontaneity." If change was inevitable and even welcomed, why was it so important to select, record, and build folklore archives? Most important, what was the Campaign for the *Defense* of Brazilian Folklore defending folklore against?

Carneiro answers this question in his essay "Protection and Restoration of Popular Festivities": a folklorist's duty was to protect folk festivities in decline or in danger of disappearing.[66] Although he considered loss as inevitable in the dynamics of folklore, Carneiro insisted on protection even while acknowledging the contradiction in this proposition. Though the act of protection constituted an "erudite interference," Carneiro, citing a UNESCO recommendation, clarifies that this interference was justified as an invaluable service to the Brazilian nation if carried out with the utmost care and discretion:

> To protect means to intervene, and usually it would be paradoxical that intervention would be advised or carried out by folklorists, but, if we are able to act with "extreme discretion," allowing the folkloric festivities "a lot of freedom," the intervention—for the imminent national interest it will acquire, returning to the people, without violating its character, its customary moments of pleasure—can be forgiven. We would be providing Brazil a service that nobody else can provide.[67]

Carneiro indeed believed that the folklorists' discreet intervention in defense of folk traditions was a matter of national interest, and thus justified, despite the paradox it presented. This essay was the basis for a list of recommendations made by the National Folklore Commission in 1957, a year before it was to become the Campaign for the Defense of Brazilian Folklore. Among these recommendations were the inclusion of folklore in school curricula, the organization of festivals and competitions with the intent of providing performance opportunities for folk ensembles, and the restoration of "lost" folk festivities in collaboration with former practitioners.[68]

The Brazilian folklore movement—focusing on advocacy and policy making at the expense of critical reflection on the complexities and paradoxes of "defending" folklore—profoundly influenced the division of capoeira, fueling the "rescue" of capoeira de Angola and redefining capoeira as folklore in the 1950s. Framed as part of Brazil's vanishing Bantu heritage, capoeira de Angola fit perfectly into this paradigm of restoration. Furthermore, by valorizing a capoeira of Bantu origins — culturally "weaker" and thus more easily hybridized than the Yoruba or "Sudanese" cultural material — Carneiro positioned capoeira closer to processes of *mestiçagem*,[69] worthy of preservation as national heritage. Brazilian folklore studies' mission of defending, protecting, and restoring culture was based on the notion of folklore as endangered, threatened by progress and modernity; even with the awareness that the idea of folklore as dying out was "itself a kind of folklore," the mission of preservation endured.

Innovation that was perceived as individual creativity or deriving from foreign borrowing, such as Capoeira Regional, fell outside the definition of folklore as "anonymous" and "collectively accepted." Although artists were allowed and even expected to innovate, "folklore bearers" (*portadores de folclore*), often browner and poorer than their artist counterparts, were not. *Bearing* folklore, folklore bearers were vessels of culture, carrying it in their bodies and transmitting it to folklorists who would protect this "patrimony" in their archives and museums. Through this model, individual acts of innovation and invention were occluded and individuals from the "folk" were reduced to "bearers" of culture. Invention and artistry by "non-erudite" individuals was permitted as long as it remained anonymous and fell within "traditional" parameters; this authorless cultural product was valued as long as it could be recorded, protected, archived, and co-opted, quite literally, as patrimony — property of the nation (*patria*).

The development of capoeira, however, challenged this model with its many innovators who openly claimed credit for their contributions. Zuma invented new kicks and proposed new rules for capoeiragem; Bimba renamed the form and claimed as his innovation moves from the past as well as borrowings from foreign martial arts; Pastinha, the guardian of capoeira's "tradition," took pride in his innovations in the institutionalization (which he called "organization") of Capoeira Angola. A movement form based on improvisation — in-the-moment decision-making based on a malleable vocabulary of attacks and defenses — in fact demands constant innovation; yet, individual innovation, a core aspect of capoeira, came in direct conflict with folklore's concept of anonymous cultural production. By framing innovations as "rescued traditions," however, capoeira de Angola practitioners syncretically appropriated folklore studies' mandate of restoration of dead or dying folk forms to legitimize innovation. As I will discuss below, the recommendations to protect and restore made by Carneiro and his cohort indeed influenced the development of capoeira de Angola in the late 1930s (referred to as Capoeira Angola since the mid-1940s), a form perceived to be threatened by the modernity and the popularity of Capoeira Regional.

MESTRE PASTINHA'S CAPOEIRA ANGOLA: GUARDING TRADITION

More than sixty years old. For sure. However, still, there is no better capoeira player . . . than Querido de Deus. Let Juvenal come, a twenty-year-old young man, let the most celebrated of all come, the most daring, the most agile, the most technically proficient, let anyone come, and Samuel, the Beloved of God shows that he is still the king of capoeira in the Bay of All Saints.
—Jorge Amado, *Bahia de todos os santos*, first edition

Mestre Vicente Pastinha is older than seventy years old. He is a small mulatto, of astounding agility, of uncommon endurance. The adversaries follow one another, one young man, another and yet another young man, disciples or colleagues of Pastinha, and he defeats them all and never gets tired, never runs out of breath.
—Jorge Amado, *Bahia de todos os santos*, tenth edition

Bimba's innovations, by his own accounts drawn from several sources to modernize capoeira, fell outside the permitted limits of folklore's dynamics, despite the "prospects of progress" purportedly welcomed in Carneiro's model. Rather than "bearing" capoeira's tradition, Bimba caused great controversy by overtly borrowing and innovating. Bahia's intellectual elite—folklorists, artists, and culture bureaucrats—openly and unambiguously disapproved of the modernity of Capoeira Regional. Writing in the late 1960s, Carneiro stressed that "the popular, folkloric capoeira, a legacy of Angola, has little [or] nothing to do with Bimba's school."[70] According to Carneiro, Bimba had distanced himself from his roots, from the "legacy of Angola." Guilherme Simões, a columnist for the newspaper A Tarde, a folklore enthusiast, and an influential presence in Salvador's Tourism Department,[71] when asked about the great capoeiristas of the past, categorically stated, "I don't [even] consider Bimba, because he wasn't an *angoleiro*."[72] One of Bimba's harshest critics was Bahian novelist Jorge Amado, the prolific modernist writer who "brought to life" Freyre's romantic notions of a Bahia made harmonious and hospitable through mestiçagem.[73] In Amado's *Bahia de todos os santos*, aptly subtitled *guia das ruas e dos mistérios da cidade do Salvador* (a guide to the streets and the mysteries of the city of Salvador), the author addresses the "problem" of Capoeira Regional:

> A great debate takes place nowadays in the capoeira community in Bahia. It happens that mestre Bimba went to Rio de Janeiro to show the people in the Lapa [neighborhood] how capoeira is played. And there he learned moves from catch-as-catch-can, jiu-jitsu, and boxing. He mixed all this with capoeira Angola, the one born out of a black dance, and returned to his city speaking of a new capoeira, "capoeira regional." Ten of the most respected capoeiristas told me, in an open and democratic debate we had about mestre Bimba's new school, that the "regional" is not to be trusted and it's a disfigurement of the old capoeira "angola," the only true [capoeira].[74]

This text exemplifies the alliances forged throughout the 1940s and 1950s between Bahia's "traditional" capoeira community—threatened by Bimba's success—and an intellectual elite intent on "preserving" Bahia's African heritage. Amado distances Bimba's innovations from Bahia, relocating them to Rio de Janeiro, where Bimba was allegedly introduced to foreign fighting techniques. The capital of Brazil at the time, Rio de Janeiro came to symbolize modernity while Bahia was refashioned as its counterpart: the cradle of Brazilian tradition. Folklorists, anthropologists, novelists, and visual artists interested in the preservation and restoration of Bahia's African heritage collaborated with "traditional" capoeira practitioners to promote capoeira de Angola, reimagining it as one of the staples of Bahia's cultural tourism experience. And even though Bimba was certainly as much of a capoeira veteran as the capoeiristas interviewed by Amado, Bimba himself was excluded from the debate and his innovations dismissed as a "disfigurement."[75]

In the first edition of *Bahia de todos os santos* (1945), Amado acknowledges, albeit reluctantly, both Bimba's acclaimed skills as a capoeirista and the success of his Capoeira Regional. He assures the reader, however, that Bimba's skills could be matched or surpassed by those of Samuel Querido de Deus, the same player repeatedly praised by Carneiro in the late 1930s. But despite favoring Querido de Deus, Amado concludes the chapter with a description of a capoeira contest between Bimba and Querido de Deus, two of Bahia's best capoeiristas: "You can see [capoeiristas] playing gracefully in popular festivals to entertain the people, showing their skills, singing their songs, the orchestra playing. It's the world's most beautiful fight[ing form] and you should consider yourself lucky if one day you're able to see mestre Bimba and Samuel Querido de Deus in a capoeira contest." While in 1945 Amado could not ignore Bimba's fame and skill even though his personal sympathies lay elsewhere, in the eighth edition of *Bahia de todos os santos*, published in 1960, this same passage is modified, and Bimba and Querido de Deus (who died not long after the publication of the first edition) are replaced by two capoeira de Angola players, Pastinha and Traíra.[76]

In this last section, I trace Pastinha's rise to the iconic status of sole guardian of capoeira's traditions, and the transformation of capoeira *de* Angola, an origin, into Capoeira Angola, a style able to compete with Capoeira Regional. As I have shown, Pastinha was the ideal candidate for the role of guardian of capoeira's "tradition"; divorced from capoeira's violent past through an alleged twenty-nine-year hiatus, Pastinha physically matched the "Angola type," an agile mulatto unencumbered by black's "brute strength." With the support of Bahia's intellectual and artistic elite, Pastinha achieved in ten years the same level of recognition and acclaim that took Bimba thirty years to attain. Pastinha found himself in the right place at the right time, and was chosen as Querido de Deus's successor after his death sometime in the late 1940s. Rather than a mere pawn of Bahia's "traditional" capoeira advocates, however, Pastinha was a clever innovator who worked within the "permitted" range of folklore's dynamics to create a "traditional" capoeira style that was nevertheless as modern as Bimba's. By framing his innovations *as* tradition, removing danger, and emphasizing ritual, Pastinha successfully transformed Capoeira Angola into the "true" capoeira.

Both Carneiro and Amado had been enamored by Querido de Deus. In *Bahia de todos os santos*, in a chapter titled "Characters" (Personagens), Amado profiled Querido de Deus, describing him as man in his sixties, with graying hair and brown, tanned skin of "indefinite" color who could, despite his age, beat any twenty-year-old capoeirista. Even "the most famous, the most daring, the most agile, the most technical" capoeirista was no match for Querido de Deus.[77] Not much is known about Querido de Deus other than the laudatory mentions and brief descriptions found in Amado and Carneiro.[78] Following her research trip to Brazil in the late 1930s, Columbia University anthropologist Ruth Landes (a student of Ruth Benedict and Franz Boas), whose local guide was Carneiro himself, wrote a detailed description of a capoeira game involving Querido de Deus—the only account of the playing style that earned the admiration of two of Bahia's most influential intellectuals. In her book *The City of Women*, Landes recounts her experience watching a game between Querido de Deus (Beloved of God) and Onça Preta (The Black Leopard):

> Watchers were crowded four deep around a wide circle.... Edison and the others helped me push front, and we were glad of the diversion. Two capoeiristas were squatting there facing the musicians. One was the champion Beloved of God, with the Christian name of Samuel. He was tall, black, middle-aged and muscular, a fisherman by trade. His challenger was The Black Leopard, a younger man, shorter and fatter. They were barefooted, wearing striped cotton jersey shirts, one with white trousers, the other with dark, one with a felt hat, the other with a cap which he later changed into a hard straw hat.... The orchestra opened the events by strumming an invocation, and this monotonous accompaniment too was essential to the occasion. It was a sort of whining nasal-toned framework within which the men executed acrobatic marvels, always to the correct beat, while the musicians chanted mocking verses.... Beloved of God swayed on his haunches while he faced his opponent with a grin and gauged his chances. The fight involved all parts of the body except the hands, a precaution demanded by the police to obviate harm. As the movements followed the musical accompaniment, they flowed into a slow-motion, dream-like sequence that was *more a dancing than a wrestling*. As the law stipulated that capoeirists must not hurt each other, blows become acrobatic stances whose balancing scored in the final check-up, and were named and classified.[79]

The game witnessed by Landes was marked by "acrobatic marvels" and a "slow-motion, dream-like" quality she recognized as belonging to the category of dance. The "precaution demanded by police" forbidding the use of the hands, and the law that "stipulated that capoeirists must not hurt each other," mentioned here, are not discussed anywhere else in the literature of the time. Although this was likely not an official "law," it may have been an informal agreement between local police and capoeira practitioners. During Landes's visits in the late 1930s, capoeira was in fact still written into the criminal code, even though police persecution had been eased (in part as a result of the advocacy of Carneiro, who undoubtedly informed Landes of capoeira's blurry legal status).[80] In *Negros bantus*, Carneiro also mentions that "the hands never work in attacks," but he lists balões as one of the exceptions to this rule.[81] While using the hands for grabbing and throwing was acceptable, using the hands for striking or handling straight razors or knives, a resource not uncommon in nineteenth-century capoeiragem, had been largely discarded.[82]

Landes was concerned by the "manner of the performance" she observed, which, she concluded, "robbed capoeira of its original sting." Landes continued: "The police had removed the sting, and the blacks had converted the remains into a weird poignant dance. Did the songs carry meaning to the people now? Did they recall the struggles that inspired them, or did they merely dramatize black men, as candomblé dramatized black women?"[83] Here Landes expresses her concern that capoeira had lost its "sting"—its efficiency as a form of combat—due to police interference and legal prohibitions. Landes's conclusion that what "remained" of capoeira had been converted into a "weird poignant dance" echoes Melville Herskovits's model of cultural survivals. However, it simultaneously acknowledges capoeira's dynamism and creative ability to adapt—a model ahead of her time (perhaps influenced by conversations with Carneiro), for which she was openly and viciously criticized.[84]

Carneiro shared Landes's assessment of capoeira as a combat tradition that shed its violence to be transformed into a harmless game: "The name capoeira is given to a game of dexterity that has its remote origins in Angola. It was a fighting tradition before, very precious in the defense of freedom or the rights of freed blacks, but both police repression and new social conditions, about fifty years ago, transformed it finally into a game, a kind of lazing around among friends. With this innocent character capoeira remains in Bahia."[85]

Writing in the late 1960s, Carneiro dated the transformation of capoeira into an "innocent" game to the 1910s and 1920s, during the height of police persecution of capoeira in Bahia. The narrative of a fighting tradition that fulfilled its destiny and *finally* "evolved" into an "innocent" game was based on an idea of progress achieved through conformity and

Figure 2.1 Prior to establishing his school at the historic Pelourinho Square,
Pastinha's Centro Esportivo de Capoeira Angola operated in temporary locations
such as the one captured here by Verger in the late 1940s. Note the flag bearing
the school's logo in the upper right corner of the photograph.
Photo Pierre Verger © Fundação Pierre Verger, c. 1947.

loss. The attribution of innocence to capoeira and comparisons to dance
feminized capoeira, further distancing it from the violence ascribed to
male bodies, particularly black male bodies. Not surprisingly, given his
advocacy to end police persecution of both candomblé and capoeira
gatherings, Carneiro expressed no desire to protect or restore the use of
weapons or the violence of capoeira.

Reimagining capoeira de Angola as an innocent, dance-like game that
had shed its violence was instrumental in dissociating capoeira from violence and criminal activity. Performances by gray-haired "old" men like
Querido de Deus and Pastinha further tamed this former combat form
into a harmless pastime. Pastinha was fifty-two years old when he returned to capoeira—hardly a young man. In the same way that Amado
highlighted Querido de Deus's physical vigor despite his age in the first
edition of *Bahia de todos os santos* (1945), in the revised tenth edition (1964)
Amado extends the same praise to Pastinha: "Mestre Vicente Pastinha

is over seventy years old. He is a small mulatto, of astounding agility, of uncommon endurance. When he starts to "play," the impression in the audience is that this poor old man, with gray hair, will fall in two minutes, taken down by the young adversary or even for being out of breath. But, oh! Big mistake!, none of this happens. The adversaries follow one another . . . and he defeats them all and never gets tired, never runs out of breath."[86] Not only did Pastinha's skin color match Querido de Deus's brown, mestiço skin, but Pastinha was similarly an "old man" whose vigor was atypical for his age. Pastinha's image as an old man—quite literally embodying the past—was instrumental in establishing Capoeira Angola as the "traditional" capoeira. Pastinha's age lent Capoeira Angola legitimacy through a connection with the past, a connection seen as lacking in Bimba's capoeira style. Through his "old" Afro-diasporic body, Pastinha further conflated Africa with the past; through his tireless and youthful performance, Pastinha restored vigor to a "dying" tradition.[87]

After teaching at various temporary locations for the previous decade, with the support of Bahia's artistic and intellectual elite Pastinha relocated his school to the historic center of Salvador in 1955. This permanent site for Pastinha's Capoeira Angola Sports Center not only assured a steady flow of students; it also provided a strategically located stage for ongoing capoeira demonstrations, attended by tourists and scholars who followed Amado's advice: "Those who go to Bahia should not miss the extraordinary spectacle of mestre Pastinha playing capoeira in the middle of the room, to the sound of the berimbau."[88]

Amado's endorsement was crucial to Pastinha's success, in the same way that Carneiro's and Amado's endorsements had been for Querido de Deus.[89] Carneiro had invited Querido de Deus rather than Bimba to demonstrate capoeira de Angola at the Second Afro-Brazilian Congress in 1937; when Ruth Landes asked to see a capoeira demonstration, Carneiro took her to watch Querido de Deus;[90] when a film crew interested in filming a capoeira game came to Amado for a recommendation, he led them to Querido de Deus.[91] Now these same recommendations were directed to an address that quickly became synonymous with capoeira's tradition: Pelourinho Square, number 19, the home of Pastinha's Capoeira Angola Sports Center, renamed Academia de Capoeira Angola in the 1960s.

Writing in the late 1960s, Carneiro uses the new term "academia" to refer to Pastinha's new school, a "proper place" for capoeira practice.[92] Having a proper, fixed place for instruction and demonstrations was crucial if Capoeira Angola was to compete with Capoeira Regional, which was taught in not one, but two permanent locations since the mid-1950s. The difference between Pastinha and Querido de Deus was precisely the fact that Pastinha, following in Bimba's footsteps, "academicized" and formalized his capoeira instruction. Like Bimba, Pastinha held formal graduation ceremonies and awarded diplomas to his students. His school was so successful that Pastinha hired other accomplished capoeiristas to teach there under the title of *contra-mestres*.[93] Like Bimba, Pastinha was referred to as a "mestre" (teacher), while Querido de Deus is always mentioned without this title, even by his ardent admirers.[94] Through teaching, Pastinha formalized and disseminated the same nonviolent, dance-like capoeira style practiced by his predecessor Querido de Deus, transforming the informal practice of capoeira de Angola into a *style* known as Capoeira Angola. Pastinha's conscious staging of his capoeira as a defined and unique style can be seen in his school's motto, written on the backdrop used in a commemorative demonstration documented by Finnish ethnographer Helinä Rautavaara in 1964: "*Academia de Capoeira, só Angola!*" (Academy of Capoeira, only Angola!), by which Pastinha meant, "For your capoeira academy, choose only Angola — accept no imitations!" (see figure 2.2).

Pastinha was the ideal candidate for succeeding Querido de Deus, not only because of his age and skin color but because of his ability to give continuity to Querido de Deus's nonviolent style of capoeira, conforming to the new classification of capoeira as a folk tradition. Pastinha, however, struggled with the losses that might ensue from this reframing of capoeira as a "weird poignant dance." Its "sting" gone, would the new capoeira "merely dramatize black men," as Landes had wondered? In his manuscripts Pastinha theorized a capoeira that could simultaneously retain its efficiency as self-defense and serve as entertainment: "Capoeira is divided into three parts, the first is the common, the one that we see, for the public, the second and third part, it is reserved in the self of those who learned and is reserved in secret, and it takes time to learn."[95] For Pastinha, the "common" capoeira, the one for the public, was distinct from the other two layers of the practice, kept in the "self" of the practitioners. The second and third layers were reached only through an embodied understanding of capoeira, the result of long-term commitment and apprenticeship. This uneven division of capoeira — one third available to the outside gaze and the other two thirds available only through practice (hidden

Figure 2.2 *The school at Pelourinho, no. 19, provided Pastinha with a permanent home for instruction and demonstrations. By the mid-1960s Pastinha's school had been renamed Academia de Capoeira Angola. Note the school's initials, ACA, at the top of the backdrop, as well as its motto, "Academia de Capoeira, só Angola!"*
Photo by Helinä Rautavaara, c. 1964. Courtesy of the Helinä Rautavaara Museum.

in the "self")—allowed for a capoeira capable of pleasing audiences as a nonviolent, feminized, dance-like acrobatic spectacle while simultaneously rehearsing its efficiency as a combat form. Having set up this simultaneity between capoeira for the "self" and capoeira as spectacle, Pastinha successfully embraced the practice of staging capoeira for tourists, filmmakers, and anthropologists and cleverly reimagined capoeira for the stage. Pastinha professionalized capoeira demonstrations and, like Bimba, began performing by invitation at clubs, hotels, and for the cameras of paying filmmakers.

The 1950s marked a time of rapid expansion for the tourism industry in Salvador. Pastinha seized this opportunity for visibility and financial gain and, with a select group of students, began exhibiting his Capoeira Angola in both formal and informal settings, both public and private functions. Sometime in the mid-1950s, Pastinha composed the following press release: "The Capoeira Angola Sports Center has the pleasure of inviting the Bahian society, the authorities, the press and the general public to watch the first Official Public Demonstration of Genuine Capoeira Angola, to take place on the 24 of this month, at 8:30 pm at the Brazilian Sport Club at the Oceania-Barra building. Tickets Cr$ 20,00."[96] Pastinha knew full well the importance of reaching out to the press, the authorities, and to "society" in order to stage a new image for "traditional" capoeira. By announcing the "first" official public demonstration of "genuine" Capoeira Angola, Pastinha implicitly dismisses previous demonstrations of capoeira de Angola as unofficial and inauthentic. Pastinha reinvents Capoeira Angola as his own, devaluing prior informal capoeira demonstrations in public spaces, such as the famous games documented by photographer Pierre Verger at the dock of the old public market in Salvador, the Mercado Modelo (Model Market), and also erasing previous formal demonstrations, such as the one by Querido de Deus and his group at the Second Afro-Brazilian Congress, organized by Carneiro in 1937.

Between 1955 and 1956 Pastinha and his students engaged in at least eight formal demonstrations, listed as follows in his manuscripts:

> The first was for the Bishop of France, at the Belvedere, the second was for some tourists at the Sé square on a stage, the third for a Medical conference from São Paulo at [blank space] in Salvador ..., the fourth [for] the Bahian Company of Navigation and Tourism ... the fifth at the Naval Base in Salvador, the sixth at the Abaeté Lagoon[97] ... the seventh on the grounds of the Vitória [club], the eighth at the ramp of the Model Market for a film recording, and more exhibitions on tour.[98]

The last performance on this list, "at the ramp of the Model Market for a film recording," was ironically a reenactment for the camera of the kind of capoeira from which both Bimba and Pastinha tried to dissociate themselves: informal performances for tourists at the dock of the public market.[99] Performing Afro-Brazilian "tradition" for foreign dignitaries (the bishop of France), navy officers, doctors from São Paulo (in Bahia

Figure 2.3 French photographer Pierre Verger documented informal
capoeira matches at Salvador's municipal Mercado Modelo (where several capoeiristas
worked as stevedores or shoe shiners). In these matches, points were often tallied and
the winner would take home the money collected from the crowd.
Photo Pierre Verger © Fundação Pierre Verger, c. 1947.

for a medical conference), and common tourists alike required Pastinha and his students to be on their "best behavior," showing control and
composure. Pastinha's "shown," held-back kicks, which barely grazed the
opponent or stopped "just before the chosen target," reassured the public that capoeira had been redeemed of its violent past of straight razors
and tough guys, having been transformed into a dance-like performance.

One of the key elements that rendered capoeira dance-like was music.
Although music surely accompanied capoeira prior to tourist demon-

strations, it is likely that the musical ensemble as we know it today—a set grouping of percussion instruments (*bateria*) present in any capoeira roda—only became a mandatory aspect of capoeira practice through its staging as a folklore. In 1964 Pastinha explained that "the musical or rhythmic ensemble is not indispensable for the practice of capoeira, but, it is evident that the 'game of Capoeira Angola' to the rhythm of the typical ensemble that accompanies the melodies and improvisations of the singers acquires grace, tenderness, charm and a mysticism that stirs the souls of the capoeira players."[100] While not indispensable, capoeira to music acquired grace, tenderness, charm, and mysticism. These dance-like qualities brought out by the musical ensemble stirred not only the practitioners' souls but undoubtedly the souls of audience members as well. In addition, grace, tenderness, and charm feminized Capoeira Angola, distancing it even further from the masculine violence with which it had been associated.

In the 1940s, before Pastinha codified the musical ensemble, informal capoeira gatherings often included a few musicians playing one or two *berimbaus* (the musical bow iconic of capoeira), one or two *pandeiros* (tambourines), and not infrequently a guitar (see figure 2.4). By the 1960s, Pastinha's ensemble contained between two and four *berimbaus*, two or three *pandeiros*, a *reco-reco* (bamboo or gourd scraper), and an *agogô* (double bell) (see figures 2.2 and 2.5).[101] Pastinha in fact turned an informal and optional approach to musical accompaniment into a mandatory, "typical" musical ensemble that has become equated with capoeira's ritual and tradition.

Aside from displaying capoeira's grace and charm, these demonstrations also included a didactic element. Pastinha created set patterns for demonstrations, which often included isolated kicks and short movement sequences performed by "the old man" himself, displaying his atypical endurance and virtuosity while simultaneously introducing the "lay" public to Capoeira Angola. Mestre João Grande (João Oliveira dos Santos, b. 1933), who began studying with Pastinha in 1950 and participated in many demonstrations, remembers that Pastinha would show a movement and state its name, introducing audiences to the movement lexicon and techniques of Capoeira Angola.[102] Displaying the strength, endurance, and agility of a much younger man, Pastinha would perform thirty to forty repetitions of the same movement, followed by a demon-

Figure 2.4 Photographer Voltaire Fraga captures an informal
street roda, c. 1940, accompanied by a guitar and two berimbaus.
Courtesy of the Arquivo Histórico Municipal de Salvador, Prefeitura Municipal Collection.

stration of attacks and defenses paired with his students.[103] Gildo Alfinete, who studied with Pastinha throughout the 1950s and 1960s, remembers, "Once I counted: he did 25 consecutive rabos de arraia."[104]

A recording made by folklorist Alceu Maynard Araújo circa 1950, as
part of a collection of scenes of Brazilian folklore entitled Veja o Brasil (See
Brazil), gives us a glimpse into Pastinha's demonstrations.[105] Maynard set
up each shot and later edited the footage, thus creating a narrative and
framing the recording according to his own research interests. Although
Maynard may have requested specific spatial arrangements or movement
sequences, it is likely that this film is representative of Pastinha's demonstrations in the early 1950s.[106]

Maynard's camera begins by zooming in on the emblem of the Centro

Figure 2.5 Pastinha (dressed in white) playing a game at a demonstration,
accompanied by his musical ensemble featuring four berimbaus.
Photo by Helinä Rautavaara, c. 1964. Courtesy of the Helinä Rautavaara Museum.

Esportivo de Capoeira Angola, clearly identifying the capoeira group in
the film. Edited footage of each percussion instrument in action catalogs
these artifacts up close, even though the available recording technology
does not capture their sound. This segmented, close-up gaze also introduces the movement footage: a pair of legs, wearing black dress pants and
leather shoes, steps from side to side in a bouncy step-hop pattern—the
ginga. A wider shot reveals these legs as Pastinha's, wearing the group's
uniform. From this initial collector's gaze, now the camera moves in and
assumes the point of view of Pastinha's contender; after repeating the
ginga a few times, Pastinha "attacks" the camera with a circular front
kick (meia lua de frente), repeating this pattern with a headbutt (cabeçada), a
straight front kick (chapa de frente), and a straight back kick (chapa de costas).

In the next scene, Maynard captures a wider view, perhaps from a second-story window or a ladder. The editing alternates between two games (one between Pastinha and a student, and another between two students) from two points of view. In both games the players exchange slow, controlled circular kicks that purposefully miss or barely graze the opponent in a dance-like performance not unlike the one observed by Landes in the late 1930s. Two players are shown briefly engaging in a *chamada*, or call.[107] The chamada today is considered capoeira angola's most significant "ritual" aspect. In a movement pattern that has been compared to ballroom dance, the players' hands meet in a momentary truce; one player challenges or "calls" the other by breaking the flow of the game and standing with raised open arms.[108] The other player answers this call by placing his palms against the caller's palms; connected, the players take a few steps back and forth until the player who initiated the call indicates an attack, prompting the responding player to resume the game.[109]

Fluidly shifting their weight from feet to hands, the players suggest rather than deliver strikes. These kicks and headbutts, now performed with grace and safety to musical accompaniment, displace capoeira's violence to the past while simultaneously rehearsing this same violence. In two moments that have stirred much controversy since this film has been posted on the video-sharing site YouTube, Pastinha and his students perform partnered throws (*balões*) for the camera. Turning his back on his student, Pastinha squats, grabs him by the arms, and flips him, safely, over his own body. In the next game, one of Pastinha's disciples, João Pequeno, steps back from the other player and raises his hands in preparation for a handstand. His contender meets João Pequeno in mid-handstand, grabs him by the waist, and momentarily anchoring his weight on his shoulder, flips him into the air.[110] The recent rediscovery and dissemination of this film destabilized the assumption, held at least since the early 1960s, that moves involving contact between players were Bimba's innovation, "connected strikes from the waist deriving from foreign fighting techniques, something not seen in traditional games, where capoeira players don't grab [each other] and they barely touch."[111]

As I have shown in chapter 1, the practice of grabbing and throwing balões was likely an intrinsic part of capoeira(gem) since at least the late nineteenth century, as described by Mello Moraes. Writing in the late 1930s, Carneiro also mentions balões as part of the movement vocabulary of capoeira de Angola,[112] and Maynard's film confirms the presence

Figure 2.6 *Two players prepare for a balão during a street roda.*
Photo by Voltaire Fraga, c.1940. Courtesy of the Arquivo Histórico
Municipal do Salvador, Prefeitura Municipal Collection.

of balões in Pastinha's capoeira in the early 1950s. However, by the time Bimba published his multimedia booklet/LP *Capoeira Regional Course* in the early 1960s, balões were no longer considered part of capoeira's "tradition."

While Bimba claimed and reimagined partnered throws as his own innovation—one that allegedly increased capoeira's efficiency as self-defense—Pastinha discarded balões for being too dangerous. Mestre João Grande, who began his apprenticeship in 1950, remembers that Pastinha removed several strikes he considered dangerous, such as *dedo nos olhos* (poking the eyes), *cotovelada* (elbow strike), as well as several balões.[113] In his manuscripts, written throughout the 1950s, Pastinha lists several movements that should be avoided in demonstrations, and balões were among them; however, a few balões are still present in the manuscripts' illustrations. In the process of shedding (or concealing) capoeira's violence, Pastinha omitted balões and foregrounded the chamada, which has since become the "trademark" of capoeira angola. While balões require contact, grabbing, and weight-bearing, chamadas *suggest* contact much in the same way that kicks are suggested in Pastinha's capoeira, coming close but "barely grazing" their target.

It is revealing that Maynard's film includes both chamadas and balões, but a film shot thirteen years later featuring Pastinha's group includes two chamadas, while balões are absent altogether. Simply titled *La Capoera*, this film by Bernard Taquet and Serge Ehrler, sponsored by the airline Panair, places capoeira as the centerpiece of a traveler's experience in Bahia.[114] Like *See Brazil*, *La Capoera* is a moving postcard of Brazil, and more specifically an invitation to visit Bahia. Using the ocean as a backdrop, the camera focuses on Pastinha's group playing a game on a beach. Like Maynard, Taquet and Ehrler zoom in on each musical instrument before showing the entire ensemble. Unlike *See Brazil*, however, this film does not include the didactic portion of the presentation where Pastinha shows each movement in isolation. Rather than overtly collecting and preserving, this short documentary assumes a voyeuristic gaze, creating the illusion of inconspicuously witnessing an unstaged, unmediated capoeira game on a deserted beach. The footage, edited from several camera angles and probably several takes, gives the viewer the impression of watching a game in its entirety. In only three minutes of edited footage, we see two chamadas: in one instance, one player opens his arms and invites the other to gesture a headbutt against his belly; in the next chamada, one player raises his right arm, palm facing out, inviting the other to meet him in a mirrored gesture. This film indicates that by the early 1960s Pastinha had renounced balões in favor of the subtle contact of the chamadas.

Today chamadas are considered to be a marker of tradition, believed to have been lost in capoeira regional.[115] While Bimba likely discarded chamadas in his process of imagining a modern, efficient capoeira, Pastinha discarded balões in his efforts to present Capoeira Angola as a nonviolent, ritualized, dance-like "folk" tradition. Although Pastinha presented himself as the guardian of "tradition," it is clear that he selected movement material, innovated, and "improved" capoeira as much as

Figures 2.7a and 2.7b Illustrations of chamadas from Pastinha's manuscripts are strikingly
similar to photos of chamadas by French photographer Pierre Verger from the late 1940s.
Photo Pierre Verger © Fundação Pierre Verger, c. 1947. Print by Vicente Ferreira Pastinha, c. 1955.

his "modern" counterpart Bimba. In the same way that Bimba invented
modernity by claiming existing movement practices as his own "improvements," Pastinha invented capoeira's tradition. Choreographing nonviolence, gentility, and respectability, Pastinha did away with the grabbing
and throwing of balões, favoring instead the more delicate, subtle, and
gentle suggestion of contact, where open hands touch lightly and never
grip, or where a head indicates a headbutt without applying force or in-
flicting harm.

The dance-like quality of chamadas may have been what attracted
French photographer and ethnographer Pierre Verger to photograph
throughout the 1940s several capoeiristas engaged in chamadas. Verger's
influence on Pastinha can be seen in several of the prints and drawings
included in Pastinha's manuscripts, where it is evident that he has traced
Verger's photographs to illustrate his musings and recommendations on
Capoeira Angola (see figures 2.7 and 2.8). (Note that the images are mirrored, which indicates that Pastinha used a kind of printing or stamping technique based on his initial tracing of the photographs.) Perhaps

Figures 2.8a and 2.8b *Verger's interest in capoeira's chamadas is reflected on the drawings and prints that illustrate Pastinha's manuscripts.*
Photo Pierre Verger © Fundação Pierre Verger, c. 1947.
Print by Vicente Ferreira Pastinha, c. 1955.

it was Verger's interest in chamadas that influenced Pastinha's choice of transforming this break in the game into a movement pattern iconic of Capoeira Angola.

By "taming" capoeira and approximating the practice to definitions of folklore—by turning it into a dance—Pastinha gained the respect and admiration of folklorists, intellectuals, artists, and bureaucrats who helped him gain recognition both for himself and for his capoeira style. Pastinha's Capoeira Angola was consistent with Carneiro's definition of a harmless capoeira: "The capoeira [players] of Bahia call their game *vadiação*—and capoeira is no more than that, in the way that it is done at public festivals in the city. The players have fun, pretending to fight."[116] Carneiro uses the term *vadiação*, literally vagrancy or loitering, a term used at the time (and still used today) to refer to capoeira. It is significant that Carneiro states the game is "no more than" *vadiação* specifically at public festivals, where "players have fun, pretending to fight." Carneiro echoes the syncretic model articulated by Pastinha, where a capoeira available to the public—gentle and dance-like—differs from other, more violent layers of the practice, hidden from public view and accessible only to insiders of the practice. Although Carneiro does list balões as part of capoeira de Angola in the 1930s, writing in the late 1960s, after Pastinha's influence had been well established, he describes a capoeira where

> the contenders don't grab each other, but, keeping their distance, free, [they] come into contact only in the precise moments of attack and defense. In particular, capoeira strikes make exclusive use of the feet, while the hands serve as support for the movements of the entire body. . . . The ginga of the capoeira [player], underscored by the songs to the sound of the berimbau and pandeiros, lends the game an appearance of dance.[117]

With help from the musical ensemble, the ginga, codified as capoeira's "basic step" by Bimba, is deployed in Capoeira Angola as a way of lending the game an *appearance* of dance. Furthermore, in this new capoeira "disguised as dance," players not only kept their distance and refrained from grabbing each other, but they refrained from using their hands at all for striking, using them instead as support.

In collaboration with Carneiro, Amado, Verger, and others, Pastinha established a dance-like capoeira that went on to be accepted as the original capoeira "from Angola," part of Brazil's Bantu legacy that should be protected and preserved. Pastinha's Capoeira Angola also embodied the gentility, cordiality, and civility ascribed to the Bahian people. In *Bahia de todos os santos*, Amado paints a portrait of "the Bahian": "[The Bahian] worships the past and dreams of the future. The Bahian who makes amiability into a true art, who is astute to the extreme, who is cordial and comprehensive, relaxed and trusting. . . . Nobody knows how to carry on a conversation like a Bahian. Slow talking, with round phrases, long clarifying pauses, with precise, careful gestures, with tame smiles and big laughs."[118] In his "guide to the streets and to the mysteries of the city of Salvador," Amado echoes the language of racial determinism when he defines the essential (and essentializing) traits of "the Bahian." Here Amado reinforces the stereotype of the unhurried (i.e. lazy), slow-talking, happy, and content (in spite of disadvantaged socioeconomic conditions) *mestiço* citizen of the tropics. With slow, rounded-out cartwheels and precise, careful kicks that barely graze the opponent, Pastinha, following on the footsteps of Querido de Deus, invented a capoeira that embodied Amado's "destination image" of both Bahia and "the Bahian."

Cordiality and amiability, indispensable traits in the hospitality industry, were foundational building blocks in the construction of both "Bahian culture" and "traditional capoeira" in the mid-twentieth century. According to Amado, writing on the flap of the cover of Pastinha's 1964 *Capoeira Angola*, Pastinha was both "a master of capoeira de Angola and of Bahian cordiality. . . . The first in his art; master of agility and courage, of loyalty and fraternal coexistence. In his School, at the Pelourinho, Mestre Pastinha constructs Brazilian culture, of the best and most real [kind]."[119] Pastinha, along with other capoeira mestres who actively participated in Bahia's tourism industry, constructed "real" Brazilian culture for tourist consumption—one marked by the gentility and conviviality of "the Bahian."

At his school, the Academia de Capoeira Angola, located in the Pelourinho historic district, Pastinha and his students held regular demonstrations for tourists. The text on the back cover flap of *Capoeira Angola* reminds readers that "the capoeira Angola academy—of Mestre Pastinha—located in the traditional Pelourinho hill, in order to cater to the numerous tourists who visit Salvador, offers special performances on Tuesdays, Thursdays and Fridays starting at 7pm. On Sundays, at 3pm."[120] Mestre João Grande remembers that during tourist season the school was often packed with tourists watching these demonstrations.[121] In the revised tenth edition of *Bahia de todos os santos* (1964), Amado refers to these demonstrations: "On Sundays well-known capoeiristas come and the celebration starts in the afternoon. Those who visit Bahia should not miss the extraordinary spectacle of Mestre Pastinha playing capoeira in the middle of the room, to the sound of the berimbau."[122]

By the mid-1960s Capoeira Angola, along with samba and candomblé, had become a staple of the Afro-Bahian tourist experience. Pastinha's school, now a tourist destination, provided both tourists and scholars with ritualized spectacles of Afro-diasporic agility. Amado describes what visitors to Pastinha's school might witness: "The string berimbaus play the ritual music, calling the players. Mestre Pastinha fills the room with his presence, his agility, his dizzying ballet. Capoeira de Angola, a Brazilian fighting form par excellence."[123] Pastinha's and Amado's emphasis on capoeira's music (and its conflation with ritual) further approximated the practice to fantasies of a "primitive" but controlled Africa, bound by ritual and tradition. Capoeira Angola, now tamed and feminized as dance, gained distinction through comparisons with Euro-

Figure 2.9 Pastinha (in white shirt) playing a game for a packed
house at his Academia de Capoeira Angola at the Pelourinho Square.
Photo by Helinä Rautavaara, c. 1964. Courtesy of the Helinä Rautavaara Museum.

pean ballet, while also retaining capoeira's status as national fighting
form "par excellence."

CONCLUSION

Bimba, regarded by Bahia's intellectual elite as the pariah of "traditional"
capoeira, was nevertheless extremely successful; in spite of relentless
criticism, his success was such that his demonstrations often filled sports
arenas and gymnasiums. Bimba cleverly co-opted Vargas's New State discourse of improvement to legitimize and promote his new capoeira style.
Like Andrade and Villa-Lobos, Bimba began with "the folk"—capoeira de
Angola—which he went on to "improve," allegedly through foreign ma-

Figure 2.10 João Pequeno
(left) and João Grande (right),
Pastinha's most famous
disciples, playing capoeira
during a fundraiser for the
aging mestre directed by Emília
Biancardi at the Mosteiro de São
Bento in 1968.
Photographer unknown.
Courtesy of Emília Biancardi.

terial from other fighting traditions. Although Bimba most likely did borrow from foreign martial arts (e.g., the hand strike to the ear, or *galopante*, which Victor H.U. protested in the 1936 matches at Odeon Stadium), he also "disguised" capoeira's tradition as improved modernity by reclaiming and codifying balões as his "abandoned waist" technique.

Pastinha embraced capoeira's "destiny"—finally "evolving" and turning into a harmless dance-like game—and downplayed its violence in public demonstrations. Embodying the gentility and cordiality through which "the Bahian" was reimagined, Pastinha removed several strikes he considered dangerous, such as *dedo nos olhos* (poking the eyes), *cotovelada* (elbow strike), and *golpe de pescoço* (strike to the neck), in addition to removing balões from Capoeira Angola in the 1960s. Even though Pastinha brought as many, if not more innovations to capoeira as did Bimba, his changes were congruent with the construction of tourist-friendly Afro-Brazilian "traditions" in mid-twentieth century Bahia. Although Pastinha insisted that the "real" capoeira (one that held on to its efficiency and violence) was kept safe from the demands imposed by the tourism industry, many of his adaptations for the stage bled through to the offstage practice of his students. For example, his removal of balões from Capoeira Angola was in fact not restricted to public demonstrations, and "Pastinian" Capoeira Angola was largely passed down to a new generation of disciples without balões.

Pastinha was one of several capoeira mestres whose work was deeply influenced by the tourism industry. He was, however, possibly one of the mestres who profited the least from the economic opportunities generated by Bahia's tourism boom. With the help of Amado, Pastinha was awarded a small retirement pension by the city of Salvador for "services rendered to the tourism industry."[124] However, this was "a meager, paltry sum for someone who gave . . . so much to Bahia."[125] Although late in Pastinha's life a few of his students began offering "shows" for tourists— which included samba, maculelê, as well as a scripted retelling of capoeira's history of violence—as a way of collecting money for their aging mestre,[126] Pastinha never joined the trend of presenting fully produced, staged folkloric shows complete with samba, dances from candomblé, and maculelê, the staples that went on to become the Brazilian "folkloric suite" of the 1970s and 1980s.

CHAPTER 3

CAPOEIRA FOR THE TOURIST STAGE
Bimba and Canjiquinha

I n the early 1950s the city of Salvador began developing strategies for organizing its nascent tourism industry.[1] In 1953 the city created the Diretoria Municipal de Turismo, or DMT (Municipal Tourism Directorate), a department charged with overseeing the development of the tourism industry, and in 1959 the DMT was renamed Departamento de Turismo e Diversões Públicas, or DTDP (Department of Tourism and Public Recreation). By the late 1950s tourism had become a national priority, and Bahia—one of the first Brazilian states to develop a tourism industry—had become one of Brazil's main cultural tourism destinations, featuring Afro-Brazilian culture as a major tourist attraction.[2]

Afro-Brazilian practices such as capoeira, samba, and candomblé became central to Bahian cultural identity during the first half of the twentieth century. As tourism in Bahia began to be organized into an industry in the 1950s, live performances of these Afro-Brazilian practices for tourists became increasingly popular, and several capoeiristas seized the opportunity to organize shows featuring capoeira. Focusing on the innovations for the stage of two influential capoeira mestres, Mestre Canjiquinha (Washington Bruno da Silva, 1925–94) and Mestre Bimba, I challenge the assumption that tourist performances necessarily entail "loss" of tradition, and propose that these tourist shows in fact offered performers a space for invention and creativity in a setting that allowed for the recontextualization of aspects of capoeira that were otherwise being phased out offstage, such as capoeira's grappling techniques known as *balões*.

The association between capoeira's participation in the tourism industry and an alleged loss of its traditions can be traced back to the influential writings of ethnographer and cultural policy maker Waldeloir Rego (1930–2001). In his oft-cited *Capoeira Angola: Socio-Ethnographic Essay*, published in 1968, Rego redirects the blame for capoeira's "loss of character" from Capoeira Regional to Salvador's ubiquitous folkloric shows for tourists.[3] Although his four-hundred-page "socio-ethnographic essay" is still considered one of the most important texts in the capoeira literature, Rego's role as a longtime functionary of Salvador's tourism department is rarely acknowledged. In this chapter I recognize Rego's role as a tourism bureaucrat and curator of city-sponsored folklore, a position that reframes his writings and sheds light on his influence in staging capoeira as folklore. Despite the title of his book, Rego does not focus exclusively on capoeira angola and offers the reader a much more nuanced analysis of capoeira than his predecessors Édison Carneiro and Jorge Amado—staunch defenders of a vanishing capoeira from Angola.

I return to Bimba's influential participation in shaping modern capoeira, this time focusing on his participation in the tourism industry, an aspect of Bimba's legacy largely ignored in much of the capoeira scholarship. While Pastinha removed contact from capoeira by practically erasing balões, Bimba and his students amplified and theatricalized this contact, creating spectacular choreographed fight sequences for the stage complete with flying kicks and machetes. Rather than downplaying violence, Bimba's students staged this violence within the safety of choreographed sequences known as *escretes*.

Unlike Bimba and Pastinha, Mestre Canjiquinha made a name for himself staging capoeira rather than defining a particular style or school of capoeira. In fact, Canjiquinha openly and vehemently denied the existence of separate styles of capoeira; he claimed that there was only one capoeira and that Angola and Regional were mere marketing strategies. These successful styles indeed resulted in a capoeira conceptualized in binary terms; most if not all capoeira practice that fell outside of this binary has been left out of the capoeira literature. By shedding light on Canjiquinha's work, I shift the discourse about capoeira away from lingering preoccupations with loss and retention and toward questions of invention, inventiveness, and authorship. I propose a revisionist reframing of Canjiquinha's work as choreography in order to foreground its originality, inventiveness, and modernity, thus disrupting the binary folklore bearer/creative artist—the former bound to "bear" unchanged tradition and the latter expected to create original, unique, and innovative works of art.

Like his predecessor Édison Carneiro, Rego had a university education in law but became a self-taught scholar of Afro-Brazilian culture. Rego's interest in Afro-Brazilian culture, like Carneiro's, was intimately connected to his own Afro-Brazilian background and his own Bahianness.[4] On the front jacket flap of Rego's *Capoeira Angola*, Jorge Amado writes that despite his book knowledge and his tendency to "devour libraries," Rego's "deepest knowledge comes from the people, from Bahian popular daily life, which is his life, his rich quotidian, his flesh and his blood."[5] Also like Carneiro, Rego worked as a cultural policy maker, occupying several administrative posts in municipal and state government from the early 1950s until his retirement in the 1990s.[6]

However, Rego's opinions diverged dramatically from those expressed by Carneiro and Amado, who praised and supported capoeira de Angola while dismissing Capoeira Regional. Writing in the late 1960s, Rego recognizes the (by then) established "tradition" of Capoeira Regional. He expresses admiration for Bimba and disagrees with Carneiro's assertion that Bimba's capoeira had nothing to do with the "legacy of Angola":[7]

> This is a rushed statement by Édison Carneiro and proof that he never watched or studied Mestre Bimba's capoeira. Even stylized capoeira, performed on theatrical stages, on television and danced in the samba groups of Bahia and [Rio de Janeiro], still has a lot of this legacy of Angola, that Édison Carneiro speaks of, and even more so with Mestre Bimba's capoeira, which, as I have said before is the very same as Capoeira Angola, only with the adoption of new Oriental and European elements, resulting in the so-called connected moves [*golpes ligados*], inexistent in Capoeira Angola.[8]

Rego expresses much greater tolerance for innovation than his predecessors, acknowledging the presence of the "legacy of Angola" even in "stylized" capoeira performed on theatrical stages and on television. Rather than fretting over Bimba's gradual innovations, Rego worried about the rapid changes he witnessed in the late 1960s: the proliferation of capoeira schools and folkloric shows in response to an expanding tourism industry. With the publication of Rego's *Capoeira Angola*, heated debates about the authenticity of Bimba's Capoeira Regional gave way to debates sur-

rounding the authenticity of folkloric shows directed by capoeira practitioners.

Despite his respect for Capoeira Regional, Rego's thinking still reflected the same model of decline and the subsequent need for protection and preservation that undergirded the folklore movement, as well
as the preoccupation with tradition that guided much of the intellectual production in Bahia. By the time Rego wrote *Capoeira Angola*, he had
worked side by side with Bahia's leading folklorists, historians, and journalists such as Hildegardes Vianna, Cid Teixeira, and Guilherme Simões.
Between 1959 and 1964 Rego was a functionary of the DTDP under the
directorship of Carlos Vasconcelos Maia, whose administration worked
closely with Bahia's intellectual and artistic elite in shaping the development of Bahia's tourism industry. Maia often consulted with novelist Jorge Amado and visual artist Carybé, in addition to being well connected in the local press. He believed that an emphasis on history and
culture was fundamental to the development of tourist activity in Salvador.[9] Consequently, Bahian tourism emerged as cultural tourism in the
early 1960s—foregrounding folk festivities, candomblé, and capoeira as
well as Bahia's African-influenced culinary traditions.

In 1964 a U.S.-backed military coup d'état deposed democratically
elected president João Goulart, replacing him with General Castelo
Branco, the first of a series of four-star generals appointed to the presi-
dency by a military junta in a period known as Brazil's *ditadura militar*
(1964–85). The first of seventeen executive orders called "institutional
acts" (*atos institucionais*), the AI-1, among other measures, suspended the
job security of public employees—mayors were replaced, and subsequently directors of several municipal agencies were replaced with legislators loyal to the military government.[10] The effects of these institutional
acts were immediately felt throughout Brazil. Shortly after the military
coup, the DTDP was reorganized and replaced by the Superintendência
de Turismo de Salvador, or SUTURSA (Superintendence of Tourism of
Salvador); Rego saw many colleagues reassigned or fired, including Maia
himself.

Rego believed that the tourism department's role should not be restricted to the promotion of tourism, but it should also strive to preserve
Bahia's traditions. The new administration, composed of politicians appointed for their loyalty to the military government rather than for their

specialized knowledge or administrative skills,[11] not only did not protect Bahia's traditions but encouraged a kind of innovation Rego saw as detrimental. Rego voices his disapproval of the new administration, which he blames for capoeira's recent decline: "The negative agent of capoeira's process of decline, sociologically and ethnographically speaking, was the municipal tourism administration. Holding the financial, material and promotional resources, it corrupted as much as possible. Although the above-mentioned division has the preservation of our traditions as its goal, its recent administrators, out of pure ignorance and incompetence, do just the opposite, directly or indirectly."[12] As evidence of capoeira's decline, Rego discusses the new uniforms worn in public demonstrations of capoeira. He dwells at length on the choices of attire sponsored by SUTURSA as examples of the failure of the tourism division to protect capoeira against "loss of character." He claims that these uniforms, consisting of soccer-type jerseys of different colors, were chosen with the intent of pleasing tourists: "With a primarily touristic concern, they choose shirts of various loud colors, in terribly poor taste, with the aim of attracting attention to the group, which looks more like a carnival group than a group of master and disciples of capoeira."[13] What made matters worse, he continues, was that these uniforms chosen by SUTURSA, which he describes as "over the top,"[14] were passively accepted by the directors of the capoeira groups. As an extreme example of these "over the top," "untraditional" attire choices, Rego mentions an instance when a capoeira mestre consulted one of the SUTURSA directors about the possibility of wearing soccer jerseys with a number on the back, like a soccer team; Rego reports with relief that, in a flash of "common sense," the director "categorically prohibited" this choice.[15]

Rego overlooks the fact that the trend of wearing soccer jerseys for public demonstrations of capoeira goes at least as far back as the late 1930s, well before SUTURSA began meddling in capoeira demonstrations. Rego's examples, rather than confirming the passivity of capoeira performers, show their ability to negotiate with the new tourism directors and adapt past practices, such as the soccer jersey trend, to current circumstances. Rego romanticized capoeiristas from the past as always wearing white suits, which he claimed to have been blacks' "preferred attire."[16] Although Bimba and his students had worn blue and white striped soccer jerseys in the 1940s,[17] by the 1960s Bimba had adopted white cotton uniforms, which may in part explain Rego's respect for him.[18] Rego condones certain kinds of innovation, such as Bimba's alleged borrowings of "Oriental and European elements," while denouncing others, such as the adoption of uniforms in "poor taste" by capoeira groups. Like the folklorists of the previous generation, Rego could not help but attempt to dictate the "acceptable" limits of innovation in an effort to protect capoeira against "loss of character."

Interestingly, Bimba's own folkloric shows steered clear of Rego's criticism. The Grupo Folclórico do Mestre Bimba operated largely without municipal subsidies, holding staged performances at Bimba's own private venue, the Sítio Caruano, and at private nightclubs such as the Boite de Ondina. Rego's respect for Bimba was undoubtedly related to the fact that Bimba's shows were independent from the tourism department. Although by the time *Capoeira Angola* was published Bimba was staging shows for tourists several times per week,[19] Rego chose to omit these shows from his book, describing instead a graduation ceremony at Bimba's school.[20] In an effort to assert the traditionality of Capoeira Regional, Rego focuses on the ceremonial aspects of this graduation ceremony and on the gravitas of Bimba's presence. He describes the order of events: speeches were followed by a formalized sequence of capoeira games, culminating in

the golden moment in the graduation ceremony—Mestre Bimba blows his whistle. Silence reigns and the ceremony begins. He quickly recounts what he knows and what he saw about capoeira and capoeiristas; and remembers passages from his life to serve as an example. After this, he invites the godmothers [*madrinhas*] to place the medals on the chest and the silk scarf around the neck of the godchildren [*afilhados*], speaking again, this time to explain about the medal[,] which is the symbol of the school[,] and the silk scarf. About the scarf . . . he explained that in the old days the greatest defense of the capoeirista against getting their necks cut by a straight razor was the use of a scarf called *esguião*, made out of pure, imported silk.[21]

In this passage Rego foregrounds the importance of Bimba's life experiences and recognizes the merit in his contributions to capoeira during the previous five decades. Bimba signaled the import of concluding his Capoeira Regional course with the conferral of medals, syncretically appropriating the distinction of military achievement; he also drew authenticity from the past through his use of the silk scarf, "rescuing" a lost tradition—an act of restoration congruent with the recommendations of the folklore movement. Bimba's invented traditions of conferring medals, tying scarves, and choosing "godmothers" (often a graduating capoeirista's girlfriend) to ceremoniously participate in this ritual had the desired effect on Rego, convincing him of the value of Capoeira Regional.

Rego further reinforces the credibility and legitimacy of Bimba's Capoeira Regional by framing the acclaimed "guardian" of Capoeira Angola as a newcomer. Rego stops just short of calling Pastinha a fraud when he attributes Pastinha's recent notoriety to the rise of the tourism industry and adds that his capoeira skills were only noteworthy considering his age: "He is not and never was the best capoeirista of Bahia.... He played like any other good capoeira, except that for his age this was something extraordinary. That's what made him well known, or rather, famous, even though this is recent, meaning starting with the advent of the official institution of tourism services in Bahia."[22] In addition to pointing out the newness of Pastinha's fame, Rego goes on to question Pastinha's capoeira credentials and suggests that Aberrê (Antônio Raymundo Argolo, 1895–1942) might have been Pastinha's *teacher* rather than his student, casting doubt over Pastinha's narrative of a triumphant return to capoeira at the urging of his student Aberrê. Rego also criticizes Pastinha's book *Capoeira Angola* (1964), taking issue with the author's explanation of capoeira's origins, which Rego believed was a task beyond Pastinha's "cultural reach": "The booklet by Pastinha should be consulted with caution due to the author's intellectual preoccupation in giving the origins and explanation of certain facts that are not, in any way, within his cultural reach."[23] It is significant that Rego also names his book *Capoeira Angola*—perhaps his attempt to correct the inaccuracies stated by Pastinha in his homonymous book, published four years earlier.

Although Rego did undertake substantial ethnographic research in the capoeira community in Salvador, his training as a historian was deeply intertwined with his role as a tourism bureaucrat. Rego completed the course on "History and Tradition of Bahia" offered by the DMT in 1954. Later he was chosen to pass on this knowledge—condensed and state-approved sound bites about Bahia's "traditions"—through workshops offered to the city taxi drivers, preparing them to interact with tourists. The "History and Tradition of Bahia" course, however, was not recognized by Bahia's education department and was not affiliated with any educational institution.[24] While in the 1950s this course was taken mostly for personal enrichment by amateur tour guides (mostly women of the Bahian elite), after the reorganization of the tourism department as SUTURSA the course was geared toward professional tour guides and travel agents.[25] Although Rego did not work officially as a tour guide himself, he was well versed in the official version of Bahia's history and tradition and was known to lecture to tourists who attended municipal folkloric shows.

Rego's writings often betray his annoyance with "unauthorized" versions of capoeira's history. He adamantly objected to the practice of including what he considered to be misinformed, fantasized retellings of capoeira's history in folkloric shows: "There is always some wiseass that claims to be a 'professor' and, in an informal tone, lectures on the origin and history of capoeira, saying the greatest heresies."[26] While the movement, music, and ritual of capoeira may have been the domain of capoeiristas, history, for Rego, was the domain of "real" professors and historians.

Discussing the 1966 show "História da capoeira e samba duro,"[27] presented by the folk ensemble Grupo Folclórico da Bahia and directed by Bimba's student Acordeon (Ubirajara Guimarães Almeida, b. 1943), Rego writes: "The group is misinformed and at times resorts to the imagination, concerning the historical and socio-ethnographic aspect of capoeira, leading to the spread of untruths to audience members. It would be better if, starting with concrete facts about capoeira, stylized as it has been, they would create their own histories [sic] and put together a show without the pretense of creating the history or ethnography of capoeira."[28] The words "history" and "story," homonyms in Portuguese, were confusing even to Rego himself, who writes that the performers of Grupo Folclórico da Bahia should "create their own histories" when he clearly meant stories. After seeing the show, Rego expressed his objections directly to Acordeon, who recounted the exchange in an interview in 2013: "I remember this as if it was today. He said: 'Listen, Acordeon, what you're showing here I wouldn't call a history of capoeira, because for a history you would have to have the sequence of a history. What you're doing here is [performing] stories of capoeira, so I think you should follow this idea of stories.'"[29] Rego also mentions this conversation in the book and goes on to praise a later show by Grupo Folclórico da Bahia where Acordeon, heeding his advice, substituted the word "story" (*estória*) for the word "history" (*história*) in the title "Vem camará 67: novas estórias de capoeira."[30] "As can be seen," Rego continues, "the term history, which designates concrete facts, consummate facts, was substituted for the term story, something made up, invented."[31] For Rego, history was the domain of historians, not practitioners, and it was a history made up of sequential and indisputable facts. During the 1937 Second Afro-Brazilian Congress, Carneiro had invited people from "the folk" to speak about their cultural practices, recognizing them as experts. Writing three decades later, Rego took on a much more conservative stance and sought to keep the "folk" from deviating from what they did best: "bearing folklore."

Folkloric shows in the urban setting of Salvador disrupted neat notions of folklore as something found in rural areas—vanishing traditions subsequently collected and studied by scholars preoccupied with their preservation. Folklore had been conceptualized as the cultural practices of "folklore bearers," "people from the people" (*gente do povo*) who were born into certain folk "traditions" and subsequently carried them, passively, in their bodies. The fact that Bimba taught several white, college-educated, middle-class students, some of whom now performed with his folkloric ensemble, disrupted class and skin color associations with "tradition," as well as the notion of "bearing" (rather than learning) folklore. Capoeiristas whose socioeconomic background and skin color did match the stereotype of the "folklore bearer" also began including music and dance forms other than capoeira in their own folkloric shows, which they had themselves learned from other "folklore bearers." Folklore was now everywhere in Salvador, borne, learned, and reinvented.

Throughout Rego's *Capoeira Angola*, his anxieties regarding innovation are palpable as he struggles with conciliating the demands of the tourism industry with the maintenance of Bahia's history and tradition. Like Amado and Carneiro, Rego takes sides. Diverging from his senior colleagues, however, he supports Bimba's eclectic approach to tradition, despite his alleged foreign borrowings, and exposes Pastinha as an "invented tradition." Rego's *Capoeira Angola* in fact marks a shift in attitude toward Bimba; however, Rego's emphasis on Bimba's rituals and ceremonies tells only part of the story. As the most comprehensive book about the state of capoeira in the late 1960s, it is telling that Bimba's folkloric shows are absent from *Capoeira Angola*. Although surely a well-intentioned choice intended to underscore the legitimacy of Capoeira Re-

Figure 3.1 Acordeon (crouching, his back to the camera) plays a game at
a public demonstration while Bimba leads the musical ensemble. Brás plays
the berimbau, and Amadeu plays pandeiro on the far right.
Photo identification courtesy of Mestre Acordeon. Photographer unknown, c. 1965.
Courtesy of the Arquivo Histórico Municipal do Salvador, Prefeitura Municipal Collection.

gional, Rego's omission has occluded this important aspect of Bimba's
work in the history of capoeira.

GRUPO FOLCLÓRICO DO MESTRE BIMBA:
STAGING VIOLENCE AND CHOREOGRAPHING
ACROBATIC CAPOEIRA

Despite Rego's 1968 acknowledgment of the worth (and the Africanity)
of Capoeira Regional, it was not until the mid-to-late 1990s that capoeira
scholarship began valuing Bimba's contributions and innovations, recognizing them as Afro-diasporic rather than dismissing them as part of a
process of co-optation and "whitening."[32] While narratives of the decline
and loss of early twentieth-century capoeira have been redirected toward
Zuma, late twentieth- and early twenty-first-century "loss of character"
(descaracterização) has been attributed to folkloric shows and the tourism
industry. However, the capoeira historiography has not adequately ad-
dressed the process of staging capoeira or its relationship with the tour-

ism industry; folkloric shows, in particular those that toured internationally, are only mentioned briefly as footnotes explaining the globalization
of the practice since the late 1970s. Undoubtedly influenced by Rego's
Capoeira Angola, subsequent research on capoeira that does acknowledge
staged capoeira performances regards tourism as both a recent influence
and a negative one, responsible for eroding capoeira's traditions.[33] Such
texts identify an increased emphasis on "acrobatics," often assumed to be
a foreign borrowing, as the clearest sign of capoeira's "loss of character."
In his 2004 book *A "capoeira" da indústria do entretenimento: corpo, acrobacia e espetáculo para "turista ver"* ("Capoeira" for the entertainment industry: body,
acrobatics and spectacle for "tourists to watch"), physical education professor Acúrsio Esteves identifies some of the "foreign" elements added
to capoeira with the intent of pleasing tourist audiences: "bright colored
clothing, acrobatics, pre-arranged movement sequences, 'rigged games,'
back flips, balances (spectacular positions for photos), . . . among other
ruses to add variety to the show and guarantee the 'vile metal.'"[34] Using
the anachronistic term "*vil metal*" (lit. vile metal, meaning "evil money"),
the author stresses the corrupting influences of monetizing capoeira.[35]
Esteves assumes acrobatics and preestablished movement sequences to
be late twentieth-century innovations, created with the intent of pleasing
tourists in overtly commercial settings.

In the preceding chapters I have shown that balões (grabbing and
throwing), often considered a foreign borrowing, had in fact been part
of capoeira practice since at least the late nineteenth century, reframed
by Bimba as innovation in his modern and efficient Capoeira Regional.
While these throws were erased by Pastinha in the process of codifying a
gentle and "folkloric" Capoeira Angola, Bimba reclaimed them as his signature move throughout the 1960s, naming them *golpes ligados* (connected
strikes) or *golpes cinturados* (strikes from the waist), collectively referred to
as *cintura desprezada* (abandoned waist). By 1968 Rego identified throws as
readily associated with Capoeira Regional, claiming that these were "different from traditional [moves]" and were "derived from elements of foreign fights, not seen in traditional strikes, where capoeiristas don't con-
nect and barely touch."[36]

I propose a direct connection between Capoeira Regional's cintura
desprezada techniques and the acrobatic assisted flips that allowed
players to gracefully fly through the air onstage. Bimba warned readers
of his *Curso de Capoeira Regional* of the dangers of these partnered throws

while at the same time listing them as part of his codified capoeira technique. Around the same time that he codified throws as his own, Bimba and his students transformed what previously had been straightforward capoeira demonstrations into shows for tourists, which included choreographed capoeira sequences featuring throws and other aerial moves—cooperative, preestablished sequences where danger and violence were reconfigured as a thrilling aerial acrobatic spectacle.

The longevity of Bimba's success was due to his ability to constantly reinvent Capoeira Regional and seize opportunities for visibility and commercial success. While in the 1930s and 1940s Bimba and his students demonstrated capoeira in sports arenas and rings, in the 1950s Bimba and his students began staging capoeira demonstrations for tourists. By the early 1950s Bimba's success was such that the activities of his Centro de Cultura Física Regional (Center for Regional Physical Culture) were divided between two locations in Salvador: one school in the historic district of the city, the Pelourinho, and another in a working-class residential neighborhood, ten kilometers to the east, called Nordeste de Amaralina.[37] This second school, also known as Sítio Caruano,[38] was used for graduation ceremonies and performances for tourists, as well as Sunday rodas, while the school located in the Pelourinho remained the place where daily instruction occurred. At the Pelourinho location, classes were offered three times a day: in the early morning, in the afternoon, and in the evening; evening classes were when Bimba's capoeira "elite"—his most advanced students—attended the school.[39] The Pelourinho location was also open to spectators, who could watch classes for a fee. Bimba charged spectators the price of a single lesson, which was also the price of tuition for a whole month of classes. Cafuné, a disciple of Bimba, initially intended only to watch a class, but after being informed of the price system, he decided to stay and learn Capoeira Regional. When he asked if he could watch a class, Bimba simply pointed to a sign posted on the door that read "class: 2,000; monthly rate: 2,000; visits: 2,000."[40] This clever pricing system kept instruction away from the eyes of casual observers and, in some instances, transformed would-be spectators into practitioners, who for the same price as watching, chose to give practice a try.

The Sítio Caruano location was where the Grupo Folclórico do Mestre Bimba (Mestre Bimba's Folkloric Ensemble) rehearsed and performed. Bimba's ensemble—a group composed of selected students, Bimba himself, and Mãe Alice[41]—also performed at nightclubs and hotels.[42] Because of the removed location of the Sítio Caruano, tourists were bused in by one of Bahia's largest travel agencies, Kontik Tourism and Travel Agency, which held an ongoing contract with Bimba.[43] In the early 1960s Bimba and his students remodeled the Sítio Caruano, adding bleacher-type seating to accommodate the growing audiences of tourists brought in three times a week to watch the Grupo Folclórico do Mestre Bimba,[44] which by that time had transformed its capoeira demonstrations into full-fledged shows.[45]

Eyewitness accounts describe Bimba as an engaging "showman" with outstanding command of the audience, who would tell jokes and entertain Brazilian and foreign visitors alike with his charisma.[46] Aside from capoeira, the shows included dances from candomblé and *samba de roda* (staged by Mãe Alice), as well as *samba duro* (a tripping samba performed by men, usually reserved for the finale of the show). The show also included *maculelê*, a mock combat dance of much-debated origins where dancers hit a pair of wooden clubs (*grimas*), rhythmically and often acrobatically, against another dancer's grimas (which were sometimes replaced by machetes).

The Sítio Caruano was also where Bimba's graduation ceremonies (*formaturas*) took place, a ritual likely borrowed from the academic institutions where many of Bimba's students were preparing to become doctors, dentists, and lawyers.[47] These ceremonies culminated in the performance of choreographed acrobatic games, a movement practice also featured in the performances of the Grupo Folclórico do Mestre Bimba. These choreographed games are referred to alternately as *esquete* or *escrete*,[48] and also spelled "schath" by Waldeloir Rego in his 1968 description of Bimba's graduation ceremonies.[49] Rego's attempt at an English spelling of the term points to a possible connection to the boxing term "scratch" (phonetically adapted and spelled "*escrete*" in Portuguese), which designates the starting position of the two contestants in a match.

Mestre Xaréu (Hélio Campos, b. 1947) explains that these escretes, which I have translated as "demonstration games," provided students with the opportunity to put in practice the abandoned waist techniques learned in class, "modifying them according to the creativity, courage and skills of the players[,] individually and as a pair."[50] Mestre Itapoan (Raimundo César Alves de Almeida, b. 1947) remembers that each student had his own set partner for demonstration games—Itapoan's own partner was Gia (Gil dos Prazeres Souza). To create each demonstration

Figure 3.2 From left to right: Gia (holding the machetes), Itapoan (in midair),
and Bimba (in white T-shirt, talking to two students, in the background).
Photographer unknown, c. 1968. Courtesy of Raimundo César Alves de Almeida.

game, two advanced students would select several partnered throws
learned in class and choreograph games that would be performed both
onstage and at graduation ceremonies. These games "were rehearsed because it was just for performance, . . . we performed during shows. Also
at graduation ceremonies there were demonstration games, which was
how we would show these throws that Mestre Bimba had introduced to
capoeira."[51] These choreographed sequences affirmed and displayed cintura desprezada as Bimba's invention, as the signature practice of Capoeira Regional. Itapoan stresses that these sequences were rehearsed
specifically for performances in front of an audience. A photo from 1968
(see figure 3.2)[52] offers a glimpse into one of these demonstration games
between Itapoan and Gia: a machete in each hand, Gia leans back as Itapoan hits his target, landing with both feet on Gia's chest—a blow called
the "bat's flight" (vôo do morcego). Although a few spectators gaze on in
amazement, the casual, even distracted demeanor of others present, including Bimba himself, points to the fairly unremarkable nature of this

seemingly astonishing feat. Whether this photo captured a rehearsal or a performance, it was clear that Bimba had seen this before and was in no way alarmed or surprised. Had this been a real confrontation, it is unlikely that Itapoan would have been allowed to deliver his "bat's flight," since Gia could have easily wounded or killed Itapoan with one or both of his machetes. In fact, the thrill of this moment is only possible through the rehearsed cooperation between these two players, who recreate and magnify violence, staging confrontation without its danger.

Flying kicks into machete-wielding opponents and acrobatic partnered throws, when not performed cooperatively in a prearranged demonstration game, had the potential of being dangerous or even deadly; in fact, the only way to execute them safely was to decide when, how, and in what order these throws and kicks were to be performed. These partnered sequences staged Capoeira Regional's potential violence and efficiency through choreographed cooperation. Bimba's demonstration games, then, performed the same labor as Pastinha's "shown," held-back kicks, which barely grazed the opponent or stopped just before making contact, reassuring the public that capoeira, now transformed into a dance-like performance, had been redeemed of its violent past of straight razors and tough guys.[53] Bimba's staged capoeira, however, was marked by daredevil flying kicks and flips that amplified and theatricalized rather than downplayed danger—a staging practice undoubtedly inherited from the rigged games (marmeladas) from the late 1930s and 1940s.

These demonstration games followed typical patterns of folkloricization: curtailed improvisation coupled with a tendency toward virtuosic, athletic, dramatic, and spectacular performance.[54] And Bimba, having embraced folkloric shows, was acutely aware of the possible consequences of folkloricization: the loss of capoeira's efficiency as self-defense. According to Acordeon, Bimba cautioned his advanced students against getting lost in the aesthetics of these demonstration games and transforming capoeira into a "mere exhibition of acrobatic elements 'for tourists to watch.'"[55] Like Pastinha, Bimba expressed a preoccupation in separating a capoeira for the stage from a capoeira practiced in "real life" situations. However, while on the surface capoeira's acrobatics may look like mere crowd-pleasing spectacle, their connection to the deadly practice of grabbing and throwing described by Mello Moraes in the late nineteenth century is evident. Staging capoeira's violence for tourists, Bimba recontextualized and reclaimed the grabbing and throwing techniques of capoeiragem.

Canjiquinha was one of the most creative capoeiristas I ever met.
The father of many things used in shows.

—Mestre Acordeon

In 1954 the Diretoria Municipal de Turismo (DMT) inaugurated its new building at the Belvedere da Sé—the same location where the Odeon Stadium once stood and where capoeira attained visibility and popularity during the 1936 pugilistic season. This building, featuring its own stage for folkloric shows, was envisioned as a tourist destination in and of itself. In addition to nightly folkloric shows, it offered tourists a privileged view of the Bay of All Saints, which could be admired with the naked eye or further explored through telescopes available at the edge of the belvedere.[56]

For nearly a decade, the folkloric shows offered at this municipal stage were directed by Washington Bruno da Silva, better known as Mestre Canjiquinha. Not as famous as Bimba or Pastinha, Canjiquinha is remembered for his participation in the tourism industry—as the capoeirista who indeed defined himself in relationship to it. The son of a single mother who worked as a washerwoman, Canjiquinha began working at age fourteen. Still a minor, he began performing odd manual jobs informally at Salvador's city hall, and was formally hired as a public functionary after he turned eighteen.[57] In the late 1950s, newspaper columnist and DMT employee Guilherme Simões invited Canjiquinha, who taught capoeira at the time at Pastinha's school, to stage folkloric shows at the Belvedere da Sé.[58] His job as a public functionary was then divided between the copy room, where he operated the mimeograph in the mornings, and the stage, where he directed Salvador's city-sponsored folkloric shows in the evenings.[59] Canjiquinha's capoeira shows mark a shift in the DMT's approach to staging folklore; having previously relied on folkloric stagings by Hildegardes Vianna,[60] now the city placed Canjiquinha, a "genuine" working-class Afro-Brazilian "folklore bearer," in charge of staging the tourism department's capoeira shows.

Canjiquinha traced his capoeira lineage to Aberrê, whose untimely death in 1942 (at age forty-seven) meant that his capoeira practice largely predated Capoeira Angola as a distinct style of capoeira.[61] Canjiquinha, perhaps influenced by the fact that his own mestre had not participated in a capoeira understood in binary terms, saw the two capoeira styles

Figure 3.3 Canjiquinha evades a kick to the chest. Photo by Baptista, published in the Diário de Notícias on September 16, 1971. Courtesy of the Arquivo Histórico Municipal do Salvador, Diário de Notícias Collection.

as marketing strategies and insisted that there was only one capoeira: "There is only one kind of capoeira. . . . There is neither capoeira regional nor capoeira angola, there is capoeira. Tell me to sing a capoeira angola song and I won't know one. I didn't learn capoeira in Angola, I learned it in Bahia, in Salvador. [Mestre Bimba] was an intelligent guy, so he created capoeira regional, which was from the region of Bahia, but [capoeira regional] doesn't exist."[62] By stating that he did not learn capoeira in Angola, Canjiquinha dismisses the story of origins circulated by Pastinha of a capoeira brought from Angola (the dance of the zebra called 'ngolo). He also dismisses the capoeira marketed as "regional" by Bimba, the savvy entrepreneur. The fact that Canjiquinha was not restricted by an affiliation to either of the two capoeira styles—he indeed exposed both as invented traditions—allowed him the freedom to reinvent capoeira for the stage.

Although Canjiquinha knew that tourists' short attention span demanded action-packed, entertaining performances, he took the time to didactically introduce the audience to capoeira. The shows at the municipal stage at the Belvedere da Sé opened with a capoeira demonstra-

STAGING BRAZIL

tion; Canjiquinha played different berimbau rhythms while his students played the types of capoeira games that each rhythm elicited. According to Mestre Brasília (Antonio Cardoso Andrade, b. 1942), who performed in Canjiquinha's ensemble from 1959 until 1966, not only were the shows didactic for audiences, but the stage was also a space where Canjiquinha's students refined their skills as players—Brasília began performing only four months after his first capoeira lesson, and much of his subsequent training happened during the nightly shows.[63] The stage was simultaneously a place for tourist spectacle and a space for honing one's skills as a capoeira player.

After this initial demonstration to the sound of the berimbau, the show progressed through three variations of capoeira invented by Canjiquinha for the stage: *muzenza, samba de angola,* and *samango.* Canjiquinha understood that the success of his shows depended on invention and creativity. He explained that "if mestre Bimba created [capoeira] regional I thought it was appropriate to create the muzenza, the samango."[64] Canjiquinha explains that he borrowed a rhythm from candomblé to create the muzenza; to this borrowed rhythm he deliberately crafted a new movement style by practicing in front of a mirror: "It came to me like this: I arrived at a candomblé [ceremony] and I heard them playing [the muzenza]. I played it on the berimbau. Then I said: how am I going to [move to] this? Then I would practice in front of a mirror. Then I had [my students] practice the movement [and] I saw that it worked."[65] In creating new movement to a candomblé rhythm, Canjiquinha authorizes his creativity and further Africanizes his capoeira performances through the Africanity of candomblé. Canjiquinha rejects his role as passive "bearer" of folklore, and instead he claims authorship and exposes his creative process—in this case, not only the transposition of a rhythm from a religious to a secular context, but the conscious movement investigation in front of a mirror in search for new movement vocabulary.

Mestre Geni (José Serafim Ferreira Júnior, b. 1947), who performed with Canjiquinha from 1955 until the late 1960s, describes the muzenza as a playful dance between two men, who would circle one another while moving their hips to the rhythm of the berimbau.[66] Waldeloir Rego affirms that the muzenza is derived from a candomblé ritual where the female initiate dances with her torso bent forward, and proposes that this bent-over position gave rise to a kind of banter with sexual overtones between two men:

The capoeirista Canjiquinha has a rhythm called Muzenza. . . . In Bahia, Muzenza is the name given to the initiate in the candomblés from the Angola "nation." When she appears in public to find out the name of her *orixá* (god), an exit song of Muzenza is sung, where she dances a choreography slightly bent forward. Based on this choreography, people and their malicious imagination decided to caricature the dance, increasing the curvature of the body, giving the impression one is about to get on all fours. With that, we see, constantly, the playfulness between two men, when one asks the other for something, and the one who doesn't want to give in answers: "only if we dance the muzenza . . . ," that is only if one gets down on all fours, to be possessed sexually.[67]

Rego adds that he asked Canjiquinha why he had named this dance muzenza, and Canjiquinha replied that he meant it as a joke. Although this homoerotic sexual innuendo was most likely included for comic effect, it is nevertheless remarkable that in the heteronormative environment of midcentury capoeira, Canjiquinha would include a dance with homoerotic overtones in his shows. And the muzenza was not the only way Canjiquinha challenged gender norms in his show; in the *festa de arromba*, the closing number where the ensemble would reenact a brawl (discussed below), Canjiquinha himself would play a damsel-in-distress who is saved by a heroic capoeirista.[68]

Canjiquinha borrowed rhythms and dances from other traditions, adding capoeira-inflected dancing to the show. In addition to the muzenza and its elements from candomblé, his samba de angola fused samba and capoeira: samba dancing that included circular kicks, cartwheels, and leg sweeps (*rasteiras*) performed to the rhythm of samba, transposed to the berimbau. Canjiquinha devised this hybrid form by "dancing samba de angola[;] playing capoeira while [dancing] samba."[69] Like Pastinha, who also danced samba de angola during his demonstrations for tourists, Canjiquinha turns capoeira into a dance by adding the festive syncopation of samba, well established in tourists' minds as the quintessential Brazilian carnival rhythm.[70]

Both the samba de angola and Canjiquinha's third variation, the samango, showcased the capoeiristas' virtuosity. For the samango, Canjiquinha created both the rhythm and the movement: "I wanted to invent a [new] rhythm[:] I created the samango. So, the dance is different. I practiced dancing sideways. The samango is very violent, it has flying scissor [kicks], it has everything."[71] Like Bimba, Canjiquinha amplified and choreographed capoeira's violence for the stage in the samango—staging violence in a hyperbolic, virtuosic fashion. Performed in pairs, like Bimba's demonstration games, samba de angola and samango games were rehearsed. Brasília remembers that games were structured to prevent injury but also to create spectacle: "The sweeps we sometimes staged, both in the samba de angola and in the samango. We would let the other [guy] complete the sweep, we would fall, get up, the audience would laugh—we performed. [In] the bat's flight we would let [the other player] hit [us], we would stagger away, and it was very beautiful, because it was just capoeira, but we had to work every rhythm with its principles."[72] Brasília uses verbs such as *encenar* (to stage) and *representar* (to perform or to act) to refer to the moments in the show when the interaction between players was orchestrated or planned in advance. From Brasília's description, it is clear that the players took pleasure in their representation of violence— an opportunity to focus on the aesthetic aspect, on the "beauty" of the game rather than on its function.

Canjiquinha's shows allowed players to learn through representation. Mestre Lua Rasta (Gilson Fernandes, b. 1950), explains that the samango "was for training; [Canjiquinha] also used it in performance, but it was [really] training so that we could improve our side kicks."[73] The festa de arromba, the show's finale, was likewise both spectacle and didactic moment. Geni explains that in the festa de arromba "Canjiquinha would put one group of capoeiristas on one side and another group of capoeiristas on the other and [we] would simulate a fight[,] everybody would fight with everybody.... It was a simulated fight where nobody got hurt."[74] According to Lua Rasta, "festa de arromba was the show's finale. It was just between us, every man for himself,... it was a fight among us. [For Canjiquinha] it was festa de arromba, for Bimba it was the esquenta-banho. Festa de arromba was what happened at a festival, it was a simulated fight at a public festival. .... Back then ... when there was a disagreement, a fight would break out, so it was a simulation of a brawl at a festival, where people would fist fight. Today nobody fights with his hands anymore; today for any reason a guy pulls out his gun."[75] Like Bimba and Pastinha, Canjiquinha transformed capoeira's violence—the very aspect of the practice that capoeira advocates had downplayed since the 1920s. Like Bimba's demonstration games, these staged brawls represented a violent encounter within the safety of the stage. Canjiquinha, however, also included the reenactment of the social context in which this violence would have taken place: a confrontation at a large public gathering (a *festa de largo*, which I have translated as "festival"). Interestingly, Lua Rasta compares Canjiquinha's festa de arromba to Bimba's *esquenta-banho* rather than to his demonstration games. Esquenta-banho (lit. shower warm-up) referred to the unstructured and often rough games that happened at the end of Bimba's advanced capoeira classes while students waited for their turn in the shower. Canjiquinha's staged brawls clearly had a significant element of improvisation, and capoeiristas were able to apply their fighting skills in a confrontation that was both "real" and staged. According to Lua Rasta, Canjiquinha would remind his performers that the festa de arromba scene was also an exercise to prepare capoeiristas for situations of conflict offstage: "We had to learn [for when we] had to defend ourselves, because at a public festival . . . you're on your own."[76] Like Bimba and Pastinha, Canjiquinha strove to maintain capoeira's efficiency as it developed as tourist spectacle.

As folkloric ensembles proliferated throughout the 1960s in Salvador, Canjiquinha realized the need to add variety to his capoeira shows. Like Bimba, he began adding *samba de roda* to his capoeira performances, as well as other "folkloric" dances: "Capoeira, maculelê, samba de roda, I was the first to put all this on the market, because I used to do [only] capoeira shows, and when I saw that it didn't work I added samba de roda, and from samba de roda I added maculelê, and from maculelê I added the *puxada de rede* [fisherman's net dance], and the maculelê I learned in 1954 from the now deceased Mestre Popó. He taught me, if I know maculelê it is thanks to him."[77] Although Canjiquinha claims to have been "the first to put all this on the market," it is difficult to establish who first created this repertory, since all ensembles at the time offered an almost identical roster of folkloric dances in their shows. By the early 1970s Canjiquinha's group, renamed Conjunto Aberrê in homage to Canjiquinha's teacher, began performing at various private tourist stages throughout the city. The entertainment listings of Salvador's main newspapers detail the various dances tourists might enjoy during a performance by Conjunto Aberrê: "samba de roda, maculelê, African dances, puxada de rede, capoeira angola, samba duro and samba de angola."[78] In these listings, Canjiquinha's capoeira is sometimes listed as capoeira regional and other times as capoeira angola, reflecting the confusion caused by his refusal to adhere to one of the two capoeira styles.[79]

This expanded repertory, which even included "African dances," was likely prompted by the increased competition Canjiquinha encountered in the late 1960s, when his show was no longer the only offering at the municipal stage at the Belvedere da Sé. The rivalry that ensued between Canjiquinha and his new competitor, Mestre Caiçara (Antônio da Conceição Morais, 1923–97), is well known among capoeiristas, and it is believed that Caiçara, who was initiated in candomblé, earned a spot at the coveted municipal stage through the intervention of an orixá.[80] Now dividing his time between the municipal stage and private nightclubs such as Boite de Ondina, Canjiquinha focused on pleasing tourists who sought performances of Brazilianness that matched the effusive, vibrant, and "over the top" destination image disseminated by Hollywood in the 1940s and 1950s.[81] Whether or not Canjiquinha was the first to create Brazil's canonic folkloric suite (with capoeira, samba de roda, and maculelê as core "numbers") is less important than his claim of (and pride in) having authored a folkloric canon, one that has endured into the second decade of the twenty-first century and remains iconic of Brazil. Canjiquinha gives continuity to the tradition of invention also seen in the contributions of capoeira innovators such as Zuma, Bimba, and Pastinha—a tradition that challenges conservative approaches to cultural production, such as the model of folklore borne by people "from the people," whose creativity must be regulated by culture experts such as Rego.

Rego and Canjiquinha both worked at the Municipal Tourism Department and knew each other well; Rego would often observe Canjiquinha's capoeira classes and folkloric shows in the evenings. In *Capoeira Angola*, Rego writes about Canjiquinha at length, often praising his singing abilities and his accomplishments in the film industry, but he only briefly acknowledges him as the main informant for his book:

> He sings like few others and has an extremely vast repertoire, including a great facility for improvisation and[,] of everyone[,] he is the one who has contributed the most to the adaptation of other folkloric songs to capoeira. A large portion of the songs in this [book] were collected from Canjiquinha. He was[,] out of all the capoeiristas in Bahia[,] the one with the most invitations for ex-

hibitions, travels to the interior and also to other states, as well as the one who most acted in films, short and full-length features[.]⁸²

Framed as a "folklore bearer" rather than a collaborator—a *source* for the songs Rego collected—Canjiquinha's contributions are downplayed in this passage, and there is no mention in the book of their close collaboration. Rego alternately praises Canjiquinha and harshly criticizes him throughout the book. Without mincing words, Rego declares a nameless folkloric group "completely prostituted":

> This [group], which by the way has a great mestre and excellent disciples, is completely prostituted. With the preoccupation of maintaining its exclusivity, against the other [group], the aforementioned [group] does everything imaginable in terms of loss of character [*descaracterização*]. At one point in the exhibition, the mestre loses his composure of mestre, tells jokes, tells anecdotes, shuffles his feet while shaking his hips [*requebros*] and brings in someone to tell a quick history of capoeira, where the greatest aberrations are said.⁸³

Although he omits Canjiquinha's name, Rego still gives the reader enough information to determine he speaks of Canjiquinha—the only one who held shows with exclusivity at the municipal folkloric stage at the Belvedere da Sé. This is a much more conservative Rego than the ethnographer who bucked the trend of blaming Bimba for causing capoeira to "lose its character." Rego asserts his authority as a capoeira historian and objects to the historical "aberrations" told onstage by someone he considers less qualified than himself (and who also remains nameless in this account).⁸⁴ Since he believed that capoeira was a creolized form born in Brazil rather than imported whole from Africa (a common debate at the time, which lasted well into the 1980s and 1990s), certainly such historical "aberrations" included stories of capoeira's African origins. Rego continues to describe this "prostituted" spectacle: "Afterwards he leads a samba de roda to the sound of capoeira musical instruments, bringing in to the circle to dance samba girls grabbed at the last minute, samba school dancers, or professional [dancers] friends of the mestre, that happened to be present at the performance. Once I asked him why all that, and he answered that it was *so that it wouldn't get monoto* (he meant to say *monotonous*) and [cause] the tourists to leave."⁸⁵ Rego undermines Canjiquinha's authority by ridiculing his shortening of the word "monoto-nous," which reveals the capoeirista's lack of formal education and his working-class status.[86] Despite Rego's ridicule—the unnecessary transcription and parenthetical explanation of the word "monotonous" as pronounced by Canjiquinha—avoiding monotony was a pressing concern in staged shows, and Canjiquinha knew that. Composure was a measure of tradition for Rego, and it was found in abundance in Bimba's demeanor. Canjiquinha's use of humor, his dancing, as well as his occasional inclusion of female samba dancers, are cited as examples of loss of both composure and tradition, even though Bimba was also known for telling jokes and entertaining his audiences, as discussed earlier.

Perhaps the height of "loss of composure" in Rego's eyes was the scene where Canjiquinha, donning a pair of high heels or just a borrowed purse from an audience member, would play the role of a woman from Rio (a *carioca*) who was visiting Bahia. Walking arm-in-arm with her new Bahian "boyfriend," who happens to be a capoeirista, the carioca tourist is approached by five men who want to rob her! Using his capoeira skills, her boyfriend fights off all attackers, but not before our protagonist faints from all the commotion. Geni and Lua Rasta remember the moment of fainting as a particularly funny moment—a part of this scene that in their youthful playfulness they helped create. In separate interviews, both Geni and Lua Rasta describe this scene. Geni recounts that: "One time, Lua and I, when Canjiquinha started to faint, we grabbed his ass, I think it was me [who grabbed it] because he expelled me, but after a while he went to find me at my house. And from this day forward, every time he fainted, either me or Lua, we grabbed [his ass], because the audience liked it, they thought it was funny to grab a woman's ass like that."[87] Lua Rasta describes Canjiquinha's transformation into the carioca tourist followed by his and Geni's humorous intervention: "He would borrow high heels from someone, would borrow a purse, and would walk swaying his hips, with his capoeira clothes still on . . . and then he did his thing of imitating a woman, imitating a carioca. Then Geni and I . . . we would grab his ass and he would go nuts! He would say 'Who was it? Who was the son of a bitch?' He would get pissed! . . . We had so much fun."[88] Of course the humor in this scene came not simply from the irreverent gesture of grabbing "a woman's ass"; this was funny because this "woman" was played by a man, and not just any man but a mestre of capoeira playing a helpless female tourist. The ass grabbing, which clearly would have been a straightforward gesture of machismo had the carioca tourist been played by a woman, is funny precisely because the gesture is simultaneously read as two men engaging in supposedly unwelcome sexual contact, while one of them is cross-dressed.[89]

Although capoeira demonstrations attracted relatively large crowds from the 1930s through the 1950s, by the mid-1960s capoeira onstage was no longer a novelty and had become standard tourist fare. Tourists' short attention span demanded brief, action-packed music and dance "numbers." Canjiquinha used all the elements at his disposal to create a fast-paced show that kept tourists engaged; not only did he innovate by incorporating samba de roda, maculelê, and puxada de rede into his shows, but he also created three new variations on capoeira: the *muzenza*, the *samango*, and the *samba de angola*.

Canjiquinha's use of humor was related simultaneously to capoeira's sense of play and to Amado's image of the happy, convivial, tropical Bahian. Using the verb *brincar* (to play, as in child's play) rather than *jogar* (to play, as in a game), Canjiquinha describes his playful approach to capoeira, both on- and offstage: "You see: I'm the happiness of capoeira. I play with one, I play with another, I play with a student, I play with the audience. . . . I am happy[,] I like to play."[90] Canjiquinha's own slogan, "I am the happiness of capoeira,"[91] was closely related to BAHIATURSA's 1979 slogan, "Bahia, land of happiness."[92] Through his playfulness and "happiness," Canjiquinha matched the destination image of Bahia as the land of happiness during his shows.

Canjiquinha was sharply aware of capoeira's importance to the tourism industry, and he knew his shows played an important role in performing Bahianness for visitors to the state—a happy, colorful, festive conviviality, not without the frisson of conflict, performed within the safety of the stage. He also knew that through his participation in several films, he played a significant role in the global dissemination of capoeira: "If today—I don't know if you'll believe me—if today capoeira is spread all over the world, you can thank me, because through films, capoeira is now all over the world."[93] Through his participation in films such as *Barravento* (The Turning Wind)[94] and *O pagador de promessas* (The Given Word, nominated for an Oscar and recipient of a Palme d'Or at Cannes),[95] both released in 1962, Canjiquinha introduced the world to capoeira.[96] In both these films, capoeira is framed as a primitive practice (and a practice of "primitives") and used as a contrast to Brazil's modernity. While in his

Figure 3.4 *Canjiquinha, holding a berimbau, in a scene from* O Pagador de Promessas.
Screenshot from O Pagador de Promessas, *Anselmo Duarte, dir., 1962.*

staged shows Canjiquinha was free to innovate and experiment with creating new rhythms and new movement styles, the directors of these films, with international audiences in mind, made sure capoeira was framed to match the destination image of Brazil, where Afro-Brazilian "natives" bore Brazil's traditions.

In *Barravento*, Canjiquinha's capoeira is removed from its urban setting and set in a fishing village, much like the place where capoeira was destined to eventually recede and disappear, as Carneiro had predicted in 1936. In *O pagador de promessas*, Canjiquinha's capoeira is staged in its urban setting, in Salvador's historic district, on the stairs of the church of the Holy Sacrament.[97] However, his fast circular kicks, along with editing that alternates rapidly between the musical instruments and the movement, gives the capoeira game a sense of chaos, of a "primitive" danger barely under control. The equation of Afro-Brazilianness and "savage" primitivism reproduced by the directors of these films continued to guide choreographies of Brazilianness onstage and on-screen throughout the 1960s and 1970s.

While Canjiquinha took capoeira to the world through his participa-

Figure 3.5 Canjiquinha, in midhandstand, plays capoeira against actor Antônio Sampaio (known today as Antônio Pitanga) in the film O Pagador de Promessas. Screenshot from O Pagador de Promessas, Anselmo Duarte, dir., 1962.

tion in films, his staged shows were performed almost exclusively inside Brazil and remained largely confined to tourist settings. Even though his creativity was limited in his work for film, Canjiquinha made the most of the relative freedom afforded to him in his nightly shows, which, as tourist entertainment, remained invisible to both theater and dance critics, and also to intellectuals writing about capoeira (except Rego), who were too preoccupied with "guardians of tradition" such as Pastinha. At a time when "tradition" circulated as the currency of legitimacy, Canjiquinha engaged creatively with capoeira, openly defying the model of folklore as static and resisting his assigned role of "bearer" of culture. Under the radar, Canjiquinha, along with his students, slowly and steadily, and certainly creatively, choreographed Brazil for hundreds of thousands of viewers during his lifetime.

CONCLUSION

Although capoeira scholarship has favored the offstage accomplishments of capoeiristas, often dismissing staged capoeira performances as a site of loss of tradition, capoeira onstage has had a profound influence on

Figure 3.6 *The author's nephew, in his capoeira uniform with the "fishing net" over his shoulder, performs a puxada de rede with his third-grade classmates, Campinas, Brazil, 2015. The fact that several capoeira schools also teach maculelê and puxada de rede today attests to the widespread and lasting influence of midcentury folkloric shows.* Family photo, used with permission.

the practice since the mid-twentieth century. Staged by capoeiristas and capoeira mestres themselves, capoeira onstage, in addition to providing entertainment and visibility, included a pedagogical aspect both for tourist audiences and for the performers themselves, who were in their majority young men at the beginning of their capoeira apprenticeship. The stage provided an opportunity for these capoeiristas to rehearse and display capoeira's violence within the safety of choreographed sequences (such as Bimba's escretes) and previously rehearsed scenes (such as Canjiquinha's festa de arromba).

Capoeiristas played a crucial role in staging capoeira as Afro-Brazilian folklore and in selecting and defining what is considered the standard repertory of Brazilian folkloric shows today: capoeira, samba de roda, puxada de rede, and maculelê. On underrated tourist stages throughout Salvador, capoeiristas disrupted the binary creative artist/folklore bearer and created their own choreographies of Afro-Brazilianness, claiming authorship and taking pride in their innovations.

CHAPTER 4

BRAZIL'S FOLKLORE FOR THE GLOBAL STAGE
Authorship, Innovation, and Spectacle

The most energetic, and for me the most thrilling item of the strangely exciting Brazilian
programme at the Roudhouse is the dance fight, the "Capoeira."
—Jane King, *Morning Star* dance critic

Throughout the 1960s, several folkloric ensembles sprang up in Salvador, performing at capoeira academies, at nightclubs, hotels and restaurants, and at Salvador's new municipal folkloric stage, the Centro Folclórico, directed by Waldeloir Rego himself.[1] While most capoeiristas staged capoeira for tourists in these informal settings, a few folkloric groups began securing spots at more prestigious "high art" venues, such as Salvador's municipal theater, the Teatro Castro Alves. Among these were Olodum Conjunto Folclórico, Grupo Folclórico Oxum, and Conjunto Folclórico Viva Bahia, directed by well-connected, educated, middle-class Bahians.[2] These groups were also able to secure funding from the municipal tourism administration, SUTURSA, to represent Brazil at international folklore festivals in the United States, Europe, and various South American and Caribbean countries throughout the 1960s and 1970s.

In this chapter I briefly discuss the work of folkloric ensembles Olodum and Oxum, continuing to an in-depth analysis of the domestic and international performances of the Conjunto Folclórico Viva Bahia between 1963 and 1974. I return to the concept of "folklore bearer," introduced in chapter 2, to examine how folkloric shows staged authenticity through the allegedly unmediated performances of cast members "from the people" (*do povo*), while simultaneously including choreography that challenged the conflation of the "folk" performer with his or her performance. The attribution of authenticity to performers from "the folk" — and the conflation of Afro-diasporic bodies with "the folk" — was central to the success of Viva Bahia's folkloric shows abroad. I examine the narratives that reinforced the audience's "unmediated" experience, disseminated through newspapers articles, reviews, and program notes, while drawing attention to the modernity of the performers, who participated in staging their own primitivism in order to meet a made-in-Hollywood "destination image" of Brazil.

While folkloric shows played into various stereotypes of Brazilians, here represented by Bahians (happy, convivial, exotic, sensual, and youthful), capoeiristas in particular also fulfilled expectations of (thrillingly) violent and primitive Afro-diasporic bodies. Capoeira performers amplified and choreographed capoeira's violence for the stage in heart-stopping choreographed sequences, directly influenced by Bimba's demonstration games (escretes) and Canjiquinha's choreographed brawl, his festa de arromba. Although these acrobatic choreographed confrontations reinforced racist associations of black male bodies with violence and hyperphysicality, they were also influential in generating a global fascination with capoeira that resulted in career opportunities, both as performers and teachers, for several capoeiristas who toured with folkloric shows in the 1960s and 1970s.

OLODUM AND OXUM:
STAGING FOLKLORE ON "HIGH ART" STAGES
In 1964 a group of Bimba's disciples, many of them university students, formed the Grupo Folclórico da Bahia, later renamed Olodum Conjunto Folclórico.[3] These capoeiristas' middle-class origins, college education, as well as the fact that most of them were not Afro-Brazilian (all markers of "non-folkness"), challenged the idea of folklore as the domain of working-class, brown or black "folklore bearers," while simultaneously lending social prestige to these ensembles. Having learned rather than passively inherited their folk knowledge, these university students staged a "secondhand" folklore that disquieted traditionalists, despite the fact that they had learned from such a well-established teacher as Bimba. In the same way that Rego objected to people from "the folk" taking on the role of historians, he also objected to middle-class university students

"infiltrating" folkloric ensembles, which as he saw it, detracted from their authenticity: "The infiltration of people with a social *status* different from [the status] of [capoeiristas] takes away [capoeira's] authenticity."[4]

The Grupo Folclórico da Bahia drew its authenticity in part from the presence of indisputable "bearers" of tradition onstage. In order to mollify criticism regarding the "non-folk-ness" of its members, the group hired Mãe Zefa (Maria Josefa das Mercês), a one-hundred-year-old "traditional Bahian woman."[5] Mãe Zefa, billed as the "spiritual mother of the group,"[6] lent authenticity to these shows through her black skin and her old age—an authenticity not sufficiently conveyed through the white, middle-class bodies of many of its performers. Acordeon (Ubirajara Guimarães Almeida) wrote and directed the group's early shows, which dealt with themes such as slavery, *quilombos* (maroon communities), famous capoeiristas, and capoeira's "social scene."[7] Like Canjiquinha, Acordeon included maculelê, puxada de rede, and samba de roda in these shows; unlike Canjiquinha, however, shows by the Grupo Folclórico da Bahia also included dances from candomblé ceremonies (discussed later in this chapter), a practice shared by many folkloric ensembles in the late 1960s and 1970s.[8]

The Grupo Folclórico da Bahia was reorganized and renamed Olodum in 1968 under the direction of Camisa Roxa (Edvaldo Carneiro e Silva) and Beijoca (Francisco Benjamin Muniz). Mãe Zefa continued to perform and tour with the group under the new directors, who complemented her presence with beautiful young *mulatas* (scantily clad, brown female samba dancers). As one enthusiastic newspaper listing warned, viewers had only one day left to "be swept away by the ecstatically beautiful mulatas in the cast."[9] In the early 1970s the group was again renamed Olodumaré, and still later Brasil Tropical, under the sole direction of Camisa Roxa. In its later iterations, the group fully embraced samba-dancing mulatas as part of the show, pairing a brown, "exotic" carnivalesque femininity with the "raw" masculine physicality of capoeira.[10]

In the late 1960s, Geni (José Serafim Ferreira Júnior)—who had studied and performed with Canjiquinha—and the brothers Cláudio and Carlito Maia (Cláudio Miranda Maia and Carlos Vasconcelos Maia Filho) founded the Grupo Folclórico Oxum, which went on to tour internationally and to perform at the Teatro Castro Alves, but not without first being turned down by the theater.[11] Founded and directed by well-connected, college-educated middle-class Bahians, the Grupo Folclórico Oxum

STAGING BRAZIL

Figure 4.1 Grupo Folclórico Olodumaré.
Photo published in the Diário de Notícias on May 10, 1976. Courtesy of the
Arquivo Histórico Municipal do Salvador, Diário de Notícias Collection.

would not be quietly left out of the programming of Salvador's most prestigious theater, and their exclusion from the 1971 season was publicized
in a prominent note in the tourism section of the Diário de Notícias. Under
a photograph of the group by renowned photographer Leão Rozenberg
(see figure 4.12), a lengthy caption denounced the injustice:

> Grupo Oxum, which is one of the best of Bahia, without a doubt,
> wrote to us stating that it was "turned down, this July, by the direc-
> tors of the TCA [Teatro Castro Alves], with the excuse that there
> was no room for them." [They] will be performing, until the 31 of

this month, in the ring of the old Red Cross, in the Campo Grande. The group is really upset, and even claimed that there is "politicking in Bahian folklore." The photo, by Leão Rozenberg, taken especially for the DN [*Diário de Notícias*], shows the sizzling bunch of Grupo Oxum, in action. We will now wait for an explanation from the people at the theater.[12]

Although I was unable to find a public response by the theater administrators, by the following year not only had the group begun to perform at the municipal theater regularly, but it had also secured sponsorship from SUTURSA for touring to Rio de Janeiro and other Brazilian cities.

The membership of Oxum and Olodum was by no means exclusively white and middle class, but the presence of these well-connected capoeiristas ensured that these groups attained the recognition, visibility, and sponsorship that allowed them to perform Bahian folklore for audiences in Brazil and abroad. The participation of Afro-Brazilian performers such as Mãe Zefa, the dancing mulatas of Olodumaré, as well as the numerous Afro-Brazilian capoeiristas who performed with these ensembles (such as Geni and Olhando p'ra Lua, today known as Mestre Lua Rasta) lent authenticity to these shows while simultaneously authorizing innovation and experimentation.

VIVA BAHIA: EMÍLIA BIANCARDI'S FOLK-POP SPECTACLES

Viva Bahia wasn't just samba de roda, maculelê, capoeira, no it wasn't. It was an experimental group that I started and I did it my way, the way I wanted.
—Emília Biancardi

While most other Bahian folkloric ensembles were directed by capoeiristas, the Conjunto Folclórico Viva Bahia was directed by Emília Biancardi, who not only was not a capoeirista; she was the only woman to direct a folkloric ensemble. Even though Viva Bahia was consistently praised by the media and received the seal of approval of Bahia's folklorists and tourism bureaucrats, Biancardi constantly struggled between a perceived need for preserving "folk" authenticity and her desire for artistic experimentation and innovation onstage. Through close analysis of the repertoire of Viva Bahia throughout the 1960s and 1970s, I trace the pro-

Figure 4.2 *The Maia brothers playing berimbau in a performance of Grupo Folclórico Oxum. Photographer unknown, c. 1975. Courtesy of the Arquivo Histórico Municipal de Salvador, Diário de Notícias Collection.*

Figure 4.3 Maculelê performed by Grupo Oxum. Geni, on the left, and Manuel Pé de Bode, on the right; Tatau can be seen in the background, center.
Photo identification courtesy of Mestre Geni. Photographer unknown.
Published in the Diário de Notícias on June 28, 1975. Courtesy of the Arquivo Histórico Municipal de Salvador, Diário de Notícias Collection.

cesses through which Afro-Brazilian "traditions" were selected, imagined, and staged both at home and abroad, and propose that Viva Bahia's performers—who were also often in charge of the choreography—purposefully and tactically met made-in-Hollywood "destination images" of a primitive and exotic Brazil in order to attain unprecedented international visibility and critical acclaim.

As examples of Viva Bahia's complex approach to preservation and innovation, tradition and modernity, I have selected four of the ensemble's most significant productions: *Aluandê* (1970), *Odoiá Bahia* (1972), *Capoeiras da Bahia* (1974), and *Festa Brazil* (1974). *Aluandê* and *Odoiá Bahia* were performed mostly in Brazil and had Biancardi as artistic director; *Capoeiras da Bahia* and *Festa Brazil*, however, were staged specifically for two separate concurrent tours abroad. For these last two shows, producers of international prestige hired artistic directors deemed more qualified than Biancardi to meet international standards, and her artistic control was diminished to "directress of the ensemble." My analysis is based on program notes, reviews, and photographs of these shows, as well as on interviews with Biancardi and former performers of Viva Bahia.

Born on April 8, 1941, Emília Biancardi Ferreira moved to Salvador with her mother from Vitória da Conquista at age thirteen, after her father's death.[13] In Salvador she studied piano at the Escola de Música da Bahia and earned a teaching certificate in Canto Orfeônico in 1960, which qualified Biancardi for her first job as a music teacher at the Instituto de Educação Isaías Alves, a public school in Salvador.[14] However, rather than follow her training in Canto Orfeônico and teach music through patriotic anthems, Biancardi decided instead to teach her students through folk songs and dances.

After the military coup d'état of 1964, Biancardi's folk ensemble—an amateur after-school activity that was gradually gaining visibility—was embraced as the official ensemble of the Inspetoria de Música e Canto Orfeônico (Inspectorate of Music and Orpheonic Song), an arm of Bahia's Secretaria de Educação (Department of Education), and the group operated under the auspices of the inspectorate until 1967. During this time, the ensemble, known simply as the folk ensemble of the Department of Education, performed regularly at the stage administered by the municipal tourism department. Biancardi's choice of the "folk" over the national in the school curriculum was in fact consonant with the increasing inter-

est in folkloric performances brought about by a growing tourism industry that demanded "authentic" representations of Bahianness. In 1967
Biancardi dissociated her ensemble from the Department of Education
and renamed it Conjunto Folclórico da Bahia, and after the success of
its two LPs, *Viva Bahia!* (c. 1967) and *Viva Bahia! Vol. 2* (1968), released by
Philips Records, the group became known as Conjunto Folclórico Viva
Bahia.

Biancardi sought the guidance of folklorist Hildegardes Vianna, who
went on to advise her research on the folkloric traditions she hoped to
stage. Although Biancardi traveled a few times with her students to the
"interior" of the state for brief ethnographic field research experiences,
the bulk of the transmission of "folk" traditions took place at Biancardi's
house, where "folklore bearers" were hired to teach maculelê, puxada de
rede, samba de roda, dances from candomblé, and capoeira. At Vianna's
recommendation, Biancardi later invited some of these "folklore bearers"
to perform with the ensemble;[15] rather than purveyors of culture merely
listed in the programs or erased altogether, these "people from the
people" (*gente do povo*) were invited to create and perform alongside her
students, many of them middle-class Bahians.[16]

Candomblé practitioners Dona Coleta (Clotildes Lopes Alves), who
taught dances from candomblé, and Seu Negão (Gilberto Nonato Sacramento), in charge of candomblé drumming, were among the "folklore
bearers" who became core members of Viva Bahia. Mestre Pastinha, by
then one of Bahia's most prestigious capoeira mestres, taught capoeira
to Biancardi's students. He did not perform with the group; instead, he
recommended one of his best students, João Grande (João Oliveira dos

Figure 4.5 Dona Coleta teaching Emília Biancardi's students at her residence in Salvador c. 1964. Photographer unknown. Courtesy of Emília Biancardi.

Santos), who became a core member of Viva Bahia and traveled with the company throughout the 1970s.

Placing "folklore bearers" on the stage—not the low-brow tourist stage but stages devoted to presenting "the arts"—lent authenticity to the material staged by Viva Bahia, while simultaneously "ennobling" the folk through high art. By 1969 the amateur troupe of teenagers had become a professional ensemble performing in Brazil's most prestigious high-art venues, such as Salvador's Teatro Castro Alves and the municipal theater of Rio de Janeiro (Teatro Municipal do Rio de Janeiro, a theater modeled after the Opera Garnier, inaugurated in 1909). Indeed, working with Viva Bahia was among the most prestigious jobs for Bahia's dancers and capoeiristas at the time: "If you danced in Emília Biancardi's show, you were the man."[17]

Folkloric shows for tourists featuring capoeira, maculelê, and various types of samba were commonplace in Salvador by the time Viva Bahia became a professional ensemble. On any given day, tourists could choose from a number of shows listed in the tourism/entertainment section of

Figure 4.6 Mestre Canapum teaching Emília Biancardi's
students at her residence in Salvador c. 1964.
Photographer unknown. Courtesy of Emília Biancardi.

Bahia's newspapers. However, as Vianna declared in a letter of support, Viva Bahia was "more than a simple folkloric ensemble. . . . Viva Bahia is not a group organized for entertaining tourists."[18] Viva Bahia's shows, categorized as art rather than entertainment, were included in the theater listings rather than in the tourism section of newspapers, available for limited engagements rather than performing on an ongoing basis. Viva Bahia's audience members sat in assigned seats facing a proscenium stage and devoted an hour or more of their undivided attention to the show, unlike audience members at tourist shows, who might sit in informal bleacher-type seating or enjoy a drink and a meal during shows held at nightclubs and restaurants.

As noted by Vianna, Viva Bahia was envisioned as "more" than an average folkloric ensemble. Biancardi explains: "Viva Bahia wasn't just samba de roda, maculelê, capoeira, no it wasn't. It was an experimental group that I started and I did it my way, the way I wanted."[19] While Canjiquinha, a "folklore bearer," was criticized for innovating, Biancardi, an urban, educated, middle-class schoolteacher, was *expected* to innovate. After the company was no longer an amateur ensemble in a school setting, Bian-

STAGING BRAZIL

cardi approached Viva Bahia's shows as a creative endeavor rather than an attempt to preserve, restore, or rescue folklore.

Biancardi's creativity was not only allowed but sanctioned by Salvador's leading folklorists, including the director of the Campaign for the Defense of Brazilian Folklore, Renato Almeida. In a note, in English, reprinted in the program for the show that commemorated Viva Bahia's tenth anniversary in 1973, Almeida expresses his full support for Biancardi's folkloric stagings:

> I hereby state that the group "VIVABAHIA," organized by the teacher Emília Biancardi Ferreira, to which she gives a secure direction, performs shows that are very close [to] folkloric authenticity, maintaining the feasible fidelity when projecting the folklore, thanks to the research she has [done on] the very origins of the popular culture. Miss Emília Biancardi Ferreira's performance deserves to be shown . . . to the Brazilian people and also to the foreign public, because it does not diminish the Folklore. [Quite] the opposite, it *gives folklore the high sense of art and love [of] national traditions.*[20]

Although Biancardi did not approach her work as a patriotic or nationalist undertaking, those working under the military dictatorship, such as Almeida, lauded her work as such. Giving folklore a "sense of art," Viva Bahia legitimized the folk through the "artistic." This and other official statements of support printed in this commemorative program, however, underscored Biancardi's ethnographic research and the "authenticity" of Viva Bahia's staged traditions rather than Biancardi's artistic input.[21] Biancardi's creativity was carefully monitored by Bahia's intellectual elite; while artistic input was allowed and welcomed, this input was expected to elevate rather than diminish Brazilian folklore—that is, artistic input should not compromise folklore's authenticity.

During the two decades of activity of Viva Bahia, Biancardi struggled with the complexities of staging folkloric traditions while preserving their "original purity." Biancardi had read Édison Carneiro's "Dinâmica do folclore" (Folklore's dynamics) and took to heart his view of folklore as always in flux. Carneiro proposed that change in folk traditions was a "natural" phenomenon, if brought about by "the folk." For him, "erudite interference" was acceptable, but any outside intervention should be carried out with "extreme discretion." This model perpetuates the erudite/folk binary, even though Carneiro had begun reconsidering this binary by envisioning folklore as a result of a dialectic process where "the whole society participates."[22] Carneiro's model, however, did not account for the changes that would result from collaborations between "folk" performers and "erudite" directors, choreographers, and producers in rechoreographing folklore for the stages of the world's major opera houses.

Aluandê (1970)

The show Aluandê, subtitled A alma e o coração da Bahia (The soul and heart of Bahia), marks Viva Bahia's first major theatrical production as a private ensemble, dissociated from the Department of Education. Although by 1969 the group was already performing at prestigious local theaters such as the Teatro Castro Alves, Viva Bahia's shows prior to Aluandê were billed generically as "folkloric shows." A specific show—one with a title—lent Viva Bahia distinction from folkloric shows performed on tourist stages, often identified only by the name of the folkloric group. A title implied that the show had been artistically conceived and authored by someone, and that it moved beyond mere reproduction of authorless, "collectively accepted" folklore.

No longer associated with the Department of Education, Biancardi was free to hire performers other than her students, thus increasing the number of "folklore bearers" in the cast. Although Viva Bahia already drew from the expertise of two respected candomblé practitioners, Seu Negão and Dona Coleta, Biancardi hired the well-known capoeirista João Grande, as well as several capoeiristas from other groups (such as Geni from Grupo Folclórico Oxum, and Olhando p'ra Lua, who also performed with Canjiquinha). Up until this point, Viva Bahia's strong suit had been maculelê, but faced with competition from the city's proliferating folkloric ensembles directed by capoeiristas whose crowd-pleasing acrobatics had become a staple of tourist entertainment, Viva Bahia strengthened its capoeira scenes through these capoeiristas' creative input and virtuosity.[23] Not only did these new additions to the cast bring expertise in an increasingly popular "traditional" movement practice, but their presence onstage authorized creativity and legitimized the show.

Although Biancardi's student-performers were not all white, many were light skinned enough, as was Biancardi herself, to be read as white, both on- and offstage.[24] Like Mãe Zefa in Grupo Folclórico da Bahia/Olodum, Viva Bahia's dark-skinned "folklore bearers," such as Seu Negão, Dona Coleta, and João Grande, brought authenticity to Viva Bahia's shows. Unlike centenarian Mãe Zefa, however, these performers were more than token symbols of Africa and the past onstage; in their thirties and forties, these "folklore bearers" were young enough to actively choreograph and perform with the ensemble for many years.

In a prominent note on the first page of the program for *Aluandê*, Biancardi asserts the legitimacy of the show by drawing attention to its "folklore bearers": "In this show we try to interpret popular expressions without letting go of their primitive and spontaneous forms. With this aim, we place individuals from the people (folklore bearers) in the main roles, allowing them to move freely, without stage blocking or any other [directions]."[25] Here Biancardi reproduces current ideas about folklore, such as the "spontaneity" proposed by Carneiro, as well as the notion of folklore as knowledge passively carried by "the folk." Biancardi downplays her own input as director by stating that these "individuals from the people" (*elementos populares*) moved freely, without stage directions. Without her stage directions, these "folklore bearers" in fact made their own choreographic decisions and adapted their own "traditions" for the stage. However, the myth of "primitive" bodies moving freely and spontaneously perpetuated by this statement does not acknowledge and, indeed, erases these "folk" performers' creativity and decision-making. In addition, this statement implicitly draws a distinction between the folklore bearers and the nonbearers in the cast, the former playing "themselves" onstage, and the latter reenacting these "traditions" learned from these and other "folk" informants.

Biancardi jokingly admits to her inexperience as a director at the time: "I accomplished my stagings through divine inspiration."[26] Since Viva Bahia did not hire a choreographer for *Aluandê*, most of the choreographic decisions were made by the performers in collaboration with Biancardi, who saw her interference as limited when it came to the dances: "I didn't have a choreographer yet; I was the one who gave it choreographic structure, but I left it the way it was taught by the folklore bearers; all I did was arrange and shorten [the dances]."[27] In addition to arranging and shortening dances, Biancardi also sought ways of making the movement larger and more spectacular—aiming to make a stronger "impact" on the audience. In the extensive program notes for *Aluandê*, Biancardi clarifies her own choreographic contributions to one of the types of samba included in the program: "The knife samba [*samba de faca*] in its true form consists of a contest between two dancers to see who is the most dexterous. Let me clarify that I added capoeira strikes for greater impact."[28] Biancardi, not a capoeirista herself, certainly collaborated with her capoeirista performers in adding movement from capoeira to this type of samba. By combining capoeira, a combat form, with a danced confrontation between two knife-wielding performers, Biancardi and her performers magnified the danger, virtuosity, and excitement of this dance, transforming it into a spectacular closing number. Not unlike the demonstration games choreographed by Bimba's students (which often included machetes), this knife samba mixed with capoeira strikes staged danger and violence to create spectacle.

The program notes for *Aluandê*, despite the stated goal of faithfully staging folklore in its "true" form, offer many indications of the show's stagedness, reminding the audience that despite its authenticity, the show was not the "real," offstage experience—a particularly important reminder in reference to the candomblé scene. In candomblé ceremonies, practitioners dance both as themselves and, after possession, as/with the *orixá* that possessed them. The candomblé scene in *Aluandê* is accompanied by a clarification in the program: "[Candomblé] is a fetishistic ritual which is performed in a didactic way [by] the ensemble." Performed in a "didactic way," these dances were divorced from possession, and audience members could rest assured that the deities would not be invoked in the theater.

Although *Aluandê* removed candomblé dances from their religious context, Viva Bahia still vowed to adhere to the recommendations of leading folklorists and culture bureaucrats at the time: staged folk performances should carefully "retain" folklore's authenticity. The group's objective is clearly stated in the program notes: "to research Bahia's folklore, reproducing [it] without letting go of its authenticity." The idea that folklore could and should be faithfully reproduced implied a stable, fixed original. Despite the fact that change was at the core of the dynamic model proposed by Carneiro, Biancardi still expressed an ongoing preoccupation with faithful reproduction and authenticity.

Odoiá Bahia (1972–1973)

Two years after *Aluandê*, Biancardi took the company in a drastically different direction. Renamed Ballet Folclórico Viva Bahia, the ensemble hired

Carlos Moraes, a ballet-trained dancer and choreographer, and brought in dancers trained in ballet, modern, and "primitive dance" from the Federal University of Bahia's dance program and from the Balé de Mercedes Baptista, based in Rio de Janeiro.

Seeking to break free from the tight boundaries dictated by Bahia's folklorists, Biancardi decided to embrace the impossibility of staging a "pure" and "authentic folklore" and joined forces with Moraes and set designer J. Cunha (José Antônio Cunha) to create *Odoiá Bahia: A Folk-Pop Spectacle*. Moraes, a former dancer with the resident ballet company of Rio de Janeiro's Municipal Theater, brought the "modernity" and prestige of ballet vocabulary, such as expansive leaps with extended legs and pointed feet.[29] Biancardi hoped that tradition and modernity could coexist onstage. In a program note for *Odoiá Bahia*, she writes, "In this show we will interpret folk forms or forms that tend towards the folkloric, in a stylized way, through elaborated choreography, maintaining, however, its true roots."[30] The term "stylized" (*estilizado/a*), as it was used at this time, refers to both a simplification and a modernization, and this modernization was intimately tied to the concept of "choreography." While "staging" (*arrumação cênica*) and "directing" (*direção cênica*) are terms often used by Biancardi to refer to her minimal interference in the movement vocabulary itself, the term "elaborated choreography" is used here to indicate new movement material derived from ballet and modern dance, dance forms considered urban, "modern," and erudite.

A listing in the daily newspaper *A Tribuna da Bahia* recommends *Odoiá Bahia*'s combination of modernity and tradition, describing it as "a modern and well thought-out production . . . where the group conceptualizes the ancient popular (folkloric) traditions within our times, employing to this end the most modern techniques of theater and dance, without, however, taking away the character of the folk dances per se, attempting, as much as possible, to stay faithful to its origins."[31] In this short note, the writer reproduces the same conflation of folklore and "ancient traditions" that Carneiro countered with his dynamic model of folklore, and praises *Odoiá Bahia* for employing "the most modern techniques of theater and dance" to usher these folkloric traditions into modernity. Biancardi and Moraes's innovations put Carneiro's dynamism into practice and tested its limits. Knowing that she had broken the cardinal rule of discreet "erudite interference," Biancardi expected the negative criticism that she and Moraes would indeed receive from the folklore establishment. In an interview for the same newspaper, the reporter points out Biancardi's anxiety:

> Concerned with the fact that it has become commonplace to label any new experimentation in this field as a disfigurement of folklore, Emília Biancardi says that the disfigurement much discussed in Bahia, is a consequence, in large part, of the perspective of traditional folklorists. She adds that "we need to get rid of the taboo that folk traditions are disappearing just because artists try to introduce more modern things," as if she was already answering in advance to any criticism that she expects to receive after the performances of the show.[32]

Anticipating the criticism she was sure to receive, Biancardi urges a rethinking of conservative views of folklore as static and endangered, and suggests that the anxieties about loss and "disfigurement" (deturpação) might be a matter of perspective. Biancardi believed that such stylized staged adaptations would not result in any kind of loss or "disfigurement" to these traditions offstage. She knew from experience that adaptations for the stage that did not rely on "elaborated choreography" were far more likely to influence "folk" practices offstage.[33]

Odoiá Bahia, like Viva Bahia's previous shows, opened with samba de roda and capoeira. The program frames these two movement forms as simple, "spontaneous" folk forms found in poor neighborhoods. Interestingly, the folk/erudite divide here is framed as a matter of socioeconomic class rather than along a rural/urban binary. This "folk" beginning gave way to increasingly balleticized and "stylized" choreography. Closing the first half of the show, the "Suite Bahiana"—a potpourri of energetic, fast-paced dances, not exclusively from Bahia—exemplifies Biancardi and Moraes's willingness to experiment. Inspired by Antônio de Castro Alves's poem "O navio negreiro" (The slave ship) and featuring set design by J. Cunha, this suite culminated in a scene called "Fantasia afro." As the title promised, this scene brought to life Hollywood-inspired fantasies of Africa, such as seminaked warriors bearing shields and spears, and grass-skirt-clad brown-skinned women, their bare breasts and torsos decorated with body paint. Viva Bahia's "Africans," however, challenged the "wildness" and primitivism that might accompany such fantasies of Africa by dancing according to a controlled, extended, and upright ballet aesthetic.[34]

Figure 4.7 A dancer leaps with extended legs and pointed feet in Odoiá Bahia, embodying a ballet aesthetic. Her bent arms and clenched fists, however, transform a potentially sylph-like gesture of lightness into a gesture of strength. Photographer unknown. Courtesy of Emília Biancardi.

The second half of the show featured some of the most controversial elements of *Odoiá Bahia*. Inspired by candomblé themes, Biancardi and Moraes combined the "folk" with the "pop," adding electric guitars (the pop) to the traditional candomblé drum ensemble (the folk). This section of the program included solos and duets based on dances performed by different orixás. The duet between Exú (the trickster, danced by Sputnick)[35] and Pomba-gira ("Exú's wife," danced by Bebé)[36] included foreign movement patterns such as the touching and lifting from a ballet pas de deux.[37] Biancardi remembers the overall reaction to this scene: "It was a scandal, everyone criticized it." According to Biancardi, *Odoiá Bahia* was criticized both by the folklore establishment and by the candomblé community for disrespecting and "disfiguring" candomblé. During an interview in 2011, still feeling the need to justify her decisions, she explains: "I wasn't a folklore bearer, I was a music teacher who experimented with folklore; what I did were *re-creations*."[38]

Odoiá Bahia was controversial precisely because it was a drastic departure from the company's previous approach, which claimed to present "folk" forms in their "original purity." No longer tied to the Department

Figure 4.8 *A dancer poses for a photo in front of the backdrop for* Odoiá Bahia *by J. Cunha. Her torso extended and arched, arms raised and fists clenched, she gazes upward and outward, defiantly. Photographer unknown. Published in the* Diário de Notícias *on October 8, 1972. Courtesy of the Arquivo Histórico Municipal de Salvador, Diário de Notícias Collection.*

of Education, Viva Bahia shed its former didactic purpose, approaching *Odoiá Bahia* as both art and entertainment. "Improving" the folk through the erudite, *Odoiá Bahia* provided an opportunity for Afro-diasporic bodies to perform as other than "themselves," even if this meant dancing out someone else's "Afro" fantasies. This collaboration between Biancardi and Moraes also provided people from disadvantaged socioeconomic backgrounds—many of them Afro-Brazilian—access to ballet training, which at the time meant increased opportunities for employment as professional dancers.[39]

Immediately after its three-day run at the Teatro Castro Alves, *Odoiá Bahia* began a tour of several Brazilian cities, followed by a trip to Guyana, where the company represented Brazil at the international music and dance festival Carifesta. However, according to Biancardi, the show was modified for the international performances: "Abroad, we took candomblé, samba de roda, in a very authentic way. We couldn't take [all this innovation] abroad."[40] Moraes's choreographic influence was nevertheless still present in the Carifesta performance, as was Biancardi's desire to go beyond the tight boundaries of tradition.

While it may have been criticized by Bahian purists, the modernity of *Odoiá Bahia* made a favorable impression on Rio de Janeiro music producers Walter Santos and Hermínio Bello de Carvalho. In 1973 Carvalho and Biancardi collaborated to create *Panorama Brasileiro*, a show aimed at foreign audiences, which like *Odoiá Bahia* combined the "folk" with the "pop." Well connected in the Rio music scene, Carvalho assembled a group of professional musicians, including emerging vocalist Simone Bittencourt de Oliveira, and the show toured Paris, Cologne, and Brussels. Despite the fact that the show included a significant element of Brazilian pop music, including the bossa nova sounds of the group Tamba Trio as well as the music of Dorival Caymmi sung by Simone, Biancardi insisted on the "primitivism" of the show. In an interview for the *Jornal da Bahia* shortly before the company's departure for Europe, Biancardi reassures the reporter that Viva Bahia would continue to honor Brazil's folk traditions: "In Brussels, Viva Bahia will perform with a minimum of elaborated forms, precisely the opposite of its previous phases, which foreground[ed] the adaptations for folklore performed on stage, with all its modern resources of set design and choreography. [This show] will have the characteristics of the early Viva Bahia, in all its primitivism, which reflects the roots that cannot be pushed aside."[41] In this interview Biancardi expresses her commitment to show Brazilian folklore "in all its primitivism," downplaying the show's pop music element for the readership of the *Jornal da Bahia*. She agreed, however, that a certain amount of sophistication was necessary for a stronger "aesthetic appeal": "In Brussels, . . . Viva Bahia will show the primitivism of our culture . . . however, the costumes will be the most sophisticated. . . . This aesthetic appeal is especially necessary abroad because the majority of the spectators is lay [and] few have heard of anything Brazilian, or more precisely Bahian, and they don't know anything about folklore."[42] Biancardi and Carvalho knew that to be successful abroad it was necessary for the "primitive" and the "folk" to be entertaining rather than merely didactic; through "the most sophisticated" costumes—elaborate carnival costumes—the directors hoped to meet a destination image of "Latin" excess established throughout the 1940s, and to please their "lay" audiences. This combination of the primitive and the sophisticated proved to be a recipe for success, and following the European performances of *Panorama Brasileiro*, Biancardi and Carvalho signed contracts for international tours to take place the following year. In 1974 Biancardi expanded and divided Viva Bahia into two groups, and the companies embarked on two simultaneous tours: *Festa Brazil*, bound for the United States and Canada, and *Capoeiras da Bahia*, for Europe and Iran.

Capoeiras da Bahia, produced by Ruth Escobar and Ninon Tallon Karlweiss, played in the most prestigious opera houses in more than ten European countries between May and October 1974;[43] *Festa Brazil*, produced by Walter Santos, took Brazilian exoticism to prestigious U.S. venues such as the Kennedy Center, the Brooklyn Academy of Music, and Madison Square Garden. These producers hired directors from Rio de Janeiro (Gilda Grillo for *Capoeiras da Bahia*, and Hermínio Bello de Carvalho for *Festa Brazil*), who replaced Biancardi as artistic director.[44] Moraes was not included in the credits for either of these shows, although sections of Moraes's choreography were reworked by the directors and the performers. No choreographer is listed in the programs, and neither are Biancardi's adaptations for the stage; absent also is the list of "folklore bearers" consulted for the show, always included in previous programs. If these shows were to construct a fiction of "primitives" spontaneously performing themselves onstage—their dances "untouched" and "pure"—any evidence of purposefully "elaborated" choreography should be carefully erased.

While *Festa Brazil* choreographed a sultry and exotic destination image of Brazil, *Capoeiras da Bahia* fulfilled European fantasies of a savage and primitive South America. Both these shows, however, staged Brazil as a high-energy, thrilling place where brown, muscular capoeiristas exuded masculine vigor, youth, and physical prowess, and strange Afro-Brazilian rituals of possession, complete with actual animal sacrifice, portrayed a culture that was both intriguing and frightening. And it was precisely the perceived danger of these two "traditions"—magnified for the stage—that provided audience members with the thrills they expected.

Festa Brazil (1974)

Under Carvalho's artistic direction, Festa Brazil drew heavily from Panorama Brasileiro, which in turn retained many choreographic elements from Odoiá Bahia. (Many of the original members of Odoiá Bahia also toured with Festa Brazil, including Bebé, Sputnick, and Seu Negão.) Even though its U.S. producer, Mel Howard Productions, based Festa Brazil's publicity on its "primitive" and spectacular aspects, featuring photos in press packets of capoeiristas flying through the air, this show continued to combine the "folk" with the "pop."

Festa Brazil was performed at Madison Square Garden's Felt Forum in April 1974 as part of the International Festival of Entertainment, a festival that featured "ethnic" performance ensembles from various countries. For New York Times dance critic Anna Kisselgoff, Festa Brazil stood out at the festival precisely for contrasting the "folk" with the "pop," which Kisselgoff interpreted as evidence that indeed Brazil was a "land of contrasts." Kisselgoff found such contrasts in the "sophisticated urban nightclub musical combo and singer" who performed "as an integral part of a program that stresses rituals of an early rural culture."[45] Here Brazil's "sophisticated" urban modernity is constructed through its juxtaposition with an "early rural culture," the vestiges of which can be seen in the rituals staged in Festa Brazil. It is not surprising that Brazil's modernity was mapped onto the bodies of light-skinned "pop" performers, such as Simone, while brown and black "folk" performers stood for Brazil's past.

A twenty-three-year-old emerging vocalist at the time, Simone was a tall Bahian with pale skin and cascading black curls. A brief bio in the program describes her as "an ideal representative of Brazil—a young and progressive country—but with a great cultural background. The Afro-European roots in Brazilian popular music have in Simone their ideal interpreter."[46] Brazil's progress and youth are embodied by Simone, as is its "cultural background," that is its blend of African and European "roots." Although Simone's skin color and hair texture clearly mark her as white in Brazil, she is framed as "the ideal interpreter" of Brazil's Afro-European musical traditions.

Kisselgoff describes Simone's sophisticated yet down-to-earth stage presence: "The studied, chic dishevelment of Simone, a popular singer who wanders around the stage barefoot, encounters no resistance from the three Maria sisters, dressed in the traditional Bahia white hoop skirts. Armed like Simone with portable microphones, they meet her on her ground in their folk material."[47] While Simone's dishevelment (her barefoot performance) is read as studied and chic, what Kisselgoff notes about the three Maria sisters (the show's Afro-Brazilian backup singers, billed as "Marias de Salvador") is that they wear "traditional" dresses and hold their own despite finding themselves out of their element, on Simone's "ground" — the modern proscenium stage equipped with portable microphones. The show successfully frames the three Marias as rural, unfamiliar with the stage, despite the fact that they came from Brazil's first capital and one of its largest cities, Salvador.

Carvalho's artistic direction sets up the contrast between modernity and tradition along skin tone. Kisselgoff notes that Carvalho "emphasizes the heritage of the black population," which provides "some of the program's most exciting sections." Kisselgoff was particularly impressed by the maculelê and capoeira scenes: "The ferocity and vigor with which these young men strike out at one another leave no room for pussyfooting, and yet they perform with choreographic precision."[48] A "ferocious" (hyper)physicality stood in stark contrast to Simone's "studied" performance of Brazilian chic. Kisselgoff identifies the vigor and youth "of a young, progressive country" in the brown bodies of the capoeiristas. Although their "choreographic precision" was as "studied" as Simone's chic dishevelment, what stood out for Kisselgoff was the capoeiristas' animalistic "ferocity" and vigorous physicality.

The masculine vigor of *Festa Brazil*'s capoeiristas stands out as the most memorable aspect of the show for *Vancouver Sun* drama critic Christopher Dafoe, whose review is titled "Vigor You Expect and Vigor You Get."[49] Dafoe, like Kisselgoff, deems the show a "curious combination of night club and folk festival." The nightclub atmosphere is created by the musical ensemble, composed of both acoustic and electric guitars, a cavaquinho, an electric bass, a synthesizer, as well as a drum set, and of course by the sultry presence of Simone. In his review, Dafoe describes the singer as a dark, statuesque beauty: "The Festa Brazil company of 35 dancers and singers provides a suitably exotic background for the two big stars of the show, guitarist Joao [sic] de Aquino and former basketball star Simone Bittencourt de Oliveira, a dark, statuesque lady with snakeskin vocal chords. De Aquino plays guitar in the great Latin pop tradition and Miss

Simone is almost overwhelming in bare feet."⁵⁰ Viva Bahia's performers are reduced to a "suitably exotic background" for Simone and Aquino, providing the "folk" roots for the Brazilian "pop." These "background" performers, most of them Afro-Brazilians, combined with the description of Simone as representative of Brazil's Afro-European culture, had a "browning" effect on Simone, who is read as "dark" by Dafoe in spite of her light skin color. While the show included some female nudity—bare breasts, as had become customary in most Brazilian folkloric shows abroad—Simone was always fully clothed. Her bare feet, however, were enough to almost overwhelm this critic in their sensuality.

Dafoe also picks up on the director's efforts to deemphasize the regional Bahian affiliation of the show and resignify Afro-Bahian music and movement as "national culture"; for this critic, the show evokes images of Rio rather than Bahia:

> Brazil ... is where the nuts come from. It is also the home of the coffee bean and the samba. Many of us would love to roll to Rio someday before we are old. Brazil, in fact, exerts a strong attraction upon many who live in these austere northern latitudes. As the cold rain pours down, they dream of mad nights in Rio, that exotic city of pleasure where everybody stays up until dawn dancing in the streets and where all the women are at least six feet tall and wear baskets of fruit on their heads.⁵¹

Referencing both the 1941 film *Charley's Aunt* ("where the nuts come from") and Carmen Miranda's signature fruit-laden headdresses, Dafoe establishes his own destination image of Brazil—a destination he hopes to reach someday before he is too old to enjoy a few pleasure-filled "mad nights in Rio." Bahia is never mentioned in this review, alluded to vaguely as "the Brazilian outback," the source of "rough" folk traditions that had been "tarted up" for the stage. In the process of being "tarted up," Bahian music and dance are made to conform to a Rio-based, made-in-Hollywood destination image of Brazil, complete with a Rio *carnaval* finale. As Dafoe concludes, "Festa Brazil strives vigorously to live up to every romantic notion of what a big, flashy Latin spectacular should be."⁵²

Through *Festa Brazil*, residents of "austere northern latitudes" could experience the excitement and exoticism of "mad nights in Rio" from the safety of their seats at the Queen Elizabeth Theater in Vancouver. As Dafoe continues to describe this contagious spectacle, he focuses on the embodied responses of those in attendance: "Toes tap, shoulders vibrate, and in the audience, one suspects, dentures click in time to the music. As all those big, strong, handsome men surge through their wild gymnastic dances one tends to feel middle-aged and badly out of condition."[53] With toes tapping and shoulders vibrating, seated audience members participate in an "austere," attenuated version of the movement onstage. Here Dafoe comments on the lack of youth he identifies both in himself and in others in the audience, whose "dentures click in time to the music." Perhaps Dafoe hoped to rescue some of this lost youth through an empathic experience with the young performers, especially those "big, strong, handsome" capoeiristas who surge through the air in their "wild gymnastic dances." This masculine vigor in fact seems central to Dafoe's experience. Although he found Festa Brazil's "Latin vibrations" excessive at times, "as if someone is beating you over the head with a pineapple," Dafoe admits that the show has met his expectations: "Vigor, however, is expected and vigor is provided in full measure. That is Brazil."[54]

Capoeiras da Bahia (1974)

Capoeiras da Bahia differed from Festa Brazil in that it staged the "folk" without the "pop." In 1973 Tallon Karlweiss, a New York-based experimental theater producer approached Escobar, a Portuguese-born actress and producer based in São Paulo, with the idea of taking a group of capoeiristas from Bahia to folk festivals in Europe, Asia, and Africa. Escobar hired emerging actress and director Gilda Grillo to direct this show and assembled a cast of dancers and capoeiristas through Biancardi's Viva Bahia. While both Biancardi and the dancers had vast creative input in this show, Grillo—a cosmopolitan, upper-class, white carioca—positioned herself as the show's innovator, and Viva Bahia's members, including Biancardi herself, took on the role of "folklore bearers" in both the publicity and the credits for the show. In London's Morning Star, Grillo is described as "tanned, blonde and beautiful and supremely articulate even in a language not her own."[55] A photograph of Grillo in an article in the British newspaper the Sunday Times shows a blonde, slender woman in her early thirties, peering at the camera over her sunglasses.[56] While Biancardi would have been at least as articulate (she was certainly more knowledgeable than newcomer Grillo about the show's material), the fact that she did not speak a foreign language meant that only Grillo's voice was heard in numerous newspaper interviews during the European tour.

In an interview for *Time Out London* magazine, Grillo takes the blame (and the credit) for altering "tradition": "I am the corruptor. The moment you present a ritual on stage you are interfering." Echoing Biancardi's earlier statements about retaining folk "purity" despite innovation, Grillo continues: "In spite of this, nothing in the Candomblé is changed. I had to find the way of capturing the essence of the rite and show it as close as possible to reality, without, however, endangering the dancers."[57] Under Grillo's direction, Viva Bahia strove to bring "raw" Afro-Brazilian primitivism to European stages. Grillo clarifies to *Time Out London* that the drummers in the show avoid the "forbidden" rhythms, but even so, "we still run some risk [of possession] every night.... We're interfering with powerful forces that should be respected."[58] In the same way that Bimba's and Canjiquinha's shows amplified and theatricalized the danger and violence of capoeira, the performers of Viva Bahia, in collaboration with Biancardi and Grillo, staged both capoeira and candomblé as thrillingly dangerous. The candomblé scene in *Capoeiras da Bahia* fulfilled the destination image of Brazil as home to a "savage," dangerous Afro-diasporic physicality, barely under the director's control.

In an interview for the *Sunday Times*, Grillo highlights the inherent violence of the movement performed in this show and the "wild" nature of the dancers:

There is bound to be a doctor in the house when the Capoeiras da Bahia—a company of Brazilian Voodoo Dancers—opens at London Round House on July 30th. In fact, he'll be permanently waiting in the wings. "The reason is that the show is so incredibly violent" said Gilda Grillo, the company director. "If we don't have three accidents a night ... we feel like celebrating." The other week one of the dancers was hauled off to hospital when—in the course of a dance called Maculele, during which the performers battle with sticks and swords—his right arm was run through with a cutlass. "He was stitched up and shot full of penicillin and told to take it easy. But as soon as my back was turned he was back on stage waving his knife about more wildly than ever."[59]

Here the dancers accidentally carry through the violence latent in combat dances such as maculelê, made more dangerous and spectacular by replacing maculelê sticks with machetes (which Grillo refers to as swords or cutlasses). The fact that this accident was featured at length in this

Figure 4.9 Loremil Machado plays the initiate in the staged ceremony that included the killing of a rooster on stage. This scene also included a live goat, pictured here. Photo by Nobby Clark, The Roundhouse, London, July 1974. © Nobby Clark/ArenaPAL.

short article (based primarily on an interview with Grillo) points to the director's awareness of the fascination of foreign audiences with the show's violence and bloodshed. Again Grillo reiterates the idea that these "wild" performers, with their machetes and their "voodoo," were only barely under the director's control.[60]

Although the bloodshed described by Grillo was an accident, the director, in collaboration with Biancardi and the performers, in fact included actual bloodshed in the show in the form of animal sacrifice (which took place in countries that did not prohibit the sacrifice as animal cruelty). Grillo explains to the readers of the *Sunday Times* that *Capoeiras da Bahia* was "a distillation of Brazilian folklore and ritual, including ceremonies of initiation, exorcism and celebration which—at other stops in their tour—has included the sacrifice of a white cockerel in full view of the audience. 'In Paris we slaughtered a cockerel every night, no trouble. In London, though, no cockerel.'"[61] Here Grillo refers to the fact that their animal sacrifice scene was not permitted in England. Her nonchalant attitude toward the sacrifice reinforces the "wildness" of the show's performers, capable of killing an animal every night, "no trouble." This animal sacrifice—anything but trivial in its religious context—emphasizes the allegedly unmediated primitivism of the performers. Critic Henri Terrière, writing for the French newspaper *Ouest-France*, describes this highly theatricalized moment of actual bloodshed: "We watch the sacrifice of a white rooster[,] which a man decapitates with this teeth to anoint the shaved head of an initiate with blood and feathers[,] who is the object of an extraordinary exaltation."[62] These "primitive" practices, barely contained by the fourth wall of the proscenium stage, allowed European theatergoers to experience the thrills of these "dangerous" rituals from the safety of their seats—an experience that reinforced their own modernity and civilization.

Rather than eliciting the desire to "roll down to Rio" expressed by Dafoe after seeing *Festa Brazil*, viewers of *Capoeiras da Bahia* might have been a bit more hesitant about planning a trip to Brazil after witnessing this violence. Perhaps for this reason, the show closed with the spectacular physicality of capoeira followed by a festive audience participation finale, where viewers were invited to go up onstage and dance the samba with "some of the most attractive and outgoing performers on any stage anywhere."[63] According to a French festival organizer, the ability to control this "extraordinarily savage and spontaneous" Afro-Brazilian physicality was what made *Capoeiras da Bahia* "a true work of art."[64]

In several interviews during their European tour, Grillo establishes her position as the creative force behind the show, while reinforcing the notion that the performers—who were said to come from a rural, "primitive Brazil"—performed "themselves" onstage with minimal interference. In an interview for the *Sunday Times*, Grillo states that the company was composed of dancers and musicians from "a small village in Bahia on the eastern coast of Brazil," even though Grillo knew perfectly well that this "small village," the city of Salvador, was at the time Brazil's fifth-largest city with a population of over one million.[65] She explains that in this village Biancardi founded a center "dedicated to preserving folk traditions." According to this narrative, Biancardi and her ensemble are stripped of any vestige of modernity or creativity; instead, they are framed as the purveyors of a "pure," unadulterated tradition which must be preserved. In several interviews Grillo stresses the idea that the company's mission was to preserve a culture in danger of disappearing. In a review of *Capoeiras da Bahia* aptly titled "A Unique Tradition Survives," *Morning*

Figure 4.10 *João Grande's opening solo in Capoeiras da Bahia*
at The Roundhouse, London, July 1974.
Photo by Nobby Clark. © Nobby Clark/ArenaPAL.

Star ballet critic Jane King informs the reader that "the authentic culture of Brazil is in danger of disappearing. [Grillo] and her associates in this venture feel it was too important to be allowed to die." [66]

And nothing could provide starker contrast to the idea of a "dying" culture than the vitality of the show's capoeira number. For King, the most energetic, "the most thrilling item of the strangely exciting Brazilian programme at the Roundhouse was the dance fight, the 'Capoeira,' from which the company takes its name." The "ritual" atmosphere established by the realistic candomblé ceremony during the first half of the show carried through to the capoeira section, characterized by King as "hypnotic": "the male dancers engage one another in fierce, rhythmical combat, dancing on their hands and taking lethal swipes and jabs at one another with their feet." [67]

This hypnotic, action-packed capoeira scene, marked by "lethal swipes and jabs," was preceded by a highly "ritualized" solo by João Grande, who solemnly entered the stage playing his berimbau. After introducing the audience to the sounds of this unusual musical bow—seen for the first time by the majority of the spectators in Europe and Iran—João Grande would lay the berimbau down on the ground and, slowly and ceremoni-

Figure 4.11 Capoeiristas
perform assisted backflips
in an unidentified show in
the early 1970s.
Photographer unknown.
Courtesy of the Arquivo Histórico
Municipal de Salvador, Diário
de Notícias Collection.

ously, "dance" capoeira around and over it in silence (see figure 4.10).[68]
After this intriguing, quiet beginning, other capoeiristas, drummers,
and berimbau players would join João Grande onstage in an explosion of
sound and movement.

For *Capoeiras da Bahia*, Biancardi remembers casting "only the best capoeiristas," those whose performance skills "could make the audience
stand up."[69] João Grande remembers that what pleased audiences were
capoeira's acrobatics, especially jumps and flips. Audiences wanted speed
and attack, bodies slashing the air with fast circular kicks and multiple
flips: "For shows onstage, you already know [what they want]: it's *vup
vup vup*."[70] The capoeiristas knew how to deliver the masculine "vigor"
expected by audience members such as Dafoe—"those big, strong, handsome men surg[ing] through their wild gymnastic dances."[71]

While the understated, slow-motion, dance-like Capoeira Angola developed by Mestre Pastinha worked well in situations where audiences
watched at close range, that capoeira style was not large enough or virtuosic enough to fit the stages of opera houses. The grabbing and throwing
of Bimba's connected moves (*golpes ligados*), choreographed by Bimba's
students for demonstration games (*escretes*) in the 1960s, turned out to be
the perfect ingredient for an expansive and spectacular capoeira suited
for proscenium stages in large theatrical venues. Figures 4.11 and 4.12
illustrate these partnered throws, now transformed into assisted flips,
where the player being "thrown" takes an active role in his own throw-

Figure 4.12 Grupo Oxum during a photo session with photographer Leão Rozenberg. Geni and Macaco perform an assisted flip in the foreground; Tatau and Olhando p'ra Lua squat, ready to begin the next game. In the background Simpatia plays atabaque and Jair plays berimbau. Photo identification courtesy of Mestre Geni. Courtesy of the Arquivo Histórico Municipal de Salvador, Diário de Notícias Collection.

ing, using the other player's body for support. These assisted flips were further transformed onstage into acrobatic solos, where each capoeirista would exhibit his most impressive jumps, flips, headspins, and upside-down balances.[72] Capoeira's spectacle of youth, vigor, and virtuosity was one of *Capoeiras da Bahia* main attractions during its European tour; in fact, Grillo decided to highlight capoeira in the title of the show because "she saw that, among all the scenes, it was the most sensational."[73]

Although staged capoeira has been blamed for an excessive emphasis on "sensational" acrobatics, often seen as the cause of capoeira's *descaracterização* (loss of character), staged acrobatics merely extended and magnified a "traditional" aerial aspect of capoeira that had been downplayed and virtually eliminated in late twentieth-century offstage capoeira practice: the practice of grabbing and throwing, known as *balões*. The stage innovation that was indeed foreign to capoeira—after all, a form of combat between two people—was the introduction of the solo format. Solos al-

lowed for expansive movement capable of moving through space, sometimes in a linear fashion, such as in sequences of multiple backflips. Solos
also divorced movement from its function—striking or tripping the adversary or avoiding strikes and sweeps—allowing for an increased attention
to the aesthetics and the visual pleasure achieved through the movement.

Grupo Folclórico Oxum's cofounder Geni, who also performed with
Canjiquinha and briefly with Viva Bahia, attributes the increased use of
floreios (flourishes) in contemporary capoeira to the adaptations made for
staged performances: "The capoeira that exists today all over the world,
it's thanks to folkloric shows. . . . Because before[,] capoeira was held
back, both angola and regional. You didn't have *floreios*, you didn't have a
thousand jumps, you didn't have these things."[74] Onstage, a "held back"
capoeira gives way to a capoeira where players are allowed to drop their
guard and be creative, indulging in *floreios* without the need to play defen-
sively. Pavão (Eusébio Lôbo da Silva), who also performed with Oxum in
the 1970s, remembers that onstage, games were "flourished, or beautiful games, in which the objective was the embodied aesthetics produced
by the capoeiristas."[75] João Grande, in an interview for the documentary
A arte da capoeira (The art of capoeira), explains that onstage, capoeira becomes free, beautiful, and playful: "On stage, it's a free game, a beautiful
game: come get me! In the roda it's different, on stage it's all pre-arranged.
In the roda you come in sure of yourself, you can't hesitate. But on stage
. . . it's for the public. . . . You open up for the other guy to come get you
and you get out of the way with a roll or a cartwheel. [It's] an open, beautiful game on stage."[76] In this statement, João Grande's pleasure in performing "open" games onstage is apparent. Rather than contributing to
capoeira's "loss of character," as has been claimed, these predetermined
movement sequences— "open" games, devoid of actual violence—in fact
released players to take pleasure in the creative process rather than focus
on survival. Since no choreographers were hired for either *Festa Brazil* or
Capoeiras da Bahia, capoeiristas were free to engage (and indeed indulge)
in a practice that has been highly valued in capoeira: individual innovation. Solos were displays of each player's best acrobatic skills, and choreographed "duets" like the one described by João Grande allowed players
to perform "open," "beautiful" games, which were not only aesthetically
pleasing but also playful and pleasurable for the players.

João Grande, today the most revered "grand master" of capoeira angola and the founder of the most sought-after capoeira angola school

Figure 4.13 Capoeiras da Bahia's open and beautiful games.
Photo by Nobby Clark, The Roundhouse, London, 1974. © Nobby Clark/ArenaPAL.

outside Brazil, looks back on the pleasure he found in performing onstage: "What I really liked were staged shows. I didn't like teaching capoeira. I liked the stage, hitting the maculelê, doing the samba, to travel
a lot, I liked it a lot, and I still like it."[77] For João Grande, the pleasure
of stage performance was intimately tied to the pleasures of traveling
and exploring new places. He adds that the performers were very well
taken care of—always staying at nice hotels, all expenses paid. At the
same time that Grillo and the European media constructed images of
primitive, "wild" performers from a "small village," the 1974 tours of both
Capoeiras da Bahia and *Festa Brazil* established Viva Bahia's capoeiristas as
transnational performing artists. Many of the cast members traveled
abroad—to Europe, Iran, and the United States—for the first time with
Viva Bahia. After seeing (and being seen by) the world, several members
of Viva Bahia emigrated to teach capoeira and/or Brazilian music, including Biancardi herself, who moved to Woodstock, New York, in 1990;[78] capoeiristas Jelon Vieira (Jelon Gomes Vieira Filho) and Loremil Machado
(Josevaldo de Souza Machado) moved to New York City in the late 1970s
and founded a Brazilian dance company, initially named after the show
Capoeiras da Bahia and later renamed Dance Brazil; Mestre João Grande has

taught capoeira angola in Manhattan since 1990, and his Capoeira Angola Center has become the global "mecca" of capoeira angola.

Festa Brazil constructed Brazilian "folk" and "pop" (tradition and modernity) along a skin-color continuum; *Capoeiras da Bahia* reinforced associations between black skin and violence, savagery, and primitivism. Both shows met the destination image of Brazil as a festive place where "happy people" stay up dancing and partying all night; where dark, statuesque barefoot women overwhelm in their sensuality and "big, strong, handsome" men share their youth and vigor with middle-aged audience members in "austere northern latitudes."

From the performers' perspective, however, the 1974 tours also provided opportunities for individual creativity and innovation, as well as the prestige that came with having toured with Viva Bahia. Folklore "bearers," such as João Grande, were freed from the burden of a tradition imposed from the outside, and seized the opportunity to be creative, choreographing solemn solos and "beautiful," playful, and open duets. While capoeira's violence was highlighted through the narratives that accompanied the performances, it was precisely its nonviolence onstage that freed performers to explore a pleasurable and creative virtuosity.

CONCLUSION

Although the Bahian folkloric ensembles that received the most visibility, state support, and critical acclaim were those led by middle-class directors, in their majority non-Afrodescendant capoeiristas, these ensembles also provided working-class Afro-Brazilian capoeiristas, dancers, and musicians with professional performance opportunities in the world's most prestigious theatrical venues. Most important, their tours sparked international interest in Afro-Brazilian culture in the 1960s and 1970s.

Biancardi's emphasis on purity and tradition in her early stagings of Afro-Brazilian folklore reinforced the notion of folklore as "borne" by *gente do povo*, whose "folk" identity was determined more by social class and skin color than by any actual rural origins. By using terms such as "folklore bearers" (*portadores de folclore*), Biancardi, echoing the nomenclature used by folklorists at the time, reinforced the distinction between folklore "borne"—transmitted unchanged from one generation to the next—and folklore learned. However, Biancardi challenged the fixity and traditionality of folklore by embracing modernity (the "pop") in works such as *Odoiá Bahia*. Rather than modernizing "the folk" by appropriating and recasting Afro-Brazilian corporeality onto mostly non-Afro-Brazilian ballet-trained bodies, Biancardi and Moraes cast Afro-diasporic performers who disrupted the folk/high art binary through their balletic performances of "Afro-fantasies."

Viva Bahia's shows in the 1960s and 1970s fulfilled made-in-Hollywood destination images of Brazil and further established this "land of contrasts" as a cultural tourism destination. Although *Festa Brazil* fulfilled expectations of Brazil's exotic primitivism—vigorous, strong brown men leaping through the air, and sultry barefoot "dark" women overwhelming in their sensuality—it also presented Brazil's modernity through its bossa nova rhythms and "nightclub" atmosphere. Lacking a "pop" element, *Capoeiras da Bahia* not only met but also magnified European audiences' fantasies of a savage, wild, barely-under-control Afro-diasporic corporeality.

Both *Festa Brazil* and *Capoeiras da Bahia* brought to life kinesthetic destination images of racially marked, othered bodies moving in "excessive" ways—overflowing with "natural" exuberance and sensuality and thrilling audiences with the "violent" physicality of capoeira and maculelê and the "dangers" of possession and animal sacrifice. While a seemingly violent capoeira was staged for audiences in "northern latitudes," the lack of actual violence onstage allowed capoeiristas to experiment with capoeira's aesthetics rather than its function, and to develop a wide vocabulary of *floreios*, including headspins, backflips, and other acrobatic moves that have since become part of offstage capoeira practice.

CONCLUSION

···

Throughout this book, I have reconsidered iterations of capoeira previously dismissed as co-optation, de-Africanization, and "loss of character" as serious objects of study, and I have identified overlooked processes through which capoeira's "traditions" were tactically rearticulated through the hegemonic discourses of modernity. By looking at capoeira angola as more than a static "survival" of a capoeira practiced in an imagined past across the Atlantic, I have been able to acknowledge both the modernity and the creativity of those responsible for choreographing capoeira's traditions.

My aim has been not only to destabilize a linear, teleological relationship between capoeira angola and capoeira regional, and thus between tradition and modernity, but also to problematize the notion that "folk" cultural production is the result of either spontaneous, collective invention or authorless continuity. My efforts to identify the "who" as well as the what, where, and when of changes in capoeira honor the repeated claims of authorship made during each innovator's lifetime—claims either downplayed or used as evidence of "loss" throughout most of capoeira historiography. Zuma's parenthetical notes taking credit for new strikes listed in *National Gymnastics*; Bimba's claim to have improved capoeira de Angola through foreign borrowings; the competing narratives of who was (or were) the first director(s) or founder(s) of the Capoeira Angola Sports Center; and Canjiquinha's claims to having invented the "folkloric suite" composed of capoeira, maculelê, puxada de rede, and samba de roda: all show a clear desire for recognition of authorship. Although the folklore studies establishment under Édison Carneiro's leadership had begun to allow for the possibility of folklore's dynamism, folklore was still understood as produced by "society as a whole." The repeated claims of authorship by various capoeiristas challenged this model of anonymous cultural production and in fact challenged the very notion of "bearing" folklore.

An analysis of the invention of capoeira's modern traditions would be incomplete without acknowledging the participation of Bahian intellectuals and culture bureaucrats who through their publications, recommendations, programming of local stages, and sponsorship of tours abroad actively shaped these traditions. As I have shown, Carneiro and Jorge Amado, as well as Waldeloir Rego, Hildegardes Vianna, Guilherme Simões, and other administrators of Salvador's tourism department, were influential in fashioning Bahia as the cradle of Afro-Brazilian tradition, and in sanctioning or rejecting specific styles of capoeira as representative of this tradition. A close look at the conflicts and alliances between folklorists, tourism bureaucrats, and capoeiristas has revealed the complexity and nuance of the process of staging capoeira in tourist contexts. The stage, as I have shown, offered both a space for learning skills which could be applied to capoeira practice offstage, such as Canjiquinha's staged brawls (*festa de arromba*), and a space for the continuity of practices that were being reframed as foreign borrowings or phased out as too dangerous, such as *balões*.

My research has reframed capoeira as a malleable practice that thrived during the tourism boom in Bahia between the 1950s and the 1970s, and has challenged analyses that have insisted on regarding capoeira as a repository of "Africanisms." Pastinha's demonstrations at the historic Pelourinho location (which Amado highly recommended to anyone visiting Salvador), Bimba's own folkloric ensemble and his contract with a travel agency, and Canjiquinha's eclectic shows at Salvador's municipal tourist stage provide ample evidence of a formative entanglement between the development of capoeira and the transformation of Bahia into one of Brazil's main cultural tourism destinations. And although capoeira mestres tried to keep capoeira for tourists separate from capoeira practiced as self-defense, the ramifications of staging capoeira — choreographed acrobatic flips or a dance-like, "well-behaved" capoeira where kicks are only suggested — bled through to a capoeira practiced offstage, resulting in what we, in the early twenty-first century, understand as capoeira.

By reading the traces of capoeira's past embodiment rather than relying on assumptions about its past, I have been able to untangle the notions of Africa, tradition, and the past and conclude that the practice we now consider "more traditional" is in fact quite different from a capoeiragem practiced by nineteenth-century capoeiras, characterized by direct and quick maneuvers interspersed with "sifting," a fidgety, hopping movement that has been transformed into the fluid *ginga* of present-day practice. Drawing conclusions about the past *from the past* rather than from "traditional" movement practices in the present allowed me to write a history of capoeira where the seams remain visible, a history that acknowledges tactical erasures, inventions, and reinventions. Most important, this history is not about an authorless practice but about the many authors of twentieth-century capoeira.

Tracing the transformation of the practice of balões, curtailed off-stage in the interest of safety, into capoeira's staged acrobatics through Bimba's demonstration games (*escretes*) allowed me to reconsider "show capoeira" as a site of invention, pleasure, beauty, and play rather than one of loss. Amplified and rechoreographed as assisted flips and solo *floreios* that thrilled audiences throughout Europe and North America, balões gave continuity to a practice discarded by "traditional" capoeira. Having been all but removed from Capoeira Angola for their excessive violence, balões, reconfigured as staged acrobatic sequences, created the illusion of danger and violence in order to meet a kinesthetic destination image of hyperphysical, "wild," and dangerous Afro-diasporic bodies. Ironically, these predetermined acrobatic sequences, devoid of actual violence, allowed performers to focus on the aesthetics and artistry of capoeira's movement, choreographing "beautiful" and "open" games. Although capoeira on international stages was largely understood as traditional— folklore borne by Brazilian "folk"—these stage performances provided a space for the creativity and innovation of capoeiristas who were as urban and as modern as Global North audience members and critics who marveled at their "wild gymnastics."

Folkloric shows introduced the world to the thrilling and spectacular staged violence and virtuosity of capoeira in the 1970s. These shows allowed theatergoers to vicariously experience the thrills of capoeira, the rituals of candomblé, and the happiness and sensuality of samba from the safety of their assigned seats. In the twenty-first century, however, a visual experience of Afro-Brazilian culture separated by a fourth wall is no longer enough. Folkloric ensembles have dwindled, and the only professional Brazilian folk ensemble that gives continuity to the stage traditions of Oxum, Olodum, and Viva Bahia at the time of this writing is the Balé Folclórico da Bahia, founded by Walson Botelho and Ninho Reis in 1988.[1]

The visual encounter provided by folkloric spectacles has been replaced, since the early 2000s, with embodied experiences of Afro-Brazilianness at retreats known as *encontros* (encounters) or *eventos* (events). At these encontros—often held in rural areas in southern Bahia where several capoeira mestres have set up "cultural centers" adjacent to near-virgin beaches, hiking paths, lakes, and waterfalls—capoeira practitioners, many from "northern latitudes," participate in week-long workshops of capoeira and Afro-Brazilian music and dance.[2] Among these retreats, held annually or semiannually, the most established are Capoeirando, organized by Mestre Suassuna (Reinaldo Ramos Suassuna, b. 1938) near Ilhéus; Dancebatukeira, organized by Mestres Cabello (Éldio Rolim, b. 1965) and Tisza (Helena Coelho, b. 1966) near the village of Serra Grande; and Permangola, organized by Mestre Cobra Mansa (Cinésio Feliciano Peçanha, b. 1960) near Valença.[3] Although they take place in relative proximity—all in southern Bahia—they each have distinct characteristics: Capoeirando, attended annually by over three hundred capoeiristas, is an encontro of large proportions that caters primarily to capoeira regional practitioners; Dancebatukeira and Permangola host between twenty and thirty participants at one time—these more intimate encontros cater to capoeiristas interested in "drinking from the fountain" of traditional capoeira (i.e., capoeira angola) and communing with nature. The schedule of classes of these encontros frequently includes maculelê, dances from candomblé, samba de roda, and capoeira, attesting to the lasting influence of the folkloric suite developed in the 1960s and 1970s through a collaboration between "folk" performers, tourism bureaucrats, local directors/choreographers, and international producers.[4]

The complex histories of these movement practices, however, are often downplayed in favor of implicit and explicit connections that add "nature" as a fourth ingredient in the authenticating equation *Africa = tradition = past*. A direct link between capoeira and an unmediated, "ancestral" nature allows "traditional" capoeira to bypass the contradictions, incongruences, and most important, the modernity of urban twentieth-century capoeira. Twenty-first-century capoeira innovators have established connections between nature and capoeira angola through encontros that combine capoeira classes and rodas with hands-on learning about environmentally sustainable agricultural practices and building techniques, creating the hybrid concepts of "permangola" (permaculture and capoeira angola) and "eco-capoeira" (ecology and capoeira). These nature-centered encontros, a growing trend in capoeira that deserves its own in-depth study, superimpose twenty-first-century anxieties about an endangered environment on early twentieth-century concerns with a "dying" capoeira in need of rescue.

When Édison Carneiro predicted in 1936 that capoeira was destined to "recede to small coastal villages," he could not have imagined that these small coastal villages would be the setting for capoeira retreats hosted by transnational mestres, offering workshops and classes derived from the repertory of midcentury folkloric shows, aimed at Global North capoeira practitioners seeking a capoeira untainted by modernity.[5] Modernity, however, is inextricable from capoeira. Twenty-first-century capoeira carries the indelible marks of its formative entanglement with staged spectacle and tourism. Quite literally seen through the eyes of others, capoeira was shaped through the lenses of photographers and filmmakers, written down and codified in manuals aimed at broadening its appeal, and staged around the world to meet a destination image of Afro-Latin excess.

NOTES

....

INTRODUCTION

1. All Portuguese-English translations are mine unless otherwise noted.

2. Mestre Jogo de Dentro (Jorge Egídio dos Santos) is a disciple of Mestre João Pequeno (João Pereira dos Santos), who was a disciple of Mestre Pastinha of the same generation as João Grande. Mestre João Pequeno taught capoeira angola in Salvador, Bahia, until his death in 2011.

3. *Angoleira/o* is a practitioner of capoeira angola. The suffix *-eiro/-eira* added to a noun refers to the doer or maker of that noun; e.g., *pão/padeiro* (bread/baker); *jardim/jardineiro* (garden/gardener); *sapato/sapateiro* (shoe/shoemaker); *angola/angoleira*.

4. In his oft-cited comparative analysis between the "traditional" capoeira and Bimba's innovations, Frigerio proposes that "we can interpret the advent of Capoeira Regional as a 'whitening' of traditional Capoeira (Angola), following a pattern similar to the one proposed by Ortiz (1978) for Umbanda." Alejandro Frigerio, "Capoeira: de arte negra a esporte branco," *Revista Brasileira de Ciências Sociais* 4, no. 10 (1989): 1.

5. The first scholar to propose an alternative to the view of capoeira regional as a "whitening" of the practice was Brazilian anthropologist Letícia Reis. Reis's analysis is groundbreaking in that it questions previous analyses of Bimba's capoeira regional as simply co-optation and "whitening" by foregrounding the fact that Bimba himself was black. Reis recasts Bimba's innovations as dynamic Africanist appropriations of hegemonic rituals and symbols, such as formal graduation ceremonies and the conferral of medals. Letícia Vidor de Sousa Reis, "Negros e brancos no jogo da capoeira: reinvenção da tradição" (PhD dissertation, Universidade de São Paulo, 1993).

6. Hobsbawm makes a distinction between "invented traditions" (purposefully fabricated new rituals framed as old and timeless) and "custom," a less structured, slow-to-develop form of "tradition." See Eric Hobsbawm and Terence Ranger, "The Invention of Tradition: The Highland Tradition of Scotland," in *The Invention of Tradition* (Cambridge: Cambridge University Press, 1983).

7. Carybé. *O jogo da capoeira*, Coleção Recôncavo n. 3. (Salvador: Livraria Turista, 1951), 1.

8. Melville J. Herskovits and Frances S. Herskovits, *The New World Negro: Selected Papers in Afroamerican Studies* (Bloomington: Indiana University Press, 1966), 57.

9. Arthur Ramos, *O negro brasileiro: ethnographia religiosa e psychanalyse*, Bibliotheca de divulgação scientifica (Rio de Janeiro: Civilização brasileira, s.a., 1951), 129–31.

10. Roger Bastide, *The African Religions of Brazil: Toward a Sociology of the Interpenetration of Civilizations*, Johns Hopkins Studies in Atlantic History and Culture (Baltimore: Johns Hopkins University Press, 1978), 283.

11. Andrew Apter, "Herskovits's Heritage: Rethinking Syncretism in the African Diaspora," *Diaspora: A Journal of Transnational Studies* 1, no. 3 (1991), 253.

12. "It is a peculiar sensation, this double consciousness, this sense of always looking at one's self through the eyes of others, of measuring one's soul by the tape of a world that looks on in amused contempt and pity." W. E. B. Du Bois, *The Souls of Black Folk*, 1st Vintage Books/Library of America ed. (New York: Vintage Books/Library of America, 1990), 9.

13. Thomas DeFrantz, "The Black Beat Made Visible: Hip Hop Dance and Body Power," in *Of the Presence of the Body: Essays on Dance and Performance Theory*, ed. André Lepecki (Middletown: Wesleyan University Press, 2004), 64.

14. Jacqueline Shea Murphy, *The People Have Never Stopped Dancing: Native American Modern Dance Histories* (Minneapolis: University of Minnesota Press, 2007), 25.

15. Susan Leigh Foster, *Choreographing Empathy: Kinesthesia in Performance* (London: Routledge, 2011), 2–6. During my interviews with directors and participants of capoeira shows in the 1970s, I came across yet another meaning of the word "choreography," one that implied the influence of a ballet aesthetic. I realized that when performers and directors stated that there was no "choreography" in the capoeira sections of the folkloric shows, they did not mean that the movement was not predetermined in advance; rather, they meant that the movement was not influenced by a ballet aesthetic (e.g., partnered lifts, leaps, and pointed feet.)

16. Rebekah J. Kowal, "Staging the Greensboro Sit-Ins," *TDR: The Drama Review* 48 no. 4 (2004): 135, 138–39.

17. Erving Goffman, *The Presentation of Self in Everyday Life* (New York: Anchor Books, 1959).

18. Dean MacCannell, *The Tourist: A New Theory of the Leisure Class* (Berkeley and Los Angeles: University of California Press, 1999).

19. Jane Desmond, *Staging Tourism: Bodies on Display from Waikiki to Sea World* (Chicago: University of Chicago Press, 1999), xx.

20. Ibid., 5.

21. Anthea Kraut, "Recovering Hurston, Reconsidering the Choreographer," in *The Routledge Dance Studies Reader*, 2nd ed., ed. Alexandra Carter and Janet O'Shea (London: Routledge, 2010), 36–37.

22. Thomas H. Holloway, "'A Healthy Terror': Police Repression of Capoeiras in Nineteenth-Century Rio de Janeiro," *Hispanic American Historical Review* 69, no. 4 (1989); Carlos Eugênio Líbano Soares, *A negregada instituição: os capoeiras no Rio de Janeiro* (Rio de Janeiro: Coleção Biblioteca Carioca, 1994).

23. Barbara Browning, *Samba: Resistance in Motion* (Bloomington: Indiana University Press, 1995); John Lowell Lewis, *Ring of Liberation: Deceptive Discourse in Brazilian Capoeira*

(Chicago: University of Chicago Press, 1992); Greg Downey, *Learning Capoeira: Lessons in Cunning from an Afro-Brazilian Art* (Oxford: Oxford University Press, 2005).

24. Cristina F. Rosa, drawing on Brenda Dixon Gottschild's "five Africanist characteristics" and Robert Farris Thompson's "canons of fine form," analyzes capoeira according to "aesthetic principles common to other West African dance endeavors and their proliferation in the New World." Cristina F. Rosa, "Playing, Fighting, and Dancing: Unpacking the Significance of *Ginga* within the Practice of Capoeira Angola," *TDR: The Drama Review* 56, no. 3 (T215) (Fall 2012): 144. She further develops her system of Africanist aesthetic principles in her book, a system she calls "the ginga aesthetic." Cristina F. Rosa, *Brazilian Bodies and Their Choreographies of Identification: Swing Nation* (New York: Palgrave Macmillan, 2015), 97.

25. Throughout *Ring of Liberation: Deceptive Discourse in Brazilian Capoeira*, John Lowell Lewis predicts that capoeira angola and capoeira regional would in fact transcend their differences and become one capoeira in the future, a prediction that almost thirty years later has not come true.

26. For Lewis, the game of capoeira is an escape valve, providing temporary relief from "social obligations and personal worries." Lewis, *Ring of Liberation*, 2.

27. Ibid., 85.

28. Browning, *Samba*, 111.

29. "Actionable assertions"—which DeFrantz derives from the ideas of J. L. Austin and Eve Sedgewick—could be exemplified by the cooperation, cunning, and creativity in the capoeira game. DeFrantz, "Black Beat Made Visible," 66.

30. The first of such dissertations was Kenneth Dossar's, followed by Greg Downey's dissertation in 1998. Both scholars were influenced by Mestre Moraes (Pedro Moraes Trindade), one of the leaders of the "revival" of capoeira angola in the 1980s. Greg Downey, "Incorporating Capoeira: Phenomenology of a Movement Discipline" (PhD dissertation, University of Chicago, 1998); Kenneth Dossar, "Dancing between Two Worlds: An Aesthetic Analysis of Capoeira Angola" (PhD dissertation, Temple University, 1994).

31. Downey proposes that capoeira angola is capable of "tearing out the shame" of white, middle-class bodies, repatterning their movement in a way that challenges the "corporeal status quo." He proposes that capoeira angola's movements may in fact be a way of restoring movements that "may have once felt natural" but which now have largely been lost in everyday life. Although Downey's work is laudable for its rigorous and extensive field research and his approach to movement as capable of effecting change, his analysis focuses on preservation and restoration of "lost" embodied patterns without historicizing this model of loss and rescue. While Downey does problematize the "traditional"/"whitened" binary, his analysis is still contained within this binary. Downey, *Learning Capoeira*, 200.

32. For recent studies that privilege capoeira angola in their analysis, see ibid.; Cristina F. Rosa, *Brazilian Bodies and Their Choreographies of Identification*; Pedro Abib, *Capoeira angola: cultura popular e o jogo dos saberes na roda* (Salvador: Editora da Universidade Federal da Bahia, 2004); Rosângela Costa Araújo, "Iê viva meu mestre: a capoeira an-

gola da 'escola pastiniana' como praxis educativa" (PhD dissertation, Universidade de São Paulo, 2004); Floyd Merrell, *Capoeira and Candomblé: Conformity and Resistance through Afro-Brazilian Experience* (Princeton: Markus Wiener, 2005); Ebony Rose Custis, "Cultural Capital, Critical Theory, and Motivation for Participation in Capoeira Angola" (master's thesis, Howard University, 2008); and Scott Correll Head, "Danced Fight, Divided City: Figuring the Space Between" (PhD dissertation, University of Texas, Austin, 2004).

33. Herskovits and Herskovits, *New World Negro*, 49.

34. Herskovits's scale was divided into the following categories: (a) very African, (b) quite African, (c) somewhat African, (d) a little African, (e) trace of African customs, or none, and (?) no report. As Apter has pointed out, the intensities themselves (such as "very," "quite," and "somewhat African") are highly relative and subjective. See Apter, "Herskovits's Heritage,"237–38.

35. Through an analysis of the Herskovitses' field diaries, the Prices shed light on their research practices and their informants, who were often their paid interpreters and servants. Richard Price and Sally Price, *The Roots of Roots: Or, How Afro-American Anthropology Got Its Start* (Chicago: Prickly Paradigm Press, 2003), 80–81.

36. Apter, "Herskovits's Heritage," 245.

37. The dance literature Thompson relied on includes the work of Alan Lomax, a folklorist who devoted his life to collecting and recording "traditional" music and dance. In 1968 Lomax, working with students of movement theorist Rudolf Laban, proposed that dances reflected "the habitual movement patterns of each culture and culture area," and went on to map and classify dances from all of the world's regions based on analysis of film recordings from twenty-one cultures—needless to say, a very small sample considering the global scale of the project. Like Thompson, Lomax reaches conclusions based on small samples of data that could not possibly accurately represent the proposed areas of study. For a review of Lomax's *Folksong Style and Culture: A Staff Report*, see Joann Wheeler Keali'inohomoku and Drid Williams, "Caveat on Causes and Correlations," *CORD News* 6, no. 2 (1975).

38. Thompson, *African Art in Motion*, 3.

39. Ibid., 5.

40. Ibid.

41. Brenda Dixon Gottschild, *Digging the Africanist Presence in American Performance* (Westport: Greenwood Press, 1996).

42. A. Cooper Albright acknowledges the important work of identifying Africanisms in dance, but warns that "we must be careful not to assume uniformity in the name of unity" and "we must also call attention to the ways in which only certain aspects of African dance (celebratory, acrobatic, presentational, energetic, etc.) get marketed as 'African.'" *Choreographing Difference*, 24. Rosa's *Brazilian Bodies and Their Choreographies of Identification* (2015) attests to the lingering influences of Thompson's Africanisms in dance studies.

43. Thompson identifies ten formal features of African dance: Ephebism: the Stronger Power that Comes from Youth; "Afrikanische Aufheben": Simultaneously Suspending and Preserving the Beat; The "Get Down Quality": Descending Direction

in Melody, Sculpture, Dance; Multiple Meter: Dancing Many Drums; Looking Smart: Playing the Patterns with Nature and with Line; Correct Entrance and Exit: "Killing the Song," "Cutting the Dance," "Lining the Face"; Vividness Cast into Equilibrium: Personal and Representational Balance; Call and Response: the Politics of Perfection; Ancestorism: Ability to Incarnate Destiny; Coolness: Truth and Generosity Regained. Thompson, *African Art in Motion*.

44. Ethnomusicologist David Ames also noticed Thompson's tendency to select fragments of movement that proved his preconceived notions of African dance. Ames

> found some aspects of the author's methodology repeatedly irritating. There was a tendency to force facts into preconceived pigeonholes, and since Thompson tends to rely a great deal on poetic statement, not infrequently this gives the reader the impression that facts are being bent by a kind of lexical sleight of hand or that conclusions were unjustifiably being extrapolated from fragmentary evidence. Not infrequently, a few ethnographic examples stand, implicitly at least, for tropical Africa as a whole, a fairly common failing of Africanists. Of course tropical Africa is an enormous area containing hundreds of societies, languages and much cultural variation—not to mention extraordinary variation in art itself.

David W. Ames, "Book review of *African Art in Motion*," *Ethnomusicology* 243 (1980): 563.

45. Although some of Thompson's categories identify movement elements that may apply to an overall "Africanist aesthetic," such as the idea of the "mask of the cool," others reinforce preconceived notions that "Africans" are somehow more connected to the earth than non-Africans, exemplified by his principle "Get-Down Quality: descending direction in melody, sculpture, dance," and the subprinciple "Stability and Straightness: personal balance," where he describes the common stance for African dance as "flat footed," while white Americans associate dancing with going "up on their toes." Thompson, *African Art in Motion*, 13, 24.

46. Thompson's ninth principle, "Ancestorism: ability to incarnate destiny," refers to the ability of African ancestors to return through dancing: "We realize that Africans, moving in their ancient dances, in full command of historical destiny, are those noble personages, briefly returned." According to Thompson, these constantly "returning" ancestors are responsible for "preserving" traits in African performance that "have been in existence for at least four hundred years." Ibid., 28–29.

47. Capoeira enthusiasts, in their eagerness to own an original newspaper clipping about a famous mestre from the past, have cut out articles about capoeira from the poorly supervised rare periodicals section of the public library of Salvador, taking the articles home as souvenirs. Newspapers from the mid-1960s onward are not considered rare: they have not been bound and are kept in slowly dissolving bundles secured with twine. As I consulted some of them, they fell apart between my fingers.

48. I consulted the following archives in Salvador during my research: the Municipal Library of Salvador (Barris), the Municipal Historical Archives of Salvador, the Pierre Verger Foundation, the Jair Moura Institute, and the private collection of photographs and newspaper clippings of Emília Biancardi. In Rio de Janeiro I con-

sulted the Museu de Folclore Édison Carneiro and the Biblioteca Nacional. I also consulted the library of the Grupo Semente do Jogo de Angola, in Campinas, São Paulo. I also consulted (remotely) the capoeira photographic archive of the Helinä Rautavaara Museum in Finland.

49. According to descriptions by Johann Moritz Rugendas (1835), Charles Ribeyrolles (1859), Alexandre Mello Moraes Filho (1901 [1893]), Manuel Querino (1916), Henrique Coelho Netto (1922), and Édison Carneiro (1937).

50. Susan Leigh Foster, "Choreographing History," in *Choreographing History*, ed. Susan Leigh Foster (Bloomington: Indiana University Press, 1995), 7.

51. Ann Cooper Albright, "Tracing the Past: Writing History through the Body," in *The Routledge Dance Studies Reader*, 2nd ed., ed. Alexandra Carter and Janet O'Shea (London: Routledge, 2010), 101.

52. The majority of academic books about capoeira in English published in the past two decades begin with the phrase "Capoeira is . . ." See Maya Talmon-Chvaicer, *The Hidden History of Capoeira: A Collision of Cultures in the Brazilian Battle Dance* (Austin: University of Texas Press, 2008); Lewis, *Ring of Liberation*; and Downey, *Learning Capoeira*. Browning's essay "Headspin: Capoeira's Ironic Inversions" uses the phrase "Capoeira is" after a brief descriptive introduction. Browning, *Samba*. Floyd Merrell actually struggles with this almost obligatory definition and writes a list of things that capoeira is, and is not, in order to illustrate its complexity. Merrell, *Capoeira and Candomblé*.

53. I am using the word "tactics" in Michel de Certeau's sense, which he opposes to strategies. Tactics, which de Certeau identifies as a "weapon of the weak," do not have a proper place or institutional localization; they operate within the stable place of strategies, in "the space of the other," constantly taking advantage of opportunities. Michel de Certeau, *The Practice of Everyday Life* (Berkeley: University of California Press, 1984).

54. Grabbing and throwing practices were first documented by Mello Moraes in the late nineteenth century and later described by Coelho Netto in 1928 and Édison Carneiro in 1937. Édison Carneiro, *Negros bantus: notas de ethnographia religiosa e folk-lore* (Rio de Janeiro: Civilização Brasileira, s.a., 1937); Alexandre José de Mello Moraes Filho, *Festas e tradições populares do Brasil*, 3rd ed. (Rio de Janeiro: F. Briguiet, 1946 [1893]); Henrique Coelho Netto, "Nosso jogo," in *Bazar* (Rio de Janeiro: Livraria Chardron, de Lello e Irmão, Ltda Editores, 1928).

55. The phrase "Afro-Brazilian art," a modification of "Afro-Brazilian martial art," is often used to describe and define capoeira. For example, the subtitle of Greg Downey's book *Learning Capoeira* is *Lessons in Cunning from an Afro-Brazilian Art*; and Ubirajara Guimarães Almeida's book (Berkeley: North Atlantic Books, 1986) is titled *Capoeira: A Brazilian Art Form*.

56. Anníbal Burlamaqui, *Gymnastica nacional (capoeiragem) methodisada e regrada* (Rio de Janeiro: n.p., 1928); Mestre Bimba, *Curso de Capoeira Regional*, sound disc, analog, 33⅓ rpm, 12 in., plus booklet (Salvador: JS Discos, c. 1963); Vicente Ferreira Pastinha, *Capoeira Angola*, 2nd ed. (Salvador: Escola Gráfica N.S. de Loreto, 1968 [1964]).

57. In his manuscripts, discussed in chapter 1, Pastinha often writes Capoeira An-

gola," with a double quotation mark at the end of the phrase, but not at the beginning. This idiosyncratic use of quotation marks may be his way of emphasizing the word "Angola." Vicente Ferreira Pastinha, "Quando as pernas fazem miserêr," in *Manuscritos do Mestre Pastinha* (unpublished manuscripts written c. 1952–57, Salvador).

1. STAGING BRAZIL'S NATIONAL SPORT

1. My English translation of Sergio Milliet's Portuguese translation (1954). Johann Moritz Rugendas, *Viagem pitoresca através do Brasil*, 5. ed., Biblioteca Histórica Brasileira (São Paulo: Livraria Martins Editôra, 1954).

2. Desch-Obi proposes that *maltas* are better described as brotherhoods than "gangs." M. Thomas J. Desch-Obi, *Fighting for Honor: The History of African Martial Art Traditions in the Atlantic World* (Columbia: University of South Carolina Press, 2008).

3. Plácido de Abreu, *Os capoeiras* (Rio de Janeiro: Typ. da Escola de Serafim José Alves, 1886), 4.

4. Katya Wesolowski. "From 'Moral Disease' to 'National Sport': Race, Nation, and Capoeira in Brazil," in *Sports Culture in Latin American History* (Pittsburgh: University of Pittsburgh Press, 2015), 165.

5. Matthias Rhörig Assunção, *Capoeira: The History of an Afro-Brazilian Martial Art* (London: Routledge, 2005), 74.

6. The coup d'état of November 15, 1889, is known and commemorated as the "proclamation of the republic," a Brazilian national holiday.

7. Gustavo Moncorvo Bandeira de Mello, *História da polícia militar do distrito federal* (Rio de Janeiro: Tipografia da Polícia Militar, 1926), 345. Cited in Soares, *A negregada instituição*, 294.

8. The Black Guard, a tightly regulated association of more than 1,500 black men, many of them capoeiras, was formed by a prominent black abolitionist, José do Patrocínio, shortly after the signing of the Golden Law (Lei Áurea) of May 13, 1888—a long-overdue decree signed by Princess Regent Isabel (daughter of Dom Pedro II) which declared the end of slavery. In the eighteen months between abolition and the coup d'état of November 15, 1889, the Black Guard supported the monarchy by confronting republican activists, often with violence, and by vowing to protect Princess Isabel at all cost. Robert Daibert, *Isabel, a "redentora" dos escravos: uma história da princesa entre olhares negros e brancos* (Bauru: Editora da Universidade do Sagrado Coração, 2001), 153.

9. Soares, *A negregada instituição*, 297–300.

10. Ibid., 29, 301–2.

11. Quoted in Waldeloir Rego, *Capoeira Angola: ensaio sócio-etnográfico* (Rio de Janeiro: Gráf. Lux, 1968), 292–93.

12. Chapter 3, Articles 156 and 157, which related to "crimes against public health."

13. Raymundo Nina Rodrigues, cited in Anadelia A. Romo, *Brazil's Living Museum: Race, Reform, and Tradition in Bahia* (Chapel Hill: University of North Carolina Press, 2010), 38–39. Nina Rodrigues actually advocated for special legislation for Afro-Brazilians, whom he believed to be incapable of following or even understanding the same laws as whites.

14. For an analysis of nineteenth-century capoeiragem in relationship to attitudes toward race, see Letícia Vidor de Sousa Reis, *O mundo de pernas para o ar: a capoeira no Brasil*, 2nd ed. (São Paulo: Publisher Brasil, 2000).

15. Mello Moraes Filho, *Festas e tradições populares do Brasil*, 455.

16. O.D.C., *Guia do capoeira ou gymnastica brazileira*, 2nd ed. (Rio de Janeiro: Livraria Nacional, 1907).

17. Antônio Liberac Cardoso Simões Pires, *Culturas circulares: a formação histórica da capoeira contemporânea no Rio de Janeiro* (Curitiba: Editora Progressiva, 2010), 138–39. Jair Moura is likely the source of the theory that O.D.C. was a navy officer named Garcez Palha. Jair Moura, *A capoeiragem no Rio de Janeiro através dos séculos* (Salvador: JM gráfica e editora, 2009).

18. The manuals that followed O.D.C.'s are, in chronological order, Anníbal Burlamaqui's *Gymnastica nacional (capoeiragem) methodisada e regrada* (1928); Inezil Penna Marinho's *Subsídios para o estudo da metodologia do treinamento da capoeiragem* (1945); Lamartine Pereira da Costa's *Capoeira sem Mestre* (self-published in 1961, and reprinted by Edições de Ouro in 1962); Mestre Bimba's *Curso de Capoeira Regional* (c. 1963); and Mestre Pastinha's *Capoeira Angola* (1964). Late twentieth-century manuals are too numerous to list here, the best known being Nestor Capoeira's *Capoeira: pequeno manual do jogador*, first published in 1981, translated as *The Little Capoeira Book* in 2003. Nestor Capoeira, *Capoeira: pequeno manual do jogador* (Rio de Janeiro: Editora Record 1986 [1981]); and Nestor Capoeira, *The Little Capoeira Book* (Berkeley: Blue Snake Books, 2003).

19. Throughout the 1930s and 1940s, intellectuals such as Jorge Amado and Édison Carneiro praised Samuel Querido de Deus, "a fisherman of remarkable corporeal agility," as the best capoeira practitioner of Bahia. Carneiro, *Negros bantus*, 159.

20. Waldeloir Rego goes as far as stating that Pastinha "is not and has never been the best capoeirista of Bahia." Rego, *Capoeira Angola*, 270.

21. Centro Esportivo de Capoeira Angola (CECA) (Capoeira Angola Sports Center), founded by Pastinha; and the Centro de Cultura Física Regional (CCFR) (Center of Regional Physical Culture), founded by Bimba.

22. Dunshee de Abranches, cited in Rego, *Capoeira Angola*, 308.

23. Coelho Netto, cited in Reis, *O mundo de pernas para o ar*, 66.

24. This lack of biographical information points to the possibility that he did not make a name for himself as a practitioner and teacher of capoeiragem like his contemporaries Bimba and Pastinha in Bahia, or Sinhôzinho in Rio de Janeiro. Lamartine Pereira da Costa, author of *Capoeira sem mestre* (1962), reported meeting Burlamaqui, who sometime around 1964 surprised him by coming unannounced to his house to inquire why *Gymnastica nacional* was not cited or even mentioned in *Capoeira sem mestre*. Da Costa claims to have been unaware of Burlamaqui and his manual prior to this meeting. Lamartine Pereira da Costa, audio-recorded interview, July 28, 2015.

25. Burlamaqui, *Gymnastica nacional (capoeiragem) methodisada e regrada*.

26. Reis's terms in Portuguese are "*branco erudito*" and "*negro popular*." See Reis, *O mundo de pernas para o ar*.

27. Ibid., 60.

28. Assunção, *Capoeira*, 131.

29. Ibid., 147.

30. Assunção, *Capoeira: The History of an Afro-Brazilian Martial Art*: 149.

31. Excerpted from a lengthy interview with Moura printed in Nestor Capoeira, *Capoeira: Roots of the Dance-Fight-Game* (Berkeley: North Atlantic Books, 2002), 204. (The translation of the original interview in Portuguese is Nestor Capoeira's).

32. Greg Downey, "Domesticating an Urban Menace: Reforming Capoeira Angola as a Brazilian National Sport," *International Journal of the History of Sport* 19, no. 4 (2002): 7.

33. Pires, *Culturas circulares*, 147.

34. Frigerio, "Capoeira," 6.

35. In the preface to the book, Mario Santos writes that Burlamaqui "is not lettered; not a doctor, not a bachelor. He is a young sportsman, a true athlete, who enjoys good health and, above all, loves his country." Burlamaqui, *Gymnastica nacional (capoeiragem) methodisada e regrada*, 3. Pires also frames Zuma as an athlete and a "sportsman." Antônio Liberac Cardoso Simões Pires, "Movimentos da Cultura Afro-Brasileira: a formação histórica da capeira contemporânea 1890–1950" (PhD dissertation, Universidade Estadual de Campinas, 2001), 98.

36. Capoeira researcher André Luiz Lacé Lopes reports Burlamaqui's birthdate as November 25, 1898. André Luiz Lacé Lopes, *A capoeiragem no Rio de Janeiro: primeiro ensaio, Sinhozinho e Rudolf Hermanny* (Rio de Janeiro: Editora Europa, 2002), 88. It is not clear whether Zuma had achieved recognition as mestre at the time of publication of his book, since he is introduced in the preface by Mario Santos as Zuma rather than Mestre Zuma. The publications by Bimba and Pastinha analyzed here date from the mid-1960s, when both were already firmly established as mestres; newspaper articles from the 1930s, however, refer to Bimba without this title. In the interest of consistency, I have chosen to refer to all three innovators without the title "mestre."

37. Burlamaqui, *Gymnastica nacional (capoeiragem) methodisada e regrada*, 3.

38. Ibid., 6.

39. Ibid., 4.

40. In English in the original, before the creolization of the word as "futebol," the contemporary Portuguese word for "soccer."

41. Burlamaqui, *Gymnastica nacional (capoeiragem) methodisada e regrada*, 18–19.

42. Ibid., 15.

43. Downey, "Domesticating an Urban Menace," 7.

44. Zuma notes that "foot-ball" playing fields "lend themselves extraordinarily well to capoeiragem [because] they break falls and do not contain dust." Burlamaqui, *Gymnastica nacional (capoeiragem) methodisada e regrada*, 20.

45. It is interesting to note that in *National Gymnastics*, the word "sport" appears in English, signaling its imported status both linguistically and conceptually. Today, the word has been fully adopted and adapted to fit Portuguese phonetic rules (*esporte*).

46. Ibid., 15.

47. *Brazil's Popular Festivities and Traditions*. I have found two possible dates for the first edition of this book, 1893 and 1895.

48. Mello Moraes Filho, *Festas e tradições populares do Brasil*, 444.

49. Ibid., 448.

50. Abreu, *Os Capoeiras*, 7.

51. A *cocada* (a headbutt, in reference to the head as a coconut) could be applied either to the chin or to the stomach of the opponent, "leaving him spread out in the middle of the street." Coelho Netto, "Nosso jogo," 135.

52. *Bahiana* means "Bahian," in this case the "Bahian move," which points to an existing exchange of movement vocabulary between Bahia and Rio de Janeiro. Ibid.

53. Burlamaqui, *Gymnastica nacional (capoeiragem) methodisada e regrada*, 35.

54. Ibid., 41.

55. Ibid., 21.

56. Ibid.

57. Zuma refers to the capoeira match as a "fight" (*luta*) but to the participants of this fight as "players" (*jogadores*).

58. Burlamaqui, *Gymnastica nacional (capoeiragem) methodisada e regrada*, 28.

59. Ibid.

60. Ibid.

61. Ibid., 24–25.

62. The upside-downness of capoeira, which has been theorized as evidence of capoeira's African origins in relationship to the cosmological system of *kalunga*, where "the ancestors walk with their feet up," is very much present in Zuma's capoeiragem. Desch-Obi explains the kalunga as a "cosmological system that understood bodies of water to be bridges connecting the lands of the living and the realm of the dead. In reference to the spiritual realm linked to these bodies of water, *kalunga* invokes an inverted world where the ancestors walk with their feet up. This gave birth to a martial art that relied on supporting one's body with the hands and kicking while upside down. Masters of the art who were forced to endure the Middle Passage spread this aesthetic of inverted kicks throughout the Americas." Desch-Obi, *Fighting for Honor*, 3–4.

63. Downey, "Domesticating an Urban Menace," 7.

64. Burlamaqui, *Gymnastica nacional (capoeiragem) methodisada e regrada*, 42.

65. I draw this analysis from my doctoral dissertation, where I analyze both Burlamaqui's *guarda* (guard) and the deceptive move *peneirando* (sifting) in chapter 1. Ana Paula Höfling, "Dancing, Fighting, and Staging Capoeira: Choreographies of Afro-Brazilian Modernity and Tradition" (PhD dissertation, University of California, Los Angeles, 2012). Cristina F. Rosa, in her 2015 *Brazilian Bodies and Their Choreographies of Identification*, a book based on her doctoral dissertation, also analyses these same moves from Burlamaqui's manual and reaches a similar conclusion. In her own dissertation from 2010, however, these details from Burlamaqui's book are not mentioned. Cristina F. Rosa, "Choreographing Identification: The Presence of Ginga in Samba, Capoeira, and Grupo Corpo" (PhD dissertation, University of California, Los Angeles, 2010).

66. Today trickery (*malandragem* or *malícia*) is considered a "foundational element" by capoeira practitioners. "*Capoeira é mandinga, é manha, é malícia*" (Capoeira is magic, it's craftiness, it's cunning) is an oft-quoted statement made by Pastinha during a

video-recorded interview included in the documentary *Pastinha! Uma vida pela capoeira—1889/1981* directed by Antônio Muricy (1981). See Adriana Albert Dias, *Mandinga, manha e malícia: uma história sobre os capoeiras na capital da Bahia (1910–1925)* (Salvador: Editora da Universidade Federal da Bahia, 2006).

67. Interestingly, this section was omitted in Penna Marinho's *Subsidies* (which otherwise reprints Zuma's book almost in its entirety). Zuma spells *tapiação* with an "i" while Plácido de Abreu spells it with an "e." For consistency, I have opted to use Abreu's spelling, which is also the current Portuguese spelling of the word: *tapeação*. Burlamaqui, *Gymnastica nacional (capoeiragem) methodisada e regrada*, 51–52.

68. Ibid., 40.

69. "With capoeiragem was born the captives' first effort for freedom in Brazil and, for this reason, its origin is, thus, sanctified." Ibid., 13.

70. For an analysis of martial traditions based on headbutting in Africa and the Americas, see Desch-Obi, *Fighting for Honor*.

71. Burlamaqui, *Gymnastica nacional (capoeiragem) methodisada e regrada*, 3.

72. Coelho Netto, "Nosso jogo," 134.

73. "*Nós, que possuimos os segredos de um dos exercicios mais ágeis e elegantes, vexamo-nos de o exhibir e, o que mais é, deixamos-nos esmurraçar em rinks por machacazes balordos que, com uma quebra de corpo e um passe baixo, de um 'ciscador' dos nossos, iriam mais longe das cordas.*" Ibid.

74. Ibid., 140.

75. Ibid., 134.

76. A. Gomes Cartusc, "Cultivemos o jogo de capoeira e tenhamos asco pelo da boxa," *O Paiz*, October 22, 1923. Reprinted in Raimundo César Alves de Almeida, *Negaça: Boletim da Ginga Associação de Capoeira*, 1994, 5.

77. Burlamaqui, *Gymnastica nacional (capoeiragem) methodisada e regrada*, 13.

78. Ibid.

79. Ibid.

80. Ibid., 15.

81. Ibid.

82. Coelho Netto's children were allowed "complete freedom, [and were] motivated to practice physical exercises in the fields, in gymnasiums and in the sea. Only then were they to know and enjoy the beauty and joys of Nature, running and playing in the sun, without the heavy clothing that was stifling their health, or throwing themselves into the ocean, with quick strokes, not infrequently returning to the sand, daringly, on the crest of a wave." Paulo Coelho Netto, *Coelho Netto e os esportes. Conferência realizada no salão nobre da Escola Nacional de Belas Artes a 25 de fevereiro de 1964* (Rio de Janeiro: Editôra Minerva, 1964), 9.

83. Burlamaqui, *Gymnastica nacional (capoeiragem) methodisada e regrada*, 15.

84. Ibid.

85. Ibid.

86. Zuma's work was published five years *before* Gilberto Freyre's *Masters and Slaves* (1933), the work credited with shaking the very foundations of early twentieth-century attitudes toward miscegenation in Brazil, and with reversing the valuation of Brazil's Afro-diasporic culture. Rather than the source of all social evil and racial

"degeneration," Freyre proposes that Afro-Brazilian music, dance, and culinary traditions should be regarded as sources of national pride.

87. Anadelia A. Romo, "Rethinking Race and Culture in Brazil's First Afro-Brazilian Congress of 1934," *Journal of Latin American Studies* 39 (2007): 35.

88. Penna Marinho studied capoeira with Mestre Sinhôzinho in Rio de Janeiro around 1937–38. Penna Marinho dedicates *Subsidies* to "the capoeiras of Brazil," making specific mentions of his teacher Sinhôzinho and Zuma, who "have worked so hard so that capoeiragem does not disappear." Penna Marinho, *Subsídios para o estudo da metodologia do treinamento da capoeiragem*, 9.

89. *Subsidies* also differs from Zuma's text in its insistence on establishing an "ideal racial type" for the practitioner of capoeiragem; neither black nor white, the ideal body for the practice of capoeiragem was found in the mulatto. Ibid., 19.

90. Ibid., 89.

91. Ibid.

92. It is not until the last three pages of the book that Penna Marinho makes his own contribution to the codification of capoeiragem, proposing supplementary exercises aimed at developing "all the physical attributes required for the practice of capoeiragem, such as elasticity, flexibility, speed and acuity." Penna Marinho, *Subsídios para o estudo da metodologia do treinamento da capoeiragem*, 83. Zuma does list additional exercises at the end of *National Gymnastics*, including weight lifting, fencing, boxing, and jiu-jitsu. Burlamaqui, *Gymnastica nacional (capoeiragem) methodisada e regrada*, 52. However, his supplementary training derives primarily from capoeiragem itself and consists primarily of jumping, falling, and standing up from a "fallen" or seated position. Penna Marinho, on the other hand, seeks to improve the body through "modern" exercises from outside capoeiragem (e.g., "analytic exercises," which worked certain body parts in isolation, such as arms and legs; or "synthetic exercises," which trained the body as a whole, such as marching, balancing, and running) — exercises derived from Penna Marinho's training as an athlete and a navy officer.

93. Esdras Magalhães dos Santos, quoted in Lopes, *A capoeiragem no Rio de Janeiro*, 161.

94. Reis proposes that "Bimba had access to erudite thought about capoeira produced in Rio de Janeiro through his disciples who were university students." I depart from her binary erudite/working class, which I believe obscures the numerous intersections between these "two worlds." Reis, *O mundo de pernas para o ar*, 105.

95. Jair Moura (1991), quoted in Frederico José de Abreu, *Bimba é bamba: a Capoeira no ringue* (Cidade da Bahia: Instituto Jair Moura, 1999), 71.

96. Abreu, *Bimba é bamba*, 67.

97. It is important to note that Zuma himself only proposes that matches could be decided through a point system but does not devise such a system. Bimba takes Zuma's ideas further and does devise a point system, where he assigns points to certain strikes. Strikes that merely touched the opponent received one point, while strikes that achieved their goal — making the adversary fall to the ground — were worth three points, adding up to a possible total of twenty-five points. See Jair Moura, *capoeira — a luta regional baiana*, Cadernos de Cultura (Salvador: Divisão de Folclore, Departamento

de Assuntos Culturais, Secretaria Municipal de Educação e Cultura, Prefeitura Municipal do Salvador, 1979), 28. Abreu cites a 1936 interview with Bimba where he describes a similar point system, but according to this account, most successful strikes were worth two points. Abreu, *Bimba é bamba*, 68. It is likely that different point systems were used throughout the 1930s; Ruth Landes, in her description of a 1938 capoeira game between Samuel Querido de Deus and Onça Preta, mentions the practice of scorekeeping. Ruth Landes, *The City of Women* (New York: Macmillan, 1947), 105.

98. Abreu, *Bimba é bamba*, 67–68.

99. It is likely that many of Bimba's matches were "rigged" and his superiority choreographed. A journalist writing in *A Tarde* (1946) asserted that cheating was commonplace in public matches (*"onde impera a marmelada"*). Reprinted in Moura, *Capoeira*, 22.

100. Although perhaps Bimba's memory, four decades later, might have embellished his prowess (being able to win a match in just over one minute), other newspaper articles confirm that Bimba's games were decided before the end of the first round. Articles from *Estado da Bahia* (1936) and *O Imparcial* (1936), quoted in Frederico José de Abreu and Maurício Barros Castro, *Capoeira* (Rio de Janeiro: Beco do Azougue Editorial, 2009), 33.

101. Burlamaqui, *Gymnastica nacional (capoeiragem) methodisada e regrada*, 13.

102. Abreu, *Bimba é bamba*, 34. According to Assunção, Bimba borrowed specific steps from Zuma such as the *queixada* (lit., a kick to the chin), listed in *National Gymnastics*. Assunção, *Capoeira*, 133.

103. No exact publication date is available. It is likely that the booklet was published after Lamartine Pereira da Costa's 1962 *Capoeira sem mestre*. Mestre Itapoan remembers that when he started studying at Bimba's Centro de Cultura Física Regional in 1964, the LP was already available for purchase. Raimundo César Alves de Almeida, audio-recorded interview, May 10, 2011. Taking into account the fact that Bimba was semiliterate, it is likely that the actual writing of this booklet was a collaborative effort between Bimba and one or more of his students. According to Waldeloir Rego, Bimba was a very intelligent man despite the fact that he lacked even an elementary school education, and he "transmitted to [his disciples] his course plan, who gave it an excellent structure and wrote it down in block letters." Rego, *Capoeira Angola*, 283.

104. Bimba, *Curso de Capoeira Regional*, 4.

105. Ibid., 1.

106. In this booklet the folkloric aspect of capoeira is equated with its music: the section where the song lyrics are listed is titled "Folklore of Capoeira" (Folclore da Capoeira), and the preface states that the booklet is "accompanied by an LP with the folklore of Capoeira." Ibid., 1.

107. It is likely that Bimba was influenced, perhaps through his academic students, by the ideas put forth by Gilberto Freyre and his Regionalist Movement in the mid-1920s. Freyre and his regionalist cohort proposed an alternative modernism to that of Rio and São Paulo, calling for a valorization of local culture, a regionalism simultaneously traditionalist and modernist. A native of Recife, the capital of the northeastern state of Pernambuco, Freyre stated in his 1926 Regionalist Manifesto: "The truth is that there isn't any other region in Brazil that exceeds the Northeast in

richness of illustrious traditions and in sharpness of character. Many of its regional values have become national." Gilberto Freyre, *Manisfeto Regionalista de 1926*, Os Cadernos de Cultura (Rio de Janeiro: Departamento de Imprensa Nacional, 1955), 19.

108. Bimba called his new technique Luta Regional Bahiana (Bahian Regional Fight [technique]), omitting the word "capoeira" altogether. Although there is a discrepancy in the literature as to whether the name of Bimba's capoeira school included the word "capoeira," it is clear that Bimba treaded carefully and understood the power of nomenclature. Raimundo C. A. de Almeida (Mestre Itapoan), Muniz Sodré, Hélio Campos, and Matthias Röhrig Assunção cite the name of Bimba's school as Centro de Cultura Física Regional (Center for Regional Physical Culture); Letícia V. de S. Reis, Waldeloir Rego, and Luiz Renato Vieira cite it as Centro de Cultura Física e Capoeira Regional (Center for Physical Culture and Regional Capoeira). Hélio Campos, *Capoeira Regional: a escola de Mestre Bimba* (Salvador: Editora da Universidade Federal da Bahia, 2009), 67; Assunção, *Capoeira*, 140; Reis, *O mundo de pernas para o ar*, 101; Rego, *Capoeira Angola*, 282; Luiz Renato Vieira, "Da vadiação à Capoeira Regional: uma interpretação da modernização cultural no Brasil" (PhD dissertation, Universidade de Brasília, 1990), 165; Muniz Sodré, *Mestre Bimba: corpo de mandinga*, Bahia Com H. (Rio de Janeiro: Manati, 2002), 67; Raimundo César Alves de Almeida, *Bimba, perfil do mestre* (Salvador: Gráfica Universitária, 1982), 27.

109. Bimba, *Curso de Capoeira Regional*, 3.

110. Ibid.

111. Most capoeira classes today, regardless of style, begin with the ginga as part of the "warm-up" for the class; its importance is emphasized and it is often referred to as the foundational or basic capoeira step.

112. Bimba, *Curso de Capoeira Regional*, 8.

113. I draw this analysis from my doctoral dissertation from 2012. Höfling, "Dancing, Fighting, and Staging Capoeira." Cristina F. Rosa, in her 2015 *Brazilian Bodies and Their Choreographies of Identification*, a book based on her doctoral dissertation, also analyses these same passages from Bimba's manual. In her own dissertation from 2010, however, these details from Bimba's booklet are not mentioned. Rosa, "Choreographing Identification."

114. Burlamaqui, *Gymnastica nacional (capoeiragem) methodisada e regrada*, 28.

115. The *esquenta-banho* was "a moment eagerly awaited by all the students, a singular moment in the learning of Capoeira Regional." Campos, *Capoeira Regional*, 220.

116. Bimba attempts to transfer this embodied pedagogical approach to *Capoeira Regional Course*, instructing the reader to "ask your colleague to take you by the hands, and practice the ginga as many times as you can." Bimba, *Curso de Capoeira Regional*, 3.

117. Ibid., 1.

118. In an interview for the *Diário de Notícias* on October 31, 1965, Bimba stated that capoeira angola "left much to be desired" because it "only shows dances and acrobatics." Reis, *O mundo de pernas para o ar*, 101.

119. Rego, *Capoeira Angola*, 32–33.

120. Moura, *Capoeira*, 23.

121. As exemplified by his *emboscadas*; held outside of the safe space of the aca-

demia, in a wooded area of Salvador known as the Chapada do Rio Vermelho, these "real-life" ambushes tested an advanced student's ability to defend himself against many attackers.

122. Rego, *Capoeira Angola*, 32–33.

123. Ibid.

124. As illustrated in Bimba's *Capoeira Regional Course*, lesson 8, figure 8-B (*asfixiante*), and lesson 13, figure 13-B (*bochecho*). Bimba, *Curso de Capoeira Regional*.

125. According to Carneiro, batuque is a "variation of capoeira," so much so that "all the contemporary capoeiristas from Bahia know how to play and [indeed] do play batuque." Carneiro, *Negros bantus*, 165.

126. Burlamaqui, *Gymnastica nacional (capoeiragem) methodisada e regrada*, 29–30; Carneiro, *Negros bantus*, 164.

127. "*Batuques lisos e sambas.*" Burlamaqui, *Gymnastica nacional (capoeiragem) methodisada e regrada*, 29.

128. Bimba, *Curso de Capoeira Regional*. The *arpão de cabeça* can be found in Bimba's fifth lesson; the *meia-lua-de-compasso* is the first strike of the sixth lesson; in the eighth and ninth lessons Bimba introduces the *banda-de-costa*, *banda traçada*, and the *rasteira*.

129. *Cintura desprezada* is often mistranslated in the capoeira literature as "despised waist." *Desprezar* means to despise or scorn, but it can also mean to toss, throw away, leave, or abandon.

130. Bimba, *Curso de Capoeira Regional*, 13.

131. Ibid., 14–15.

132. See Vieira, "Da vadiação à Capoeira Regional," 180.

133. Mello Moraes Filho, *Festas e tradições populares do Brasil*, 449.

134. Ibid.

135. Bira Almeida notes that this passage does not describe the game of capoeira as he knows it, and explains that this may be a result of transformations in the practice or the fact that Mello Moraes, not a capoeirista himself, was unable to interpret what he saw. Ubirajara Almeida, *Capoeira*, 23.

136. Sodré, *Mestre Bimba*, 69.

137. Carneiro, *Negros bantus*, 150.

138. Interview from *A Tarde*, March 16, 1936, reprinted in Abreu, *Bimba é bamba*, 67–68.

139. Ibid.

140. Bimba, *Curso de Capoeira Regional*, 19.

141. Moura, *Capoeira*, 22–23.

142. Reis proposes that these graduations transposed academic, religious, and military rituals and symbols to the world of capoeira. Reis, *O mundo de pernas para o ar*, 108.

143. Ruth Landes famously concludes the foreword of her 1947 ethnography of Bahian candomblé with the declaration: "This book about Brazil does not discuss race problems there because there were none." Landes, *City of Women*, vi.

144. Carneiro believed that capoeira, along with all "elements of black folk-lore" was destined to "recede to small coastal villages." Carneiro, *Negros bantus*, 159–60.

145. Pastinha, *Capoeira Angola*, 30.

146. Ibid. Although capoeira regional (in the broad sense of the term, including styles that deviate from Bimba's pedagogy) may still be the dominant form of capoeira at the time of this writing, being found in private clubs, gyms, and schools, both in Brazil and abroad, the late twentieth and early twenty-first centuries have seen a pronounced increase in popularity of capoeira angola. Perhaps not yet sought by "legions" of people, capoeira angola has spread to most major urban centers around the world, and it is not uncommon for practitioners of capoeira regional to switch to capoeira angola after a few years of practice.

147. Burlamaqui, *Gymnastica nacional (capoeiragem) methodisada e regrada*, 13.

148. Pastinha, *Capoeira Angola*, 31–32.

149. Ibid., 35.

150. Carneiro, *Negros bantus*, 149. Ironically, Carneiro chooses the hybrid, "diluted" Bantu heritage (over Ewe/Yoruba heritage) as the flag-bearer of capoeira's tradition. The relationship between Bantu heritage and capoeira de Angola is further discussed in chapter 2.

151. Pastinha, *Capoeira Angola*, 8.

152. Summarized from an interview by Roberto Freire published in the magazine *Realidade* in 1967. Reprinted in Abreu and Castro, *Capoeira*, 25.

153. Pastinha states that he distanced or removed himself ("*me afastei*") from capoeira between 1912 and 1941. Pastinha, "Quando as pernas fazem miserêr," 5, 24.

154. Pastinha, "Quando as pernas fazem miserêr," 5–6. See Assunção, *Capoeira*, 154–55, for a more detailed analysis of the process of founding the Centro Esportivo de Capoeira Angola in the 1940s and 1950s.

155. Waldeloir Rego proposes yet another possibility to Pastinha's capoeira "lineage": rather than having learned from an African from Angola named Benedito, he speculates that Aberrê might have been Pastinha's teacher rather than his student. Rego, *Capoeira Angola*, 270–71. Mestre Cobrinha Verde (Rafael Alves França, 1917–83) questions Pastinha's version of events: "I [had] never heard of Pastinha. Never, only after Aberrê's death. Before Aberrê died, Pastinha was often accompanied by Aberrê. It was only afterwards that Pastinha started directing the school and saying that he had been Aberrê's teacher. Aberrê never told me who his teacher was." Quoted in Marcelino dos Santos, *Capoeira e mandingas: Cobrinha Verde* (Salvador: Gráfica Santa Bárbara, 1990), 18.

156. Noronha's manuscripts were written in the mid-1970s, but many of the entries consist of the author's memories of Bahia's capoeira scene going back to the first decades of the century. Daniel Coutinho, *O ABC da capoeira de Angola: os manuscritos do Mestre Noronha* (Brasília: CIDOCA, 1993).

157. Ibid., 17. The name of the group is mentioned elsewhere in the manuscript as Conjunto de Capoeira Angola Conceição da Praia (Capoeira Angola Ensemble Conceição da Praia). Ibid., 52–53.

158. Paulo Santos Silva was one of several men who supported Pastinha's efforts of creating and maintaining a capoeira center. These supporters and enthusiasts, who also supported Pastinha's project financially (akin to the role of *ogan* in candomblé),

were sometimes granted the honorary title of "president" or "vice president." In his manuscripts Pastinha acknowledges that Paulo Santos Silva was elected president one month before the statute was published. Clearly this supporter mistook the honorary title given to him for license to claim the CECA as his own.

159. Coutinho, *O ABC da capoeira de Angola*, 17.

160. I have followed Pastinha's spelling of the names of these founders. Pastinha, "Quando as pernas fazem miserêr," 30–31.

161. In 1840 the Brazilian monarchy created the Navy Apprentice Company, whose purpose was to remedy the lack of navy personnel by training boys and young men (ages ten to seventeen) to become sailors. These young boys were, in theory, to be brought in voluntarily by their parents, but in practice many of these boys were sent to Navy Apprentice Companies by police if found orphaned or abandoned, or for engaging in "disorderly conduct." After the military coup d'état of 1889 these "companies" began to be referred to as "schools" but continued to function as a kind of reformatory for poor, "deviant" youth, employing severe corporal punishment such as public floggings. Navy apprentices received instruction in arithmetic, calligraphy, Portuguese language, carpentry, as well as a variety of sports. In Salvador one of the mandatory texts used at the Navy Apprentice School was a collection of Benjamin Franklin's (aka Richard Saunder) maxims translated as "Bom Homem Ricardo," which also served as a way of indoctrinating students in the value of work and the dangers of alcohol consumption and idleness. See Silvia Capanema P. Almeida, "A modernização do material e do pessoal da marinha nas vésperas da revolta dos marujos de 1910: modelos e contradições," *Estudos Históricos* 23, no. 45 (2010): 155–66.

162. The original founders of the first center of capoeira angola, according to Noronha, felt pushed out by Pastinha. In his manuscripts, Noronha expresses his profound disappointment and regret in their choice of Pastinha as the new leader for their Capoeira Angola Center, claiming that after officially registering the center and bringing in several students, Pastinha ostracized the original founders from the center, "because his good friends were the owners and even his own wife a certain Ms. Nice [was] the origin of our distancing from the center at the Pelourinho n. 19. We the owners didn't have the right to anything." Coutinho, *O ABC da capoeira de Angola*, 61.

163. It is unclear whether Pastinha's father was indeed Spanish-born or if he was the descendant of Spaniards. Some contemporary capoeira scholarship spells Pastinha's name with an ñ, Pastiña, thus emphasizing Spanish origins. I found no evidence of this alternate spelling in the early twentieth-century primary sources I consulted.

164. Braz do Amaral, quoted in Penna Marinho, *Subsídios para o estudo da metodologia do treinamento da capoeiragem*, 14.

165. Carneiro, *Negros bantus*, 147.

166. Penna Marinho, *Subsídios para o estudo da metodologia do treinamento da capoeiragem*, 7.

167. Ibid., 19, 7.

168. Photographic evidence shows both Bimba's and Pastinha's groups (as well as other capoeira groups, such as Caiçara's and Samuel Querido de Deus's) wearing soccer jerseys with broad vertical stripes in the 1930s and 1940s; later, in the 1950s,

Pastinha's disciples can be seen wearing polo shirts with the embroidered emblem of his school, often complemented by white smoking jackets. See chapter 2 for further discussion of uniforms.

169. Paulo Santos Silva, "Estatuto do Centro Esportivo de Capoeira Angola" (Salvador: Centro Esportivo de Capoeira Angola, 1952), 9.

170. *Contra-mestre* today is a rank immediately preceding the rank of *mestre*, or master teacher. It is likely that this is also what Pastinha meant here, although the term also means "foreman." Pastinha, "Quando as pernas fazem miserêr," 4.

171. Vicente Ferreira Pastinha, "Pensamentos," in *Manuscritos do Mestre Pastinha* (unpublished manuscripts written c.1952–57, Salvador), 34–35.

172. Ibid., 9–15.

173. Pastinha, "Quando as pernas fazem miserêr," 52.

174. Written by Paulo Santos Silva, who was criticized by Pastinha for usurping the title of founder of the center in this same statute. Nevertheless, he echoed Pastinha's preoccupations with good behavior, expressed elsewhere. Silva, "Estatuto do Centro Esportivo de Capoeira Angola," 2.

175. Pastinha, *Capoeira Angola*, 27–28.

176. Ibid., 33. In the early twenty-first century, most if not all capoeira angola groups continue to advocate for safety, vehemently condemning excessive violence. Mestre João Grande, a disciple of Pastinha, stated that Pastinha habitually removed dangerous elements from capoeira, citing some *balões* as examples. João Oliveira dos Santos, audio-recorded interview, November 14, 2011.

177. Charles Ribeyrolles, an exiled French journalist who moved to Brazil in 1858, compares capoeira to dance in *Brasil pitoresco*, a bilingual French/Portuguese book divided into several volumes, published in 1859. In a chapter titled "The Farm," Ribeyrolles briefly discusses the "Games and Dances of Negros": on weekends and holy days, he notes, "blacks are allowed one or two hours for dancing. . . . Here, [we find] capoeira, a kind of pyrrhic dance, of daring and combative maneuvers, to the sound of the drum from the Congo." Ribeyrolles describes a less violent, dance-like capoeira practiced to "the sound of the drum from the Congo" since he probably witnessed capoeira as part of rural life practiced at "The Farm," away from the maltas of the cities. Charles Ribeyrolles, *Brasil pitoresco: história, descrições, viagens, colonização, instituições*, 3 vols., Coleção Reconquista do Brasil (Belo Horizonte and São Paulo: Editora Itatiaia; Editora da Universidade de São Paulo, 1980 [1859]), 51. It is significant that Rugendas does not refer to capoeira as a dance—a label popularized by the caption of his famous lithograph *Jogar Capoëra ou Danse de la Guèrre*—but as a war game (*Kriegsspiel*). Johann Moritz Rugendas, *Malerische Reise in Brasilien* (Paris: Herausgegeben von Engelmann & Cie., 1835), 26, cited in Rego, *Capoeira Angola*, 59.

178. Pastinha, *Capoeira Angola*, 28.

179. As previously noted, Bimba believed that capoeira angola "left much to be desired" because it was reduced to "dances and acrobatics." Interview for the *Diário de Notícias* on October 31, 1965, quoted in Reis, *O mundo de pernas para o ar*, 101.

180. Pastinha quoted in Abreu and Castro, *Capoeira*, 21.

181. Landes, *City of Women*, 103. Samuel Querido de Deus is further discussed in chapter 2.

182. Pastinha, "Quando as pernas fazem miserêr," 4.

183. Pastinha, *Capoeira Angola*, 50.

184. Ibid.

185. Ibid. This is almost identical to Zuma's stated aim for "sifting": "to disturb the attention of the adversary and better prepare the decisive blow." Burlamaqui, *Gymnastica nacional (capoeiragem) methodisada e regrada*, 42.

186. Pastinha, *Capoeira Angola*, 34.

187. *Maldade* is used by Pastinha as a synonym for *malícia*, but the word can also mean "meanness" or "evil deed." Drawings of the *chamada* (call), a challenge issued during the game that has become iconic of capoeira angola, are labeled in Pastinha's manuscripts as "*maldade.*"

188. This is Pastinha's spelling of *drible*, from the English "dribble," a term that migrated from soccer to capoeira, meaning to dodge, evade, or deceive.

189. While the photos illustrate eleven different moves, Pastinha lists seven attacks as the "main moves of Capoeira Angola": *cabeçada* (headbutt), *rasteira* (leg sweep), *rabo de arraia* (stingray's tail), *chapa de frente* (front kick), *chapa de costas* (back kick), *meia lua* (half moon, a circular kick), and *cutilada de mão* (a strike with the hands). Several of these moves are the same as those described by early twentieth-century observers. It is interesting to note that the hand strike listed by Pastinha has been omitted from capoeira angola practice today. Pastinha, *Capoeira Angola*, 35.

190. Ibid., 68–71.

191. Ibid., 68.

192. Pastinha, quoted in Abreu and Castro, *Capoeira*, 23.

193. "The capoeirista is not seen anymore as a troublemaker—he is a sportsman." Pastinha, *Capoeira Angola*, 30.

194. Pastinha, "Quando as pernas fazem miserêr," 12.

195. Ibid., 1.

196. Burlamaqui, *Gymnastica nacional (capoeiragem) methodisada e regrada*, 15.

197. Reis, *O mundo de pernas para o ar*, 101.

2. FIGHTING AND DANCING

1. Interview for the newspaper *A Tarde*. "A 'luta regional' não é meio de 'cavação,'" *A Tarde*, February 7, 1946.

2. See chapter 1 for a discussion of Article 402 of the Brazilian penal code of 1890, which prohibited the public practice of capoeiragem.

3. Interview with Bimba, cited in Reis, *O mundo de pernas para o ar*, 103. These were likely permits established by local police chiefs. To my knowledge, there were no amendments to Article 402 and the prohibition of capoeira in public spaces remained until 1940. *Contos de réis* refers to one thousand *mil-réis* or one million *réis*, the plural of *real*, the Brazilian currency until 1942.

4. Noronha's "memories" of these conflicts—many ending in gun or knife vio-

lence—may have been derived from stories he heard growing up. Written down more than fifty years later (in the 1970s), these memories often refer to the period between 1917 and 1922, when Noronha, born in 1909, was between eight and thirteen years old. Daniel Coutinho, *O ABC da capoeira de Angola*, 30–31.

5. Bimba's first "school" was conceptualized as a club, the Club União em Apuros, located in the Salvador neighborhood of Engenho Velho de Brotas.

6. Reis, "Negros e brancos no jogo da capoeira," 87.

7. In 1927 Bimba and his students participated in "an exhibition in honor of former Congressman Simões Filho, founder of the newspaper *A Tarde*." *A Tarde*, March 23, 1968, quoted in Abreu, *Bimba é bamba*, 30. In 1934 Bimba and his group performed at the Brotas Stadium in Salvador during a benefit for the city's homeless shelter. Raimundo César Alves de Almeida, *A Saga do Mestre Bimba* (Salvador: Ginga Associação de Capoeira, 1994), 23.

8. In an interview for the *Diário de Goiânia* in 1973, Bimba stated, "The person who took the Capoeira of Brazil from under the claws of police, I think[,] aside from God[,] was me." Abreu and Castro, *Capoeira*, 33.

9. Mestre Itapoan writes that Bimba initially tried attending public rodas with his students, but his capoeira was so intimidating that rodas would disperse at the mere sight of Bimba and his students. Almeida, *A Saga do Mestre Bimba*, 20–21.

10. Known as Bahia's Independence Day, July 2 (Dois de Julho) marks the day when Brazilian military forces took back the province of Bahia from Portuguese control (July 2, 1823)—almost one year after all other Brazilian provinces had been independent from Portugal (September 7, 1822).

11. *A Tarde*, July 1, 1936, quoted in Abreu, *Bimba é bamba*, 31.

12. This document also recognizes Bimba as "director of the physical education course" at his now registered school. Almeida, *Bimba, perfil do mestre*, 17.

13. "Bahia's policy at the time forced *terreiros* [candomblé houses] to apply to the police for permits to celebrate each religious festival. The police charged a fee for this permission, which could apparently vary in scale." Romo, *Brazil's Living Museum*, 81.

14. The matches continued until December 12, 1936, but from July until December they were held at another location, at the Campo da Graça, due to the closure of the stadium at Parque Odeon in July. Abreu, *Bimba é bamba*, 43–44.

15. Ibid., 62.

16. Jorge Amado, *Bahia de todos os santos: guia das ruas e dos mistérios da cidade do Salvador*, 10th ed. (São Paulo: Livraria Martins Editôra, 1964), 56–57.

17. Abreu, *Bimba é bamba*, 43.

18. The fact that the stadium was dismantled less than six months after it was built suggests a modest, temporary building, much smaller than the soccer stadium where Bimba and his students had recently staged matches.

19. "Capoeira is a kind of backwards Jiu-Jistu, its goal is to eliminate the adversary, with moves that are agile, violent and in their majority decisive." Abreu, *Bimba é bamba*, 64.

20. *O Imparcial*, February 7, 1936, quoted in ibid., 54.

21. *Diário de Notícias*, March 9, 1936, quoted in ibid., 63.

22. Ibid., 64–65. Zey (spelled Zehyr) is mentioned by Pastinha in 1964 as one of the greatest living capoeiristas. Pastinha, *Capoeira Angola*, 25.

23. *O Imparcial*, March 12, 1936, quoted in Abreu, *Bimba é bamba*, 65. At least two other similar challenges were printed by local newspapers, one by Américo Pequeno and another by Aberrê. See *Diário de Notícias*, March 13, 1936, quoted in ibid. *Diário da Bahia*, March 25, 1936, quoted in ibid., 77.

24. Bimba challenged Samuel Pescador (probably the same person as the player known as Samuel Querido de Deus, cited by Jorge Amado, Édison Carneiro, and Ruth Landes as the greatest player of capoeira de Angola at the time) as well as the capoeiristas Eugênio and Henrique Bahia. *Diário da Bahia*, January 6, 1936, quoted in ibid., 50.

25. Victor H.U. and Aberrê are listed as cofounders, with Pastinha, of the Capoeira Angola Sports Center in 1941. Pastinha, "Pensamentos," 30–31.

26. The press condemned the unsuccessful fight as a "joke," pointing to its lack of polish and professionalism by derisively comparing it to an informal soccer match among friends (*um baba*). *O Imparcial*, February 19, 1936, quoted in Abreu, *Bimba é bamba*, 58.

27. According to Pastinha, Aberrê (Antônio Raymundo Argolo, 1895–1942), also spelled ABR, had been his student in the early 1910s. Other sources, such as Mestres Waldemar da Paixão, Canjiquinha, and Cobrinha Verde, state that Aberrê was Pastinha's teacher, not his student. See Rego, *Capoeira Angola*, 270–71; and Paulo Andrade Magalhães Filho, "Jogo de discursos: a disputa por hegemonia na tradição da Capoeira Angola bahiana" (master's thesis, Universidade Federal da Bahia, 2011).

28. In a *demonstration* rather than a fight, Bimba and Aberrê engaged in a process of selection in order to show the public only the most spectacular aspects of the practice. This collaborative demonstration suggests the existence of established "conventions" for semichoreographed capoeira demonstrations. *O Estado da Bahia* and *O Imparcial*, February 19, 1936, quoted in Abreu, *Bimba é bamba*, 58.

29. Ibid., 57.

30. According to Aberrê's former student Mestre Caiçara (Antônio Conceição Moraes), Bimba and Aberrê were good friends and often practiced capoeira together. Magalhães Filho, "Jogo de discursos," 63.

31. *Diário da Bahia*, March 28, 1936, quoted in Abreu, *Bimba é bamba*, 79–80.

32. In 1940 George Gracie, of the Gracie family responsible for developing the Brazilian style of jiu-jitsu, confessed that he had participated in rigged matches, and went on to state that such matches were commonplace. He stated, "I realized, indignant, that sports fans like spectacle and decided to accept the [rigged] matches, since only in a simulated fight can you achieve spectacle." "Porque, cada vez mais, se desmoraliza o profissionalismo . . . ," *A Tarde*, July 30, 1940.

33. "A 'luta regional' não é meio de 'cavação.'"

34. Published on June 9, 1936, and reprinted the following year in Édison Carneiro, *Negros bantus*, 149.

35. Anthropologist Simone Pondé Vassallo notes that Bahian intellectuals such as Édison Carneiro and Jorge Amado championed the preservation of cultural forms deemed pure, and saw capoeira regional as a threat to capoeira's integrity. Simone

Pondé Vassallo, "Capoeiras e intelectuais: a construção coletiva da capoeira 'autêntica,'" *Estudos Históricos* 32 (2003): 111.

36. Landes, *City of Women*, 13–14.

37. Romo, *Brazil's Living Museum*, 65.

38. Carneiro, *Negros bantus*, 159.

39. Ibid.

40. Ibid.

41. All capoeiristas listed here were most likely of African descent. I have not been able to find other references to Oséas, but I believe he too may have been Afro-Brazilian.

42. The physical characteristics of the "Angola type" are discussed in chapter 1. Carneiro, *Negros bantus*, 150.

43. Ramos refers to the superiority of the "Sudanese" cultural influence in Brazil, which he subdivides into *"'yorubas,' 'gêges,' 'haussás,' 'minas.'"* Ramos, *O negro brasileiro*, 21.

44. In 1934, the same year Freyre published *Casa grande e senzala* (The masters and the slaves), Ramos published the influential *O negro brasileiro* (The Brazilian Negro).

45. Among Bantu cultures, Ramos lists *"angolas," "cabindas," "congos," "benguelas"* and other "provinces of the vast southern African territory." Ramos, *O negro brasileiro*, 22.

46. Ibid., 88.

47. Ramos considered Bantu myths to be "disfigured and transformed, . . . almost unrecognizable due to the fast work of the symbiosis of mythic species" (*deturpados e transformados, . . . quase irreconhecíveis pela obra rápida da simbiose das espécies míticas*). Ibid., 89.

48. Although the capoeira designation "from Angola" precedes the publication of Carneiro's book by at least one year, already present in the news reports of the 1936 matches at Odeon Stadium, it is absent from the capoeira record prior to the mid-1930s, suggesting a direct relationship between Carneiro's interest in Brazil's Bantu heritage and the capoeira style that became known as capoeira de Angola.

49. The text of this chapter was first published in *O Estado da Bahia* in 1936.

50. Capoeira historian Matthias Röhrig Assunção notes that even though Angola identity was considered "impure" in candomblé, Carneiro associated it with a capoeira style he believed to have retained the "purity" of African traditions. This inversion may have resulted from an alleged Bantu retention of "play and games, whereas the serious Sudanese retained their religion." Matthias Röhrig Assunção, "Angola in Brazil: The Formation of *Angoleiro* Identity in Bahia," in *African Heritage and Memories of Slavery in Brazil and the South Atlantic World*, ed. Ana Lúcia Araújo (Amherst: Cambria Press, 2015), 135–36.

51. Carneiro's classification of capoeira betrays his limited knowledge of the practice; in his list of nine "species" of capoeira, he includes the names of capoeira musical rhythms (São Bento Grande, São Bento Pequeno) as well as names of places where capoeira was practiced in Salvador (Conceicão da Praia). From this list, he declares capoeira "de Angola" the purest form. Carneiro, *Negros bantus*, 149.

52. Cited in Romo, *Brazil's Living Museum*, 67; Waldir Freitas Oliveira and Vivaldo da

Costa Lima, *Cartas de Édison Carneiro a Artur Ramos: de 4 de janeiro de 1936 a 6 de dezembro de 1938*, Baianada (São Paulo: Editora Corrupio, 1987), 128.

53. This performance, which featured many of the same players who had recently participated in the matches at Odeon Park, was held at the tennis courts of the Itapagipe Regatta Club. Assunção, *Capoeira*, 151; Romo, *Brazil's Living Museum*, 74.

54. For a detailed analysis of both the first and the second Afro-Brazilian Congresses, see Romo, *Brazil's Living Museum*.

55. Oliveira and Lima, *Cartas de Édison Carneiro a Artur Ramos*, 131; Assunção, "Angola in Brazil," 131.

56. Daryle Williams, *Culture Wars in Brazil: The First Vargas Regime, 1930–1945* (Durham: Duke University Press, 2001), 98–100.

57. The "interior" was an imagined collective of geographic spaces that included small coastal towns as well as rural areas located inland.

58. Ricardo Goldenberg, "Educação musical: a experiência do canto orfeônico no Brasil," *Proposições* 6, no. 3[18] (1995): 105.

59. Teachers of Canto Orfeônico were trained in music theory, music history, and aesthetics, as well as ethnography and folklore. See ibid.

60. Carneiro, *Negros bantus*, 159–60.

61. Renato Almeida, quoted in Luís Rodolfo Vilhena, *Projeto e missão: o movimento folclórico brasileiro, 1947–1964* (Rio de Janeiro: Fundação Getulio Vargas Editora; Ministério da Cultura, FUNARTE, 1997), 186.

62. Édison Carneiro, *Dinâmica do folclore* (Salvador: Editora Civilização Brasileira, 1965), 3.

63. Ibid., 16.

64. Édison Carneiro, *Folguedos tradicionais* (Salvador: Conquista, 1974), 195.

65. Text from the back cover of the Campaign for the Defense of Brazilian Folklore's journal, *Revista Brasileira de Folclore* (May–August 1963).

66. Carneiro, *Dinâmica do folclore*, 99–111.

67. Ibid., 111.

68. Ibid., 112–13.

69. Mestiçagem, or racial miscegenation, was being established as the defining element of Brazilian national identity at the time.

70. I estimate that this text was written in the late 1960s, since it is absent from the collected essays published in 1965 in *Dinâmica do folclore*. It was published posthumously in the early 1970s in two sources, with minor modifications. The phrase "legacy of Angola" is written "*de Angola*" (from Angola) in *Capoeira*, and "*do Angola*" (of the Angola type) in *Folguedos tradicionais*. Édison Carneiro, *Capoeira*, Cadernos de folclore (Rio de Janeiro: Campanha de Defesa do Folclore Brasileiro, 1975), 14; Carneiro, *Folguedos tradicionais*, 140.

71. Guilherme Simões was a nephew of the founder of the Bahian newspaper *A Tarde*, where he worked as a columnist; he also worked at the Superintendência de Turismo da Cidade de Salvador (City of Salvador Tourism Superintendence), SUTURSA, created in 1964.

72. The term *angoleiro/a* today refers to practitioners of capoeira angola. The term was widely disseminated during the renaissance of capoeira angola in the 1980s. Simões added that Bimba had indeed been an angoleiro but too long ago, "when the Dead Sea was still in the ICU." Guilherme Simões, audio-recorded interview, June 1, 2011.

73. For an analysis of the connections between Amado and Freyre, see Patricia de Santana Pinho, "Gilberto Freyre e a baianidade" in *Gilberto Freyre e os estudos latino-americanos*, ed. Joshua Lund and Malcolm McNee, Série Críticas (Pittsburgh: Instituto Internacional de Literatura Iberoamericana, 2006).

74. Amado, *Bahia de todos os santos*, 183.

75. I am translating the word *"deturpação"* as "disfigurement." In a more general sense, it can also mean purposeful misrepresentation.

76. In the first edition of *Bahia de todos os santos* (1945), Jorge Amado describes Samuel Querido de Deus as a Bahian fisherman in his midsixties. By the eighth edition of this same book (published in 1960), we know that Querido de Deus was no longer alive, because Amado includes a note to say that his portrait of Querido de Deus was written while he was still living. In *O jogo da capoeira*, published in 1951, Carybé lists Querido de Deus as a capoeirista of the past, indicating he was no longer alive at the time, thus placing his death between 1945 and 1950.

77. Amado, *Bahia de todos os santos*, 234–35.

78. If he is indeed the same Samuel who wrote a letter to the newspaper *O Imparcial* during the 1936 pugilistic season, challenging Bimba's portrayal by the media as Bahia's capoeira champion, his family name would be de Souza. See Abreu, *Bimba é bamba*, 65.

79. Landes, *City of Women*, 102–3. Italics mine.

80. Landes and Carneiro were romantically involved, a fact that was later used to discredit Landes's work and tarnish her reputation as a scholar. Romo, *Brazil's Living Museum*, 119–29.

81. Carneiro, *Negros bantus*, 151.

82. Mestre Waldemar da Paixão reported being specifically asked by police (probably sometime in the 1940s) not to teach his students to use "knife, machete, straight-razor and sword." Quoted in Magalhães Filho, "Jogo de discursos'."

83. Landes, *City of Women*, 106.

84. For a discussion of the personal attacks on scholars who in the 1940s dared to propose that Bahia was not an unaltered product of the past, but instead a site of dynamic change, see Romo, *Brazil's Living Museum*, chapter 4.

85. This text was published posthumously in both Carneiro, *Folguedos tradicionais*, 141; and Carneiro, *Capoeira*, 3.

86. Amado, *Bahia de todos os santos*, 209.

87. In his manuscripts Pastinha often refers to himself as "the old man" (*o velho*). In this passage, using the third person, he speaks of the success of his performances: "People see him an applaud. . . . His behavior adds respect to his age[;] see it to believe it." Pastinha, "Quando as pernas fazem miserêr."

88. Amado, *Bahia de todos os santos*, 209.

89. Curiously, Carneiro does not mention Pastinha at all in his 1950 description

and analysis of capoeira in *Dinâmica do folclore*. He does mention Samuel Querido de Deus, Maré, Aberrê, Juvenal, Polu, and Onça Preta. For Carneiro, Querido de Deus was not as easily replaceable as he was for Amado. Carneiro, *Dinâmica do folclore*, 53.

90. Landes, *City of Women*, 102.

91. Amado, *Bahia de todos os santos*, 235.

92. Carneiro, *Folguedos tradicionais*, 140.

93. By several accounts, Pastinha "outsourced" much of the teaching in his academy. Cobrinha Verde (Rafael Alves França), who is mentioned by Amado in the first edition of *Bahia de todos os santos*, is known to have taught at Pastinha's school. See Marcelino dos Santos, *Capoeira e mandingas: Cobrinha Verde* (Salvador: Gráfica Santa Bárbara, 1990).

94. Visual artist Carybé does list Querido de Deus among Bahia's *mestres* of the past. Carybé, *O jogo da capoeira*, n.p.

95. This three-part division, perhaps influenced by Comte's three-part models—his three "states" (theological, metaphysical, and positive) and the three principles of his religion of humanity (love, order, and progress)—is also expressed by Pastinha in his division of capoeira into "past, present and future." Pastinha, "Quando as pernas fazem miserêr," 26.

96. Ibid., 54.

97. The performance at the Abaeté Lagoon may have been a joint invitation to Bimba and Pastinha. In his manuscripts, Pastinha cites a 1957 performance at the "Bahiete," which according to Angelo Decânio is Pastinha's spelling of Abaeté. Angelo Decânio, *A herança de Pastinha*, Coleção São Salomão (self-published, Salvador, 1997), 52.

98. Pastinha, "Quando as pernas fazem miserêr," 54.

99. One year before this demonstration, both Bimba's and Pastinha's students were hired to participate in Alexandre Robato's 1954 film *Vadiação*, a film shot on a set (at the Cine Guarany) that attempted to reproduce a dock ambiance such as the one at the ramp of the Model Market. Curiously, while Bimba is featured playing berimbau, Pastinha himself is absent from the film. Both *Vadiação* and the film recording mentioned by Pastinha suggest a nostalgic valorization of the informal capoeira performances such as the ones at the ramp of the market, perhaps by then a thing of the past. See Ana Paula Höfling, "Capoeiras of Bahia," in *Axé Bahia: The Power of Art in an Afro-Brazilian Metropolis*, ed. Patrick A. Polk et al. (Los Angeles: Fowler Museum at UCLA, 2017).

100. It is significant that Pastinha states that the music is important not for rendering capoeira more appealing to outside audiences but for "stirring the souls" of the players themselves. Pastinha, *Capoeira Angola*, 27–28.

101. The *agogô* seems to have been added to the ensemble only in the 1960s. A gourd shaker (*ganzá*) and a small drum can be seen in earlier versions of the ensemble, e.g., in Alceu Maynard's early 1950s recording. Pastinha is also known for having experimented with other musical instruments, such as the guitar, castanets, and wood blocks.

102. João Grande (João Oliveira dos Santos), audio-recorded interview, November 14, 2011.

103. Interview with João Grande, quoted in Assunção, *Capoeira*, 166.

104. Interview with Gildo Alfinete (Gildo Lemos Couto), quoted in José de Jesus Barreto and Otto Freitas, *Pastinha: o grande mestre da Capoeira Angola*, Coleção Gente da Bahia (Salvador: Assembléia Legislativa do Estado da Bahia, 2009), 141.

105. Maynard was a member of the National Folklore Commission and a capoeira enthusiast. He had been a student of a capoeira teacher from Rio de Janeiro called Menê, who during the Republican persecution of the late 1890s had been "deported" to Maynard's hometown of Botucatu, São Paulo, at the end of the rail line known as Sorocabana. Alceu Maynard Araújo, *Folclore nacional*, 3 vols., Série Cultura e Ciência (São Paulo: Edições Melhoramentos, 1964), 314. It is unclear if or how this film was originally exhibited or broadcast. The capoeira footage surfaced around 2009 on the video-sharing site YouTube.

106. The sounds of this demonstration were not captured along with the images. There are two versions of this film circulating among capoeira enthusiasts and researchers: one without sound, and another with narration recorded over a highly orchestrated version of Ary Barroso's "Na Baixa do Sapateiro," also known as "Bahia"—a song whose lyrics express a longing for a Bahia that "will not leave my thoughts." A mistake made by the narrator attests to Bimba's fame at the time, despite Pastinha's rising popularity. As the camera zooms in on Pastinha's face, the narrator identifies him: "Mestre Bimba, who today has a famous school in Salvador, Bahia, transformed the old capoeira into the Bahian regional fight [technique]" (0:49). He later repeats his mistake, stating that Mestre Bimba was "the sexagenarian who performed in this capoeira exhibition." I obtained a copy of *Veja o Brasil* (without sound) from capoeira scholar Frede Abreu. The version with sound is available on YouTube. Alceu Maynard Araújo, "Capoeira de Angola," in *Veja o Brasil* (DVD) c.1950. www.you tube.com/watch?v=QrLNIwZ1x50.

107. This may be the same movement referred to as *passo a dois* (two-person step) in the late nineteenth century: "Passo a dois is a quick foot shuffle that precedes the head butt and the leg sweep." Mello Moraes Filho, *Festas e tradições populares do Brasil*, 448.

108. Greg Downey writes: "When spectators ask about the chamada, veteran players sometimes offer historical explanations of its origin. One instructor, for instance, suggested that it was a parody of European ballroom dancing. He explained that slaveholders sometimes danced with enslaved women, but also beat them. . . . Players who cannot offer any historical explanation, however implausible, for the chamada—probably the majority—still assert that it is 'traditional.'" Downey, *Learning Capoeira*, 107.

109. Although Maynard's choppy editing does not show the viewer what follows a chamada, contemporary practice indicates that the game would resume after each chamada.

110. Emília Biancardi has suggested that Maynard may have specifically requested a performance of balões. She reports never having seen Pastinha teaching or performing such throws at his school during her visits in the 1960s. Emília Biancardi, personal communication, 2011.

111. Maria Isabel, "Folclore: o dengo do povo está perdendo a pureza original,"

Diário de Notícias August 23, 1976. Waldeloir Rego also affirms that "connected strikes" (*golpes ligados*) were inexistent in Capoeira Angola. Rego, *Capoeira Angola*, 269.

112. "The hands almost never work in attacks, except in the several throws [balões], where the hands support the body of the adversary so as to throw him, over [one's] head, backwards." Carneiro, *Negros bantus*, 150.

113. João Grande (João Oliveira dos Santos), audio-recorded interview, November 14, 2011.

114. Broadcast as part of the French television series *Les coulisses de l'exploit* (Behind the scenes of exploits) on May 15, 1963. Produced by Henri Carrier, images by Bernard Taquet and Serge Ehrler, commentary by Georges de Caunes. www.ina.fr /video/CPF04007124 (accessed January 20, 2016).

115. Downey explains that "one of the most dramatic, 'traditional' sequences in the roda is the chamada or 'call,' a formalized challenge enacted through gesture." Downey, *Learning Capoeira*, 105.

116. Carneiro, *Capoeira*, 9.

117. Carneiro, *Folguedos tradicionais*, 143.

118. Amado, *Bahia de todos os santos*, 22.

119. Pastinha, *Capoeira Angola*, front cover flap.

120. Ibid., back cover flap.

121. João Oliveira dos Santos, audio-recorded interview, November 14, 2011.

122. Amado, *Bahia de todos os santos*, 209.

123. Jorge Amado, "Conversa com Buanga Fêlê, também conhecido como Mário de Andrade, chefe da luta de Angola," *Tempo Brasileiro* 1, no. 1 (September 1962), quoted in Rego, *Capoeira Angola*, 275.

124. Barreto and Freitas, *Pastinha*, 146.

125. Jota Bamberg, quoted in "Mestre Pastinha Doente: 'Agora eu quero morrer,'" *Tribuna da Bahia*, November 19, 1979, 5.

126. Luis Vitor Castro Jr., "Campos de visibilidade da capoeira baiana: as festas populares, as escolas de capoeira, o cinema e a arte (1955–1985)" (PhD dissertation, Pontifícia Universidade Católica de São Paulo, 2008), 104.

3. CAPOEIRA FOR THE TOURIST STAGE

1. In 1952 the city of Salvador published the first *Roteiro Turístico da Cidade de Salvador* (Tour guide of the city of Salvador); in the following year, the bilingual English/ Portuguese *Bahia de Ontem e de Hoje* (Bahia of yesterday and today), also published by the municipality of Salvador, introduced visitors to the notable sites and sights of the city through photographs and illustrations, highlighting the contrast between the old (Bahia of yesterday) and the new (Bahia of today). Anadélia Romo notes that the framing of Bahia as both traditional and modern dates back to initiatives that began during Vargas's New State, as early as 1939, such as the publications and exhibitions sponsored by the Office of Culture and Promotion of the State of Bahia. Romo, *Brazil's Living Museum*, 89–90.

2. In partnership with the United States government, Brazil formed a commission to develop strategies for the promotion of tourism to Brazil—the Tourism Project for

Brazil. For a detailed account of the development of the tourism industry in Bahia, see Lucia Maria Aquino de Queiroz, *Turismo na Bahia: estratégias para o desenvolvimento* (Salvador: Secretaria da Cultura e Turismo, 2002), 30–69.

3. Rego, *Capoeira Angola*. The book was reissued as part of the Capoeira Viva Collection through the Gregório de Mattos Foundation in 2015 after almost five decades out of print. Waldeloir Rego, *Capoeira Angola: ensaio sócio-etnográfico*, Coleção Capoeira Viva, 2nd ed. (Salvador: Fundação Gregório de Mattos, 2015). All citations here follow the page numbers of the first edition. I have maintained the original punctuation, capitalization, and italicization of the original.

4. In an interview, Emília Biancardi corrected my own U.S.-centered and historically inaccurate description of both Rego and Carneiro as *negros* (blacks): "They were *mulatos*," she said, emphasizing the last word. Biancardi, who knew both Carneiro and Rego personally, continues to explain how even though they were mulattos, they were light-skinned enough to identify as white: "Back then, *mulatos* did not admit they were *mulatos*. Today they do because the world has changed." Emília Biancardi Ferreira, audio-recorded interview by author, May 9, 2011.

5. Jorge Amado's text on front jacket flap of the second edition of Rego's *Capoeira Angola*.

6. Rego's tenure spanned all three iterations of Salvador's tourism department: DMT, DTDP, and SUTURSA. See Lucia Maria Aquino de Queiroz, "A gestão pública e a competitividade de cidades turísticas: a experiência da cidade do Salvador" (PhD dissertation, Universitat de Barcelona, 2005); Queiroz, *Turismo na Bahia*.

7. Carneiro, *Capoeira*; Carneiro, *Folguedos tradicionais*.

8. Rego, *Capoeira Angola*, 269.

9. Queiroz, *Turismo na Bahia*, 60.

10. *Atos institucionais* were known by their numbers (AI-1, AI-2, etc.). These decrees gradually gave the military unlimited executive powers and voided the democratic political process. The AI-1gave the president power to easily pass constitutional amendments, suspend the job security of civil servants for six months, and "suspend for 10 years the political rights of any citizen and to cancel the mandates of federal, state, and municipal legislators." The AI-2 abolished all political parties and instituted the practice of "indirect elections" for president, amplified by the AI-3, which extended "indirect elections" to state governors and mayors. Thomas E. Skidmore, *The Politics of Military Rule in Brazil* (Oxford: Oxford University Press, 1988), 20, 46. These institutional acts paved the way to the most repressive of all executive orders, the AI-5, the decree that intensified torture, assassinations, and "disappearances" aimed at annihilating the opposition to the military regime.

11. The new tourism administration was harshly criticized in the Bahian press. The newspaper *A Tarde* accused the new director of SUTURSA of doing nothing but traveling back and forth between Bahia and Rio all year, and ridiculed him as "the tourist of the year." A journalist by the name of Menezes, writing in *A Tarde* in 1965, stated that SUTURSA was only concerned with "dreaming up plans impossible to implement, forgetting the basics of the development of our tourism." Quoted in Queiroz, *Turismo na Bahia*, 81.

12. Rego, *Capoeira Angola*, 361.

13. Ibid., 45.

14. What I am translating as "over the top" is Rego's use of the adjective *amacaca-do(a)* in his phrase *"camisas amacacadas."* *Amacacado(a)* is an adjective deriving from the word *macaco*, Portuguese for "monkey." To compare someone to a monkey usually refers to an inability to think for oneself; it is someone who is only able to imitate, "like a monkey." Rego's comparison could also refer to a monkey's supposed clownish behavior.

15. Rego, *Capoeira Angola*, 361–62.

16. Ibid., 45.

17. Pastinha's colors were yellow and black and Bimba's were blue and white. By the 1950s both Bimba and Pastinha had their own emblems embroidered on their students' uniforms, marking their respective affiliations. By the early 1960s Pastinha's ensemble can be seen wearing smoking jackets.

18. In the mid-to-late 1940s, because of the inconvenience of having to buy soccer jerseys in lots of eleven (the number of players in a soccer team) and the lack of choice in sizes, Bimba decided to switch to plain white shirts with the emblem of the CCFR (Centro de Cultura Física Regional) designed by his student Angelo Decânio and embroidered by one of his wives, Mãe Bena. Angelo Decânio, *A herança de Mestre Bimba: filosofia e lógica africanas da capoeira*, 2nd ed., Coleção São Salomão (self-published, Salvador, 1997), 44–45.

19. Campos, *Capoeira Regional*, 128.

20. Graduation ceremonies nevertheless included some of the same elements as folkloric shows, such as acrobatic demonstration games, samba duro, and samba de roda. The fact that the demonstration games were clearly choreographed was not condemned by Rego as a "loss" (in fact he barely mentions these games, referring to them only through his attempt at an English spelling of *escrete*: "schath"). The addition of samba to the ceremony seemed traditional enough for Rego and met no objections. Rego, *Capoeira Angola*, 286.

21. Ibid.

22. Rego, *Capoeira Angola*, 270.

23. Rego, *Capoeira Angola*, 271.

24. This course was taught by local experts on Bahia's history and culture, such as Luiz Monteiro, Carlos Ott, Hildegardes Vianna, Alberto Marinho, and Wanderley Pinho, and also included visits to local candomblé temples and to the Pelourinho. Queiroz, *Turismo na Bahia*, 47, 60.

25. Queiroz, "A gestão pública e a competitividade de cidades turísticas," 319, 45.

26. Rego, *Capoeira Angola*, 290.

27. According to Mestre Acordeon, the title of this show was "Vem camará: histórias de capoeira" (Come Friend: Histories of Capoeira). *Camará* (from *camarada*, or comrade) means "friend" or "buddy." Ubirajara Guimarães Almeida, audio-recorded interview by author, August 4, 2013. Mestre Acordeon moved to Northern California in the late 1970s and was the first capoeira mestre to begin teaching Bimba's Capoeira Regional on the West Coast of the United States.

28. Rego, *Capoeira Angola*, 323.

29. Ubirajara Guimarães Almeida, audio-recorded interview by author, August 4, 2013.

30. "Come Friend 67: New Stories of Capoeira."

31. Rego, *Capoeira Angola*, 323.

32. Letícia Vidor de Sousa Reis and later Matthias Röhrig Assunção have acknowledged Bimba's innovations as dynamic Africanist appropriations of hegemonic rituals and symbols. Reis, "Negros e brancos no jogo da capoeira"; Assunção, *Capoeira*.

33. See Barreto and Freitas, *Pastinha*; Acúrsio Pereira Esteves, *A "capoeira" da indústria do entretenimento: corpo, acrobacia e espetáculo para "turista ver"* (Salvador: Bureau Gráfica e Editora, 2004); Castro, "Campos de visibilidade da capoeira baiana." Castro concurs with Esteves's assessment of a tourism industry that necessarily incurs "loss" to capoeira.

34. Esteves, *A "capoeira" da indústria do entretenimento*, 128.

35. Cristina F. Rosa similarly sees commodification as a threat, claiming that capoeira is currently "facing one of its biggest threats in the age of globalization: commoditized exoticism." Cristina F. Rosa, "Risk Taking Bodies and Their Choreographies of Protest," in *Moving (across) Borders: Performing Translation, Intervention, Participation*, ed. Brandstetter and Hartung (Bielefeld: Transcript Verlag, 2017).

36. Rego, *Capoeira Angola*, 32.

37. The revitalization of the historic center of Salvador did not take place until the 1980s; in the 1950s and 1960s this area was far from being a prime location or one with easy access by tourists or residents of more affluent neighborhoods.

38. Mestre Itapoan remembers that in the early 1950s Carlos Senna and a few other disciples pooled the money to buy a house on a street called Sítio Caruano in the neighborhood of Nordeste de Amaralina, which they then gave to Mestre Bimba. Raimundo César Alves de Almeida, e-mail communication, September 7, 2011. Rego lists the address as R. Sítio Caruana [sic], 49. Rego, *Capoeira Angola*, 286.

39. Campos, *Capoeira Regional*, 158.

40. Ibid., 210. The currency was likely the *Cruzeiro* (Cr$) before its devaluation and renaming as *Cruzeiro Novo* (NCr$) in 1967.

41. Bimba is known to have had several "wives" (simultaneous common law marriages). Mãe Alice, one of his wives, was a candomblé priestess who brought in other women from her candomblé house for singing and dancing in the show.

42. The group performed regularly at the Boite de Ondina. Almeida, *A saga do Mestre Bimba*, 47; Campos, *Capoeira Regional*, 128.

43. Agência Kontik de Viagens e Turismo was founded in the early 1950s as a travel agency named Cliper (pronounced "clipper"). The airline PanAmerican, which owned airplanes named Clipper, sued Cliper in 1958 demanding a name change. In 1958 the agency was renamed Kontik and became one of the largest travel agencies in Bahia; it is still in existence today. Queiroz, *Turismo na Bahia*, 50.

44. Raimundo César Alves de Almeida, audio-recorded interview, May10, 2011.

45. Mestre Acordeon remembers that Mestre Bimba's demonstrations were transformed into full-fledged folkloric shows at the urging of his students, following the

success of other folkloric ensembles in the mid-1960s. Ubirajara Guimarães Almeida, audio-recorded interview, August 4, 2013.

46. Campos compares Bimba's command of the audience to that of legendary Brazilian variety show host Silvio Santos. Castro, "Campos de visibilidade da capoeira baiana," 95.

47. Letícia Reis has interpreted these formal graduations, complete with medals and godmothers, as transpositions of hegemonic symbols (academic, religious, and military) to the world of capoeira. Reis, *O mundo de pernas para o ar*, 108.

48. In an interview, Itapoan explained to me that "learned" people think this practice should be referred to as *esquete*, the Portuguese spelling for the borrowed English term "sketch," which refers to a set scene in theater. However, he reminded me that they didn't have "this kind of vocabulary" at that time, and that the correct term is *escrete*. Raimundo César Alves de Almeida, audio-recorded interview by author, May 10, 2011. Hélio Campos, however, also a disciple of Bimba's, uses the term *esquete*. Campos, *Capoeira Regional*, 56.

49. "After [an explanation about the ritual elements of the ceremony] and [other] social obligations, a demonstration of schath [sic] follows." Rego, *Capoeira Angola*, 287.

50. Campos also quotes Gato Branco (José Luiz Pinto Filho) on his experience with demonstration games: "The demonstration games at the graduation ceremony[,] I thought they were incredible, because it taught you how to fall, with all those throws, you had a sense of balance it gave you a great sense of balance." Campos, *Capoeira Regional*, 55–56.

51. Raimundo César Alves de Almeida, audio-recorded interview, May 10, 2011.

52. This photograph is dated July 9, 1968, in Almeida, *A saga do Mestre Bimba*, 180; and 1971 in Raimundo César Alves de Almeida, *Capoeira: retalhos da roda* (Salvador: Ginga Associação de Capoeira, 2005), 17.

53. Pastinha, *Capoeira Angola*, 27–28.

54. Barbara Kirshenblatt-Gimblett, *Destination Culture: Tourism, Museums and Heritage* (Berkeley: University of California Press, 1998), 64–65.

55. Ubirajara Guimarães Almeida, *Água de beber, camará: um bate-papo de capoeira* (Berkeley: United Capoeira Association, 1999), 52.

56. Goli Guerreiro describes the sculpture by Mario Cravo placed outside the DMT building as a soapstone mermaid in a lake, and explains that "the idea was to transform the monument in an attraction peculiar to Bahia, similar to the Fountain of Trevi, in Italy, where tourists could throw coins for good luck." Goli Guerreiro, "A cidade imaginada: Salvador sob o olhar do turismo," *Revista Gestão e Planejamento* 6, no. 11 (2005): 8; Queiroz, "A gestão pública e a competitividade de cidades turísticas," 318.

57. Video-recorded interview with Canjiquinha by Raimundo César Alves de Almeida and Luis Renato Vieira, c. 1988, unpublished. See also Antônio Moreira et al., *Canjiquinha: a alegria da capoeira* (Salvador: Fundação Cultural do Estado da Bahia, c. 1989), 28, 46.

58. Moreira et al., *Canjiquinha*, 59. Several capoeira players who had not been Pastinha's disciples, including Canjiquinha and Cobrinha Verde (Rafael Alves França),

taught at the Capoeira Angola Sports Center in the 1950s. See Santos, *Capoeira e man-dingas*.

59. Moreira et al., *Canjiquinha*, 63.

60. Vianna staged folkloric shows performed at various professional conferences held in Bahia. Queiroz, *Turismo na Bahia*, 62.

61. Aberrê's participation in the 1936 pugilistic season is discussed in chapter 2. Pastinha states that Aberrê died in September 1942, shortly after the formation of the Capoeira Angola Sports Center in 1941. Pastinha, "Quando as pernas fazem miserêr," 7. Canjiquinha's biographers state that Canjiquinha studied with Aberrê until 1951, but I believe this is a typo and the date should read 1941. Moreira et al., *Canjiquinha*, 59.

62. Mercia Queiroz and Ricardo Ottoni, "Capoeira em cena" (Salvador: Instituto de Radio Difusão Educativa da Bahia, 1982).

63. Antonio Cardoso Andrade, audio-recorded interview, December 28, 2013.

64. Canjiquinha, quoted in Moreira et al., *Canjiquinha*, 40.

65. "It is played [*se toca*] differently, it is played [*se joga*] differently. It occurred to me like this: I arrived at the candomblé and I heard they playing: it's muzenza, it's muzenza. I played it on the berimbau. Then I said: how am I going to play [*jogar*] this? Then I would practice in front of the mirror. Then I had [my students] practice the movement. I saw that it worked." Canjiquinha, quoted in ibid.

66. José Serafim Ferreira Júnior, audio-recorded interview by author, July 20, 2015. Mestre Geni's nickname, as given by Canjiquinha in jest, was initially Madame Geni (Madam Geni), in reference to a popular soap opera. He is listed in early programs of folkloric shows as Madame Geni.

67. Rego, *Capoeira Angola*, 64.

68. *Festa de arromba* is an expression from the 1960s and 1970s, still in limited use today in Brazil, that can be loosely translated as "a blowout party." Canjiquinha's use of the phrase is probably related to a popular song titled "Festa de Arromba," recorded by rock/pop singer Erasmo Carlos in 1964.

69. Canjiquinha, quoted in Moreira et al., *Canjiquinha*, 41.

70. Jorge Amado, in his 1960 edition of *Bahia de todos os santos*, mentions that Pastinha would dance the "samba de Angola" in his demonstrations for tourists. Amado, *Bahia de todos os santos*, 209.

71. Canjiquinha, quoted in Moreira et al., *Canjiquinha*, 40.

72. Antonio Cardoso Andrade, audio-recorded interview, December 28, 2013.

73. Mestre Lua Rasta's nickname, as given by Canjiquinha, was Olhando P'ra Lua (Looking at the Moon). Gilson Fernandes, audio-recorded interview, July 13, 2015.

74. José Serafim Ferreira Júnior quoted in Castro, "Campos de visibilidade da capoeira baiana," 113.

75. Gilson Fernandes, audio-recorded interview, July 13, 2015.

76. Gilson Fernandes, quoted in Castro, "Campos de visibilidade da capoeira baiana," 114.

77. Video-recorded interview with Canjiquinha by Raimundo César Alves de Almeida and Luis Renato Vieira, c. 1988, unpublished. It is unclear whether he was "the first to put all this on the market"; Emília Biancardi's folkloric ensemble (at the time called

Conjunto Folclórico da Secretaria de Educação) performed maculelê shows at the municipal stage at the Belvedere da Sé from 1964 to 1967, and Bimba and Pastinha had been including samba in their capoeira demonstrations at least since the early 1960s.

78. *Tribuna da Bahia*, March 3, 1972. In the 1970s, the ensemble included *danças africanas* (African dances) in its already varied repertory—a choice that foregrounded the Africanity of Bahian culture and established a link to an imagined ancestral Africa.

79. I consulted entertainment listings from several Bahian newspapers at the Biblioteca Pública dos Barris, Salvador, BA (*Tribuna da Bahia, A Tarde, Jornal da Bahia, Diário de Notícias*, among others).

80. Antonio Cardoso Andrade, audio-recorded interview by author, December 28, 2013.

81. In fact it was Carmen Miranda, the embodiment of Brazilian excess in Hollywood films at this time, who provided the inspiration for the nickname "Canjiquinha," given to Washington Bruno da Silva because of his habit of singing one of Miranda's popular songs, "Canjiquinha quente" (1937). Rego, *Capoeira Angola*, 275.

82. Ibid., 275–76.

83. Ibid., 362.

84. Canjiquinha's shows often included a brief lecture about capoeira, delivered either by Rego or by two other capoeira experts, Salvador D'Avila and Dr. Protázio. José Serafim Ferreira Júnior, audio-recorded interview, July 20, 2015.

85. Rego, *Capoeira Angola*, 362. Italics in original.

86. In the chapter "Comentário às cantigas" (Commentary on songs), Rego lists and annotates in alphabetical order more than one hundred words used in capoeira songs, many of them nonstandard pronunciation of standard Portuguese words, such as "*açúca*" for "*açúcar*," and "*chamá*" for "*chamar*." His explanation of Canjiquinha's pronunciation of the word "*monótono*" should be understood in this context. It does, nevertheless, frame Canjiquinha as an uneducated informant whose speech needs to be translated for the erudite reader. Rego, *Capoeira Angola*, 362.

87. José Serafim Ferreira Júnior, audio-recorded interview, July 20, 2015.

88. Gilson Fernandes, audio-recorded interview, July 13, 2015.

89. Gay men in the audience might have relished a queer reading of the gesture, or alternatively might have felt uncomfortable by the display of homophobia (a same-sex advance being met with anger), even if in jest. During my research in Bahia in the summer of 2016, a source who wished to remain anonymous confirmed the well-known rumor that Rego was gay. This information may be relevant in understanding Rego's disapproval of this scene, namely his objection to the ridicule of same-sex desire and cross-dressing.

90. Canjiquinha, quoted in Moreira et al., *Canjiquinha*, 71.

91. Ibid., 72.

92. Eufrázia Cristina Menezes Santos, "Performances culturais nas festas de largo da Bahia," in *30th Annual Encontro da Anpocs, Performance Drama e Sociedade Working Group* (Caxambu, 2006), 6.

93. Video-recorded interview with Canjiquinha by Raimundo César Alves de Almeida and Luis Renato Vieira, c. 1988, unpublished.

94. Written and directed by Glauber Rocha and produced by Rex Schindler.

95. Written by Anselmo Duarte and Dias Gomes and directed by Anselmo Duarte.

96. Although Canjiquinha received credit for "original music" in *The Turning Wind*, his performance in the film goes uncredited; for his role in *The Given Word*, Canjiquinha is credited as "capoeira fighter."

97. Igreja do Santíssimo Sacramento da Rua do Passo. In the film, the church is referred to as Igreja de Santa Bárbara.

4. BRAZIL'S FOLKLORE FOR THE GLOBAL STAGE

1. Shortly after the publication of Rego's *Capoeira Angola* in 1968, the SUTURSA acquired a second folkloric stage, the new Centro Folclórico at the Castro Alves Square (the former location of the famous Tabaris nightclub and brothel). According to Mestre Geni, Rego was in charge of the programming of that stage. Magalhães Filho, "Jogo de discursos," 91.

2. The folkloric ensemble Olodum discussed here bears no relation to the samba-reggae musical group Olodum created in the late 1970s.

3. The Grupo Folclórico da Bahia was founded by Acordeon (Ubirajara Guimarães Almeida), Itapoan (Raimundo César Alves de Almeida), Camisa Roxa (Edvaldo Carneiro e Silva), and Beijoca (Francisco Benjamin Muniz).

4. Rego, *Capoeira Angola*, 290. Emphasis in original. Rego dwells at length on what he considered an ill-advised attempt by this group to stage the history of capoeira (see chapter 3). Ibid., 322–23.

5. Mãe Zefa had been a live-in nanny with Acordeon's family for two generations. Almeida, *Capoeira*, 46, 133. The presence of a centenary performer made headlines in the publicity of the shows she participated in; however, her age may have been "rounded up" in order to heighten her appeal as a bearer of ancient African traditions.

6. "Mãe Zefa é a força do grupo," *Jornal J.C.*, July 19, 1970.

7. Almeida, *Capoeira*, 46.

8. Ibid. In 1970 Acordeon directed an experimental show titled *Camarax—um folclore pra frentex* at the Teatro Castro Alves, which included a slideshow featuring images of bombs exploding, a real motorcycle onstage, and a duet titled "Capoeira do amor" (Capoeira of love), danced to the sound of a saxophone and a berimbau. Acordeon envisioned this show as a type of social critique intended to break molds. Ubirajara Guimarães Almeida, audio-recorded interview, August 4, 2013.

9. Jurandir Ferreira, "Olodum sai de cartaz," *Diário de Notícias*, July 17, 1970.

10. Brasil Tropical hired choreographer Domingos Campos, who had been a student of Mercedes Baptista. According to the program for their 1979 show at the Teatro Castro Alves, capoeira was presented in two different ways in the program: a pas de deux titled "Capoeira do amor" (Capoeira of love), and the "traditional" capoeira scene, which was influenced by Canjiquinha's *festa de arromba*, his choreographed brawl discussed in chapter 3. Edvaldo Carneiro e Silva and Domingos Campos, "Brasil Tropical," playbill (Teatro Castro Alves, Salvador, 1979).

11. Carlos Vasconcelos Maia Filho and Cláudio Miranda Maia are sons of the renowned Bahian writer Carlos Vasconcelos Maia. A newspaper article written by their

father details the Maia brothers' involvement with Grupo Oxum: having performed briefly in the late 1960s with the folk ensemble Afonjá, directed by Vermelho (Maurício Lemos de Carvalho), as well as with the ensemble Olodum, the brothers cofounded the group with Geni and Aristides Pupo Mercês (known today as Mestre Aristides), both of whom had studied and performed with Canjiquinha. Carlos Vasconcelos Maia, "Grupo Oxum: 10 anos de folclore na Bahia," A Tarde, July 9, 1978, 3. According to Geni, the group was founded by himself and Carlito Maia. José Serafim Ferreira Júnior, audio-recorded interview, July 20, 2015.

12. "Órgãos de turismo devem promover Feira de Artes," Diário de Notícias, July 22, 1971, 5.

13. Biancardi, personal communication. Her father was a mulatto lawyer from Vitória da Conquista, and her mother was the daughter of Italian immigrants. Despite the fact that Biancardi's father was Afro-Brazilian, she is light skinned and is considered "white" in Bahia. Although her second surname, Ferreira, is her father's family name, she chose the more unique Italian last name from her mother's side as her professional and stage surname.

14. Canto Orfeônico, a form of choral singing based on patriotic themes, instilled discipline and collectivity in schoolchildren. See Goldenberg, "Educação musical"; and Flávio Oliveira, "Orpheonic Chant and the Construction of Childhood in Brazilian Elementary Education," in Brazilian Popular Music and Citizenship, ed. Idelber Avelar and Christopher Dunn (Durham: Duke University Press, 2011).

15. Emília Biancardi, Raízes musicais da Bahia (Salvador: Secretaria de Cultura e Turismo da Bahia, 2006), 14.

16. Although Biancardi's students were not wealthy, the fact that they were finishing their secondary education indicates a middle-class socioeconomic status.

17. Mestre Renê, quoted in Magalhães Filho, "Jogo de discursos," 87.

18. Hildegardes Vianna, open letter in support of Viva Bahia (Emília Biancardi, private archive, Salvador, 1969).

19. Emília Biancardi Ferreira, audio-recorded interview, May 9, 2011.

20. Text by Renato Almeida, then-president of the Campaign for the Defense of Brazilian Folklore, printed in the program for the show Viva Bahia 10 anos (1973) sponsored by Bahia's culture department. Original text in English; italics mine.

21. In addition to statements by Almeida and Vianna, the program includes statements of support by heavyweights such as Édison Carneiro and Jorge Amado.

22. Carneiro, Dinâmica do folclore, 16.

23. Maculelê, a dance largely "restored" by one person from an allegedly dead African tradition from the interior of Bahia, lent itself perfectly for stage adaptations and performances by "non-bearers." Mestre Popó (Paulinho de Almeida Andrade) is believed to have singlehandedly given maculelê a second life by passing it on to his sons and later teaching it to performers of several folkloric ensembles in the capital, including Viva Bahia and Canjiquinha's Conjunto Aberrê. Mestre Popó's account of the "restoration" of maculelê is quoted in the program for Aluandê: "My mother told me that maculelê came from Africa. As a boy I danced maculelê with João Obá and Barão here in Santo Amaro, [but] after these old black slaves died I held on [to it], [and] only

after [my] boys [were old enough] I asked if they wanted to know this game from the past." Emília Biancardi, "Aluandê: alma e coração da Bahia," playbill (Teatro Municipal do Rio de Janeiro, 1970).

24. For a discussion of the complex understandings of whiteness in Brazil, see Patricia de Santana Pinho, "White but Not Quite: Tones and Overtones of Whiteness in Brazil," SX 29 (2009).

25. Biancardi, "Aluandê."

26. Emília Biancardi Ferreira, audio-recorded interview, May 9, 2011.

27. Ibid.

28. Biancardi, "Aluandê."

29. Moraes found in the partnership with Viva Bahia a way of accessing a wide array of Afro-Brazilian folk traditions as sources for his choreography, which he would go on to develop as director of the Ballet Brasileiro da Bahia. In the early 1970s, Moraes was invited to teach at the Ballet School of the Teatro Castro Alves (EBATECA) in Salvador and began directing and creating choreography for the folk-inspired ballet company Ballet Brasileiro da Bahia, where Afro-Bahian themes were danced using ballet technique, including pointe work. In 2011, I visited him in Salvador and listened as he reminisced about his long career; he died in 2015 at age seventy-nine.

30. Emília Biancardi, "Odoiá Bahia: espetáculo folk-pop," playbill (Teatro Castro Alves, Salvador, 1972).

31. "Ballet Folclórico Viva Bahia," Tribuna da Bahia, July 13, 1972.

32. "Um folclore moderno que não deturpa o tradicional," Tribuna da Bahia, July 12, 1972.

33. In retrospect, Biancardi discusses the impacts of staging maculelê for Viva Bahia. Writing in 1989, she notes, "In the past few years, [we can see] the introduction [into maculelê] of moves from capoeira, hip movements from samba, steps from frevo, and especially [from] dances of candomblé, as well as some acrobatics and spontaneous steps, created by the dancers." Biancardi quotes from Vianna, who states that "maculelê grew and was transformed.... It moved to a new land, new conditions, unable to continue with the same characteristics of yore. . . . It is now a dance for shows." Emília Biancardi, Olelê maculelê (Brasília: Edição Especial, 1989), 22.

34. Several dancers in this cast were trained in ballet, and some were brought in from the Katherine Dunham-influenced Balé Mercedes Baptista, based in Rio de Janeiro, to perform in Odoiá Bahia. Some of the male dancers were also Moraes's ballet students at the Ballet School of the Teatro Castro Alves (EBATECA).

35. "Sputnick" was the stage name for Marcos Aurélio Fernandes (after the Soviet satellite Sputnik), who went on to study ballet with Moraes and dance with the Ballet Brasileiro da Bahia.

36. "Bebé" was the stage name for Neusa Saad, one of Biancardi's former students, who teaches Afro-Brazilian folk dances at the Federal University of Bahia.

37. This description is based on information obtained during interviews with Saad and Biancardi. No visual documentation is available for this duet, although I was able to refer to photos of a later restaging of the duet for performances abroad.

38. Emília Biancardi Ferreira, audio-recorded interview, May 9, 2011.

39. Several of the dancers in *Odoiá Bahia* went on to perform in Moraes's Ballet Brasileiro da Bahia in addition to their work with Viva Bahia. Afro-diasporic bodies onstage dancing ballet, a dance technique known to require specialized, rigorous training, disrupted associations between these racially marked bodies and "natural," "spontaneous" movement.

40. Emília Biancardi Ferreira, audio-recorded interview, May 9, 2011.

41. "Viva Bahia: 10 anos de folclore sem auxílio," *Jornal da Bahia*, August 19 and 20, 1973.

42. Ibid.

43. According to a framed tour schedule, displayed proudly on one of the walls of the Capoeira Angola Center of Mestre João Grande in Manhattan, *Capoeiras da Bahia* performed in Spain, France, Italy, England, Switzerland, Belgium, Yugoslavia, Turkey, Greece, Germany, and Iran.

44. In the program for the Canadian performances of *Festa Brazil*, Biancardi's role is reduced to "director of the Viva Bahia ensemble"; for the performances at Royce Hall at the University of California, Los Angeles, she is listed as "Directress and Folklorical Researcher for the Viva Bahia Folk Ensemble"; in the French-language program for *Capoeiras da Bahia*, she is credited with having "trained" the company: "*La compagnie a été entraînée par Émilia [sic] Biancardi Ferreira.*"

45. Anna Kisselgoff, "The Dance: Festa Brazil," *New York Times*, April 10, 1974, 34.

46. Hermínio Bello de Carvalho and Walter Santos Productions, "Festa Brazil," playbill (New Madison Square Garden Attractions, Inc., New York, 1974).

47. Anna Kisselgoff, "The Dance: Festa Brazil," *New York Times*, April 10, 1974, 34.

48. Ibid.

49. Christopher Dafoe, "Vigor You Expect and Vigor You Get," *Vancouver Sun*, May 16, 1974, 41.

50. Ibid.

51. Ibid.

52. Ibid.

53. Ibid.

54. Ibid.

55. Jane King, "A Unique Tradition Survives," *Morning Star*, August 30, 1974, 4.

56. Philip Oakes, "Doing a Voodoo," *Sunday Times*, July 28, 1974, 32. Photo credit: Bryan Wharton.

57. Interview by Jan Murray for *Time Out London*, August 1974, quoted in Rofran Fernandes, *Ruth Escobar: 20 anos de resistência* (São Paulo: Global Editora, 1985), 177.

58. Ibid.

59. Philip Oakes, "Doing a Voodoo," *Sunday Times*, July 28, 1974, 32.

60. The use of the word "voodoo" in this article is likely Oakes's rather than Grillo's.

61. Philip Oakes, "Doing a Voodoo," *Sunday Times*, July 28, 1974, 32.

62. Henri Terrière, "Sensationnel depart de Festival hier soir à la maison de la Culture," *Ouest-France*, May 21, 1974.

63. "Audience participation is decidedly encouraged, providing a rare opportunity to dance with some of the most attractive and outgoing performers on any stage

anywhere." Jane Murray for *Time Out London*, August 1974, quoted in Fernandes, *Ruth Escobar*, 177.

64. "It's a fantastic show ... this troupe is absolutely stunning physically speaking. It's an extraordinarily savage and spontaneous expression, but perfectly controlled afterwards. One could say it's truly [a work of] art." Interview with Danielle Delorme, *Ouest-France*, May 21, 1974. Quoted in Fernandes, *Ruth Escobar*.

65. Philip Oakes, "Doing a Voodoo," *Sunday Times*, July 28, 1974, 32.

66. Jane King, "A Unique Tradition Survives," *Morning Star*, August 30, 1974, 4.

67. Ibid.

68. In a capoeira retreat I attended in 2010 (Dancebatukeira), where both João Grande and Biancardi were honored guests, João Grande reenacted this opening dance and taught it to one of his students from New York. My description is based on having observed this brief revival, as well as on conversations about this scene with both João Grande and Biancardi.

69. Emília Biancardi Ferreira, audio-recorded interview, May 9, 2011.

70. "*[Capoeira] em show de palco, já sabe, é vup vup vup.*" "*Vup vup vup*" refers to the sound of the capoeiristas' bodies slashing the air with flips and kicks, like the English "whoosh" or "swoosh." João Oliveira dos Santos (João Grande), audio-recorded interview, November 14, 2011.

71. Christopher Dafoe, "Vigor You Expect and Vigor You Get," *Vancouver Sun*, May 16, 1974, 41.

72. Mestre Pelé da Bomba (Natalício Neves da Silva, b. 1934), who performed with Viva Bahia in the 1960s but did not tour abroad with the ensemble, remembers that the capoeira scene included flying scissor kicks (*tesoura voadora*) and backflips (*salto mortal*). He adds that he created his own choreography and so did all the capoeiristas in the group. Natalício Neves da Silva, audio-recorded interview, June 5, 2011.

73. Emília Biancardi Ferreira, audio-recorded interview, May 9, 2011.

74. Mestre Geni, quoted in Magalhães Filho, "Jogo de discursos," 85.

75. Lôbo is an emeritus professor in the dance department at the State University of Campinas (Unicamp), in Brazil. Eusébio Lôbo da Silva, *O corpo na capoeira* (Campinas: Editora da Unicamp, 2008), 25.

76. Frede Abreu, Josias Pires Neto, and Hans Herold, *A arte da capoeira* (Salvador: Instituto de Radio Difusão Educativa da Bahia, 2010,) documentary film.

77. João Grande laughed at the irony in this statement, since teaching has been his main relationship to capoeira for the past thirty years. João Oliveira dos Santos (João Grande), audio-recorded interview, November 14, 2011.

78. Biancardi spent a decade in the United States teaching Brazilian music and leading an all-women musical ensemble called Iabás, in collaboration with Geralyn Burke. She has returned to Brazil and now lives in Salvador.

CONCLUSION

1. In 2011 I attended a Balé Folclórico da Bahia performance in Los Angeles, which included several "numbers" that entered the Brazilian folkloric repertory in the 1960s — dances from candomblé, puxada de rede (fisherman's net dance), the ca-

poeira do amor (capoeira of love) duet, and a version of Canjiquinha's capoeira brawl. The show also included bare breasts decorated by white body paint, a costume choice used in several of Viva Bahia's shows. For an analysis of the Balé Folclórico da Bahia, see Meredith A. Ahlberg, "Dancing Africa in Bahia: Dance, Embodied Authenticity and the Consumption of 'Africa' in Bahia, Brazil" (master's thesis, University of California, San Diego, 2011).

2. In the summers of 2007, 2008, and 2010, I attended Dancebatukeira, held at the Fazenda Cultural Ouro Verde, directed by Mestres Cabello and Tisza. I also attended three different encontros organized by Mestre Jogo de Dentro (Jorge Egídio dos Santos), in 2006, 2007, and 2008, held both in Salvador and in the area known as the Vale do Capão, an ecotourism destination in inland Bahia sought for its hiking paths and waterfalls. Today Mestre Jogo de Dentro also directs a cultural center, Espaço Cultural Casa Grande da Ilha, in the area known as Cacha Pregos on the island of Itaparica, accessible by ferry or motorboat from Salvador.

3. Mestres from other capoeira groups are invited as guest instructors for each of these encontros, and such participation increases the international visibility of these mestres and facilitates invitations for teaching workshops overseas. Interestingly, Capoeirando invites mestres of capoeira angola as guest teachers, but the other encontros, which focus on capoeira angola, do not typically invite mestres of capoeira regional.

4. Capoeirando also includes workshops and performances of puxada de rede, dança guerreira (warrior dance), and dança do fogo (fire dance). In an interview, Suassuna stated that he created the warrior dance (with the assistance of a choreographer) to add diversity (diversidade) to the capoeira shows he directed in the 1970s in São Paulo, a justification similar to Canjiquinha's for adding variety to his own shows. He explained that a "warrior" dance was the perfect theme to get his students, primarily men, to agree to dancing onstage, an activity seen as the domain of women. Reinaldo Ramos Suassuna, audio-recorded interview by author, August 17, 2011. Although Suassuna lived in Itabuna, in southern Bahia, he reported going to Salvador often in the 1960s to learn from various capoeira mestres, including Canjiquinha, and to watch folkloric shows. His warrior dance shares several of the primitivist elements of these shows' African-themed dances, such as its costumes and props (leopard-print loin cloths and shields and spears), which hark back to a Hollywood-inspired view of a primitive Africa populated by seminaked, spear-brandishing warriors. At Capoeirando, the fire dance, similar to fire dances performed in Polynesian-themed tourist shows, is often performed in conjunction with maculelê, itself a "warrior-like" dance performed with clubs, which are sometimes replaced by machetes.

5. Carneiro, Negros bantus, 159–60.

BIBLIOGRAPHY

Abib, Pedro. *Capoeira Angola: cultura popular e o jogo dos saberes na roda*. Salvador: Editora da Universidade Federal da Bahia. 2004.

Abreu, Frede, Josias Pires Neto, and Hans Herold. *A arte da capoeira*. Salvador: Instituto de Radio Difusão Educativa da Bahia, 2010.

Abreu, Frederico José de. *Bimba é bamba: a capoeira no ringue*. Cidade da Bahia: Insituto Jair Moura, 1999.

Abreu, Frederico José de, and Maurício Barros Castro. *Capoeira*. Rio de Janeiro: Beco do Azougue Editorial, 2009.

Abreu, Plácido de. *Os capoeiras*. Rio de Janeiro: Typ. da Escola de Serafim José Alves, 1886.

Ahlberg, Meredith A. "Dancing Africa in Bahia: Dance, Embodied Authenticity and the Consumption of 'Africa' in Bahia, Brazil." Master's thesis, University of California, San Diego, 2011.

Albright, Ann Cooper. *Choreographing Difference: The Body and Identity in Contemporary Dance*. Middletown: Wesleyan University Press, 1997.

———. "Tracing the Past: Writing History through the Body." In *The Routledge Dance Studies Reader*, 2nd ed., ed. Alexandra Carter and Janet O'Shea. London: Routledge, 2010.

Almeida, Raimundo César Alves de. *A saga do Mestre Bimba*. Salvador: Ginga Associação de Capoeira, 1994.

———. *Bimba, perfil do mestre*. Salvador: Gráfica Universitária, 1982.

———. *Capoeira: retalhos da roda*. Salvador: Ginga Associação de Capoeira, 2005.

———. *Negaça: Boletim da Ginga Associação de Capoeira*, 1994, 3–6.

Almeida, Renato. *Folclore*. Rio de Janeiro: Ministério da Educação e Cultura, Departamento de Assuntos Culturais, Programa de Ação Cultural, 1976.

———. *Inteligência do folclore*. Rio de Janeiro: Livros de Portugal, 1957.

———. *Vivência e projeção do folclore*. Rio de Janeiro: Livraria AGIR Editôra, 1971.

Almeida, Silvia Capanema P. "A modernização do material e do pessoal da marinha nas vésperas da revolta dos marujos de 1910: modelos e contradições." *Estudos Históricos* 23, no. 45 (2010): 147–69.

Almeida, Ubirajara Guimarães. *Água de beber, camará: um bate-papo de capoeira*. Berkeley: United Capoeira Association, 1999.

──────. *Capoeira: A Brazilian Art Form*. Berkeley: North Atlantic Books, 1986.

Amado, Jorge. *Bahia de todos os santos: guia das ruas e dos mistérios da cidade do Salvador*. São Paulo: Livraria Martins Editôra, 1945.

──────. *Bahia de todos os santos: guia das ruas e dos mistérios da cidade do Salvador*, 10th ed. São Paulo: Livraria Martins Editôra, 1964.

Ames, David W. "Book Review of *African Art in Motion*." *Ethnomusicology* 243 (1980): 561–63.

Apter, Andrew. "Herskovits's Heritage: Rethinking Syncretism in the African Diaspora." *Diaspora: A Journal of Transnational Studies* 1, no. 3 (1991): 235–260.

Araújo, Alceu Maynard. *Folclore nacional*. 3 vols. Serie Cultura e Ciência. São Paulo: Edições Melhoramentos, 1964.

──────. *Veja o Brasil*. DVD. Distributor unknown, c. 1950. Author's private collection, copy obtained from the Instituto Jair Moura, Salvador.

Araújo, Rosângela Costa. "Iê viva meu mestre: a capoeira angola da 'escola pastiniana' como praxis educativa." PhD dissertation, Universidade de São Paulo, 2004.

Assunção, Matthias Röhrig. "Angola in Brazil: The Formation of Angoleiro Identity in Bahia." In *African Heritage and Memories of Slavery in Brazil and the South Atlantic World*, ed. Ana Lúcia Araújo. Amherst: Cambria Press, 2015.

──────. *Capoeira: The History of an Afro-Brazilian Martial Art*. London: Routledge, 2005.

Barreto, José de Jesus, and Otto Freitas. *Pastinha: o grande mestre da Capoeira Angola*. Coleção Gente da Bahia. Salvador: Assembléia Legislativa do Estado da Bahia, 2009.

Bastide, Roger. *The African Religions of Brazil: Toward a Sociology of the Interpenetration of Civilizations*. Johns Hopkins Studies in Atlantic History and Culture. Baltimore: Johns Hopkins University Press, 1978.

Biancardi, Emília. "Aluandê: alma e coração da Bahia." Playbill. Teatro Municipal do Rio de Janeiro, 1970.

──────. "Odoiá Bahia: espetáculo folk-pop." Playbill. Teatro Castro Alves, Salvador, 1972.

──────. *Olelê maculelê*. Brasília: Edição Especial, 1989.

──────. *Raízes musicais da Bahia*. Salvador: Secretaria de Cultura e Turismo da Bahia, 2006.

Bimba, Mestre. *Curso de Capoeira Regional*. Sound disc, analog, 33 ⅓ rpm, 12 in., plus booklet . Salvador: JS Discos, c. 1963.

Bogéa, Inês, and Moira Toledo. *Figuras da dança: Carlos Moraes*. São Paulo: São Paulo Companhia de Dança, 2010.

Browning, Barbara. *Samba: Resistance in Motion*. Bloomington: Indiana University Press, 1995.

Burlamaqui, Anníbal. *Gymnastica nacional (capoeiragem) methodisada e regrada*. Rio de Janeiro: n.p., 1928.

"Campanha de Defesa do Folclore Brasileiro." *Revista Brasileira de Folclore*, May–August 1963.

Campos, Hélio. *Capoeira Regional: a escola de Mestre Bimba*. Salvador: Editora da Universidade Federal da Bahia, 2009.

Capoeira, Nestor. *Capoeira: pequeno manual do jogador*. Rio de Janeiro: Editora Record, 1986 [1981].

———. *Capoeira: Roots of the Dance-Fight-Game*. Berkeley: North Atlantic Books, 2002.

———. *The Little Capoeira Book*. Berkeley: Blue Snake Books, 2003.

Carneiro, Édison. *Capoeira*. Cadernos de folclore. Rio de Janeiro: Campanha de Defesa do Folclore Brasileiro, 1975.

———. *Dinâmica do folclore*. Salvador: Editora Civilização Brasileira, 1965.

———. *Folguedos tradicionais*. Salvador: Conquista, 1974.

———. *Negros bantus: notas de ethnographia religiosa e folk-lore*. Rio de Janeiro: Civilização Brasileira, s.a., 1937.

Carrier, Henri, et al. "La Capoera." In *Les coulisses de l'exploit*. Paris: Institut National de l'Audiovisuel, 1963. www.ina.fr/video/CPF04007124.

Cartusc, A. Gomes. "Cultivemos o jogo de capoeira e tenhamos asco pelo da boxa." *O Paiz*, October 22, 1923.

Carvalho, Hermínio Bello de, and Walter Santos Productions. "Festa Brazil." Playbill. New Madison Square Garden Attractions, Inc., New York, 1974.

Carybé. *O jogo da capoeira*. Coleção Recôncavo n. 3. Salvador: Livraria Turista, 1951.

Castro Jr., Luis Vitor. "Campos de visibilidade da capoeira baiana: as festas populares, as escolas de capoeira, o cinema e a arte (1955–1985)." PhD dissertation, Pontifícia Universidade Católica de São Paulo, 2008.

Certeau, Michel de. *The Practice of Everyday Life*. Berkeley: University of California Press, 1984.

Coelho Netto, Henrique. "Nosso jogo." In *Bazar*. Rio de Janeiro: Livraria Chardron, de Lello e Irmão, Ltda Editores, 1928.

Coelho Netto, Paulo. *Coelho Netto e os esportes. Conferência realizada no salão nobre da Escola Nacional de Belas Artes a 25 de fevereiro de 1964*. Rio de Janeiro: Editôra Minerva, 1964.

Coutinho, Daniel. *O ABC da capoeira de Angola: os manuscritos do Mestre Noronha*. Brasília: CIDOCA, 1993.

Custis, Ebony Rose. "Cultural Capital, Critical Theory, and Motivation for Participation in Capoeira Angola." Master's thesis, Howard University, 2008.

da Costa, Lamartine Pereira. *Capoeira sem mestre*. Rio de Janeiro: Edições de Ouro, 1962.

———. *Capoeiragem: a arte da defesa pessoal brasileira*. Self-published, Rio de Janeiro, 1961.

Daibert, Robert. *Isabel, a "redentora" dos escravos: uma história da princesa entre olhares negros e brancos*. Bauru: Editora da Universidade do Sagrado Coração, 2001.

Debret, Jean Baptiste. *Voyage pittoresque et historique au Brésil ou séjour d'un artiste français au Brésil, depuis 1816 jusqu'en 1831 inclusivement, époques de l'avenement et de l'abdication de S.M. Don Pedro, premier fondateur de l'empire brésilien*. Paris: Didot Frère, 1834–39.

Decânio, Angelo. *A herança de Mestre Bimba: filosofia e lógica africanas da capoeira*, 2nd ed. Coleção São Salomão. Self-published, Salvador, 1997.

———. *A herança de Pastinha*. Coleção São Salomão. Self-published, Salvador, 1997.

DeFrantz, Thomas. "The Black Beat Made Visible: Hip Hop Dance and Body Power." In *Of the Presence of the Body: Essays on Dance and Performance Theory*, ed. André Lepecki. Middletown: Wesleyan University Press, 2004.

Desch-Obi, M. Thomas J. *Fighting for Honor: The History of African Martial Art Traditions in the Atlantic World*. Columbia: University of South Carolina Press, 2008.

Desmond, Jane. *Staging Tourism: Bodies on Display from Waikiki to Sea World*. Chicago: University of Chicago Press, 1999.

Dias, Adriana Albert. *Mandinga, manha e malícia: uma história sobre os capoeiras na capital da Bahia (1910–1925)*. Salvador: Editora da Universidade Federal da Bahia, 2006.

Dossar, Kenneth. "Dancing between Two Worlds: An Aesthetic Analysis of Capoeira Angola." PhD dissertation, Temple University, 1994.

Downey, Greg. "Domesticating an Urban Menace: Reforming Capoeira Angola as a Brazilian National Sport." *International Journal of the History of Sport* 19, no. 4 (2002): 1–32.

———. "Incorporating Capoeira: Phenomenology of a Movement Discipline." PhD dissertation, University of Chicago, 1998.

———. *Learning Capoeira: Lessons in Cunning from an Afro-Brazilian Art*. Oxford: Oxford University Press, 2005.

Du Bois, W. E. B. *The Souls of Black Folk*. 1st Vintage Books/Library of America ed. New York: Vintage Books/Library of America, 1990.

Escobar, Ruth, and Ninon Tallon Karlweis. "Les Capoeiras de Bahia." Playbill. Les Publications Willy Fischer, Le Théatre de la Porte Saint-Martin, Paris, 1974.

Esteves, Acúrsio Pereira. *A "capoeira" da indústria do entretenimento: corpo, acrobacia e espetáculo para "turista ver."* Salvador: Bureau Gráfica e Editora, 2004.

Fernandes, Rofran. *Ruth Escobar: 20 anos de resistência*. São Paulo: Global Editora, 1985.

Foster, Susan Leigh. *Choreographing Empathy: Kinesthesia in Performance*. London: Routledge, 2011.

———. "Choreographing History." In *Choreographing History*, ed. Susan Leigh Foster. Bloomington: Indiana University Press, 1995.

Freyre, Gilberto. *Manisfeto Regionalista de 1926*. Os Cadernos de Cultura. Rio de Janeiro: Departamento de Imprensa Nacional, 1955.

Frigerio, Alejandro. "Capoeira: de arte negra a esporte branco." *Revista Brasileira de Ciências Sociais* 4, no. 10 (1989).

Goldenberg, Ricardo. "Educação musical: a experiência do canto orfeônico no Brasil." *Pro-posições* 6, no. 3[18] (1995): 103–9.

Gottschild, Brenda Dixon. *Digging the Africanist Presence in American Performance: Dance and Other Contexts*. Westport: Greenwood Press, 1996.

Guerreiro, Goli. "A cidade imaginada: Salvador sob o olhar do turismo." *Revista Gestão e Planejamento* 6, no. 11 (2005): 6–22.

Head, Scott Correll. "Danced Fight, Divided City: Figuring the Space Between." PhD dissertation, University of Texas, Austin, 2004.

Herskovits, Melville J., and Frances S. Herskovits. *The New World Negro: Selected Papers in Afroamerican Studies*. Bloomington: Indiana University Press, 1966.

Hobsbawm, Eric, and Terence Ranger. "The Invention of Tradition: The Highland Tradition of Scotland." In *The Invention of Tradition*. Cambridge: Cambridge University Press, 1983.

Höfling, Ana Paula. "Capoeiras of Bahia." In *Axé Bahia: The Power of Art in an Afro-*

Brazilian Metropolis, ed. Patrick A. Polk et al. Los Angeles: Fowler Museum at UCLA, 2017.

———."Dancing, Fighting, and Staging Capoeira: Choreographies of Afro-Brazilian Modernity and Tradition." PhD dissertation, University of California, Los Angeles, 2012.

Holloway, Thomas H. "'A Healthy Terror': Police Repression of Capoeiras in Nineteenth-Century Rio de Janeiro." *Hispanic American Historical Review* 69, no. 4 (1989): 637–76.

Keali'inohomoku, Joann Wheeler, and Drid Williams. "Caveat on Causes and Correlations." *CORD News* 6, no. 2 (1975): 20–29.

Kirshenblatt-Gimblett, Barbara. *Destination Culture: Tourism, Museums and Heritage.* Berkeley: University of California Press, 1998.

Kowal, Rebekah J. "Staging the Greensboro Sit-Ins." *TDR: The Drama Review* 48, no. 4 (2004).

Kraut, Anthea, "Recovering Hurston, Reconsidering the Choreographer." In *The Routledge Dance Studies Reader*, 2nd ed., ed. Alexandra Carter and Janet O'Shea. London: Routledge, 2010.

Landes, Ruth. *The City of Women.* New York: Macmillan, 1947.

Lewis, John Lowell. *Ring of Liberation: Deceptive Discourse in Brazilian Capoeira.* Chicago: University of Chicago Press, 1992.

Lopes, André Luiz Lacé. *A capoeiragem no Rio de Janeiro: primeiro ensaio, Sinhozinho e Rudolf Hermanny.* Rio de Janeiro: Editora Europa, 2002.

MacCannell, Dean. *The Tourist: A New Theory of the Leisure Class.* Berkeley: University of California Press, 1976. Reprint, 1999.

Magalhães Filho, Paulo Andrade. "Jogo de discursos: a disputa por hegemonia na tradição da Capoeira Angola bahiana." Master's thesis, Universidade Federal da Bahia, 2011.

Maia, Tatyana de Amaral. "O patrimônio cultural brasileiro em debate: a ação do Conselho Federal de Cultura (1967–1975)." *Revista CPC (Centro de Preservação Cultural USP)* 11 (2011): 60–86.

Matos, Consuelo de Almeida. "A Bahia de Hildegardes Vianna: um estudo sobre a representação de mulheres negras." Master's thesis, Universidade do Estado da Bahia, 2008.

McMains, Juliet. *Spinning Mambo into Salsa: Caribbean Dance in Global Commerce.* New York: Oxford University Press, 2015.

Mello Moraes Filho, Alexandre José de. *Festas e tradições populares do Brasil*, 3rd ed. Rio de Janeiro: F. Briguiet, 1946 [1893].

Merrell, Floyd. *Capoeira and Candomblé: Conformity and Resistance through Afro-Brazilian Experience.* Princeton: Markus Wiener, 2005.

Moreira, Antônio, et al. *Canjiquinha: a alegria da capoeira.* Salvador: Fundação Cultural do Estado da Bahia, c. 1989.

O.D.C. *Guia do capoeira ou gymnastica brazileira*, 2nd ed. Rio de Janeiro: Livraria Nacional, 1907.

Oliveira, Waldir Freitas, and Vivaldo da Costa Lima. *Cartas de Édison Carneiro a Artur*

Ramos: de 4 de janeiro de 1936 a 6 de dezembro de 1938, Baianada. São Paulo: Editora Corrupio, 1987.

Oliveira, Flávio. "Orpheonic Chant and the Construction of Childhood in Brazilian Elementary Education." In Brazilian Popular Music and Citizenship, ed. Idelber Avelar and Christopher Dunn. Durham: Duke University Press, 2011.

Pastinha, Vicente Ferreira. Capoeira Angola, 2nd ed. Salvador: Escola Gráfica N.S. de Loreto, 1968 [1964].

———. "Pensamentos." In Manuscritos do Mestre Pastinha. Unpublished manuscritps written c. 1952–57, Salvador. https://portalcapoeira.com.

———. "Quando as pernas fazem miserêr." In Manuscritos do Mestre Pastinha. Unpublished manuscritps written c. 1952–57, Salvador. https://portalcapoeira .com.

Penna Marinho, Inezil. Subsídios para o estudo da metodologia do treinamento da capoeiragem. Rio de Janeiro: Imprensa Nacional, 1945.

Pinho, Patricia de Santana. "Gilberto Freyre e a baianidade." In Gilberto Freyre e os estudos latino-americanos, ed. Joshua Lund and Malcolm McNee. Série Críticas. Pittsburgh: Instituto Internacional de Literatura Iberoamericana, 2006.

———. "White but Not Quite: Tones and Overtones of Whiteness in Brazil." SX 29 (2009).

Pires, Antônio Liberac Cardoso Simões. Culturas circulares: a formação histórica da capoeira contemporânea no Rio de Janeiro. Curitiba: Editora Progressiva, 2010.

———. "Movimentos da Cultura Afro-Brasileira: A formação histórica da capoeira contemporânea 1890–1950." PhD dissertation, Universidade Estadual de Campinas, 2001.

Price, Richard, and Sally Price. The Roots of Roots: Or, How Afro-American Anthropology Got Its Start. Chicago: Prickly Paradigm Press, 2003.

Queiroz, Lucia Maria Aquino de. "A gestão pública e a competitividade de cidades turísticas: a experiência da cidade do Salvador." PhD dissertation, Universitat de Barcelona, 2005.

———. Turismo na Bahia: estratégias para o desenvolvimento. Salvador: Secretaria da Cultura e Turismo, 2002.

Queiroz, Mercia, and Ricardo Ottoni. "Capoeira em cena." Salvador: Instituto de Radio Difusão Educativa da Bahia, 1982.

Ramos, Arthur. O negro brasileiro: etnographia religiosa, 3rd ed. Bibliotheca Pedagógica Brasileira. São Paulo: Companhia Editora Nacional, 1951 [1934].

Rego, Waldeloir. Capoeira Angola: ensaio sócio-etnográfico. Coleção Baiana. Rio de Janeiro: Gráf. Lux, 1968.

———. Capoeira Angola: ensaio sócio-etnográfico. Coleção Capoeira Viva, 2nd ed. Salvador: Fundação Gregório de Mattos, 2015.

Reis, Letícia Vidor de Sousa. "Negros e brancos no jogo da capoeira: reinvenção da tradição." PhD dissertation, Universidade de São Paulo, 1993.

———. O mundo de pernas para o ar: a capoeira no Brasil, 2nd ed. São Paulo: Publisher Brasil, 2000.

Ribeyrolles, Charles. Brasil pitoresco: história, descrições, viagens, colonização, instituições.

BIBLIOGRAPHY

3 vols. Coleção Reconquista do Brasil. Belo Horizonte and São Paulo: Editora Itatiaia; Editora da Universidade de São Paulo, 1980 [1859].

Romo, Anadelia A. *Brazil's Living Museum: Race, Reform, and Tradition in Bahia.* Chapel Hill: University of North Carolina Press, 2010.

———. "Rethinking Race and Culture in Brazil's First Afro-Brazilian Congress of 1934." *Journal of Latin American Studies* 39 (2007): 31–54.

Rosa, Cristina F. *Brazilian Bodies and Their Choreographies of Identification: Swing Nation.* New York: Palgrave Macmillan, 2015.

———. "Choreographing Identification: The Presence of Ginga in Samba, Capoeira and Grupo Corpo." PhD dissertation, University of California, Los Angeles, 2010.

———. "Playing, Fighting, and Dancing: Unpacking the Significance of *Ginga* within the Practice of Capoeira Angola." *TDR: The Drama Review* 56, no. 3 (T215) (Fall 2012).

———. "Risk Taking Bodies and Their Choreographies of Protest." In *Moving (across) Borders: Performing Translation, Intervention, Participation,* ed. Brandstetter and Hartung. Bielfeld: Transcript Verlag, 2017.

Rugendas, Johann Moritz. *Viagem pitoresca através do Brasil,* 5th ed. Biblioteca Histórica Brasileira. São Paulo: Livraria Martins Editôra, 1954.

Santos, Eufrázia Cristina Menezes. "Performances culturais nas festas de largo da Bahia." In *30th Annual Encontro da Anpocs, Performance Drama e Sociedade Working Group.* Caxambu, 2006.

Santos, Marcelino dos. *Capoeira e mandingas: Cobrinha Verde.* Salvador: Gráfica Santa Bárbara, 1990.

Shea Murphy, Jacqueline. *The People Have Never Stopped Dancing: Native American Modern Dance Histories.* Minneapolis: University of Minnesota Press, 2007.

Silva, Edvaldo Carneiro e, and Domingos Campos. "Brasil Tropical." Playbill. Teatro Castro Alves, Salvador, 1979.

Silva, Eusébio Lôbo da. *O corpo na capoeira.* Campinas: Editora da Unicamp, 2008.

Silva, Paulo Santos. "Estatuto do Centro Esportivo de Capoeira Angola." Salvador: Centro Esportivo de Capoeira Angola, 1952.

Silva Junior, Paulo Melgaço da. *Mercedes Baptista: a criação da identidade negra na dança.* Brasília: Fundação Cultural Palmares, 2007.

Skidmore, Thomas E. *The Politics of Military Rule in Brazil.* Oxford: Oxford University Press, 1988.

Soares, Carlos Eugênio Líbano. *A Capoeira escrava e outras tradições rebeldes no Rio de Janeiro (1801–1850).* Campinas: Editora Unicamp, 2001.

———. *A negregada instituição: os capoeiras no Rio de Janeiro.* Rio de Janeiro: Coleção Biblioteca Carioca, 1994.

Sodré, Muniz. *Mestre Bimba: corpo de mandinga.* Bahia Com H. Rio de Janeiro: Manati, 2002.

Talmon-Chvaicer, Maya. *The Hidden History of Capoeira: A Collision of Cultures in the Brazilian Battle Dance.* Austin: University of Texas Press, 2008.

Thompson, Robert Farris. *African Art in Motion: Icon and Act in the Collection of Katherine Coryton White.* Los Angeles: University of California Press, 1974.

Vassallo, Simone Pondé. "Capoeiras e intelectuais: a construção coletiva da capoeira 'autêntica.'" *Estudos Históricos* 32 (2003): 106–24.

Vianna, Hildegardes. *A Bahia já foi assim.* Coleção Baiana. Salvador: Editora Itapuã, 1973.

———. *Antigamente era assim.* Salvador: Editora Record, 1994.

———. Open letter in support of Viva Bahia. Emília Biancardi, private archive, Salvador, 1969.

Vieira, Jelon. "Dance Brazil." Jaki Levi and Arrow Root Media. www.dancebrazil.org (accessed April 9, 2011).

Vieira, Luiz Renato. "Da vadiação à Capoeira Regional: uma interpretação da modernização cultural no Brasil." PhD dissertation, Universidade de Brasília, 1990.

Vilhena, Luís Rodolfo. *Projeto e missão: o movimento folclórico brasileiro, 1947–1964.* Rio de Janeiro: Fundação Getulio Vargas Editora; Ministério da Cultura, FUNARTE, 1997.

Wesolowski, Katya. "From 'Moral Disease' to 'National Sport': Race, Nation, and Capoeira in Brazil." In *Sports Culture in Latin American History.* Pittsburgh: University of Pittsburgh Press, 2015.

Williams, Daryle. *Culture Wars in Brazil: The First Vargas Regime, 1930–1945.* Durham: Duke University Press, 2001.

INTERVIEWS

Almeida, Raimundo César Alves de. Audio-recorded interview by author. May 10, 2011.

Almeida, Ubirajara Guimarães. Audio-recorded interview by author. August 4, 2013.

Andrade, Antonio Cardoso. Audio-recorded interview by author. December 28, 2013.

Biancardi Ferreira, Emília. Audio-recorded interviews by author. August 15, 2010; May 9, 2011.

Borges, Aricelma. Audio-recorded interview by author. May 18, 2011.

da Costa, Lamartine Pereira. Audio-recorded interview by author. July 28, 2015.

Lopes, André Luis Lacé. Video-recorded interview by author. July 29, 2015.

Fernandes, Gilson. Audio-recorded interview by author. July 13, 2015.

Ferreira Júnior, José Serafim. Audio-recorded interview by author. July 20, 2015.

Moraes, Carlos. Audio-recorded interview by author. May 16, 2011.

Saad, Neusa. Audio-recorded interview by author. May 25, 2011.

Santos, João Oliveira dos. Audio-recorded interview by author. November 14, 2011.

Silva, Natalício Neves da. Audio-recorded interview by author. June 5, 2011.

Silva, Washington Bruno da. Video-recorded interview by Raimundo César Alves de Almeida, c. 1988.

Simões, Guilherme. Audio-recorded interview by author. June 1, 2011.

Suassuna, Reinaldo Ramos. Audio-recorded interview by author. August 17, 2011.

INDEX

Photographs and illustrations in the text are indicated in italics.

Aberrê (Antônio Raymundo Argolo),
50, 66, 106, 115, 184n155, 189n27–30,
200n61
Abreu, Frederico José de, 36, 66
Abreu, Plácido de, 19–20, 29, 43
Academia de Capoeira Angola. See Capoeira Angola Sports Center
Acordeon, Mestre, 107–8, 109, 114, 130
acrobatics, 44–45, 79, 84, 109–14,
157–59, 165
actionable assertions, 10, 171n29
aerial moves. See acrobatics
African Art in Motion (Thompson), 11
African dances, 121, 172–73nn43–46,
201n78
Africanity, 5, 9–12, 34–35, 58, 117
African origins of capoeira, 24–26, 46,
50–51, 68–69, 122, 178n62
Afro-Brazilian culture, 68–71, 161–62,
164–66
Afro-Brazilian folklore, 127, 161
Afro-Brazilian performers, 125, 132,
151–55. See also Conjunto Folclórico
Viva Bahia
Afro-Brazilian tradition, 46, 85–86, 98,
148–49
Afro-diasporic corporeality, 27, 49, 58,
59–60, 129, 146, 162
Alfinete, Gildo, 88
Alice, Mãe, 111–12

Almeida, Raimundo César Alves de. See
Itapoan, Mestre
Almeida, Renato, 73, 139
Almeida, Ubirajara Guimarães. See Acordeon, Mestre
Aluandê (theatrical production), 135,
140–42
Alves, Antônio de Castro, 144
Alves, Clotildes Lopes (Dona Coleta),
136, 136, 140–41
Amado, Jorge, 64, 77–79, 81–82, 95–96,
102–3
Amaral, Braz do, 52
Andrade, Antonio Cardoso. See Brasília,
Mestre
Andrade, Mario de, 71–72
angoleira/o, 169n3, 192n72
animal sacrifices, 148–49, 154–55, 162
appropriation, 5, 24, 34, 38–39, 47,
49–50, 58–60, 75–76, 105–6
Apter, Andrew, 5
Aquino, João de, 150–51
Araújo, Alceu Maynard, 88–92, 194n105
Argolo, Antônio Raymundo. See Aberrê
arpão de cabeça, 43
The art of capoeira (A arte da capoeira),
159
Assunção, Matthias Röhrig, 24–25,
190n50
atos institucionais. See institutional acts

attacks and defenses, 24–32, 39–45, 56–57, 66, 70, 88–90, 187n189. *See also* violence

aú, 10, 43

authenticity, 39, 67–69, 102–3, 129–30, 132, 136–37, 139, 141–43

authorship, 30, 117, 121, 127, 163–64. *See also* innovation

backflips, 157–58

Bahia, 52, 62–63, 68–71, 76–82, 92–96, 100, 103–4, 106–8, 124

Bahia, Henrique, 64–66

Bahia de todos os santos (Amado), 64, 77–79, 81–82, 95–96

Bahian regional fighting style (*luta regional Bahiana*), 65–66, 68, 182n108

balão-de-lado, 43

ballet aesthetic, 144, 145–46, 170n15, 205n39

Ballet Folclórico Viva Bahia, 142–49

balões: Bimba's use of, 47; documentation of, 174n54; movement description, 43–45; Pastinha's use of, 90–93, 98; photo of, 91; in *See Brazil*, 194n110; transformation of, 165; and use of hands, 80

bamboleio, 35

banda, 43

banda forçada, 32

Bantu culture, 61, 69–70, 75, 95, 184n150, 190nn45–47

Barravento (film), 125

Bastide, Roger, 4–5

batuque, 42–43, 47, 183n125

Bazar (Coelho Netto), 29–30

Beijoca (Francisco Benjamin Muniz), 130

Belvedere da Sé, 115–17, 121–22

Bentinho, Mestre, 46

berimbau (musical bow), 82, 87, 95–96, 117–18, 133, 156–57

Biancardi Ferreira, Emilia: *Aluandê*, 140–42; on *balões*, 194n110; *Capoeiras da*

Bahia, 152–61; credits, 205n44; *Festa Brazil*, 149–52; heritage of, 203n13; on maculelê, 204n33; and modernity, 161–62; on *mulatos*, 196n4; *Odoiá Bahia*, 142–49; overview, 132–40

Bimba, Mestre: Africanist innovations of, 24–26; and Capoeira Regional, 36–47, 62–67, 110–14; *Capoeira Regional Course*, 39–47, 181n103, 182n116; Carneiro on, 67–69; criticisms of, 76–78; ensemble of (Grupo Folclórico), 111–14; overview, 36–38, 59; partnered throws, 43, 66, 90–92, 110–14, 157–58; photo of, 109, 113; point system, 180–81n97; and Rego, 102–9; students of, 129, 180n94

Black Guard (Guarda Negra), 20, 175n8

boxing, 28, 33, 63–64

boxing ring (*tablado*), 64

Branco, Castelo, 103

Brasília, Mestre, 117, 119

The Brazilian Negro (Ramos), 69

Browning, Barbara, 10

Burlamaqui, Anníbal (pseud. Zuma): and Bimba, 36–43; biographical information, 176n24, 177nn35–36; criticisms of, 24–26; *National Gymnastics*, 26–35, 41–42; overview, 58–59; and Pastinha, 48–49; photo and illustration of, 37; point system, 180n97

cabeçada, 29, 57, 89

Caiçara, Mestre, 121

Camisa Roxa (Edvaldo Carneiro e Silva), 130

Campaign for the Defense of Brazilian Folklore (Campanha de Defesa do Folclore Brasileiro), 73–74

Campos, Hélio. *See* Xaréu, Mestre

Canapum, Mestre, 138

candomblé, 68, 70, 71, 81, 117–18, 142, 145, 153, 156

Canjiquinha, Mestre, 100, 115–26, 116, 125–26, 153

Capoeira Angola, 48–60, 82–97, 165
capoeira angola: and Canjiquinha, 115–16, 120–21; and *chamada*, 90–92; connection with nature, 166–67; Downey on, 10, 171n31; efficacy of, 41–42; and innovations, 46; and Pastinha, 48–60; popularity of, 184n146; Reis on, 24; retention/loss binary, 9
Capoeira Angola (Pastinha), 48–58, 96, 106
Capoeira Angola: Socio-ethnographic Essay (Rego), 41, 101, 102–9, 121–22
Capoeira Angola Sports Center (CECA), 50–53, 81, 82–83, 88–89, 96
A "capoeira" da indústria do entretenimento ("Capoeira" for the entertainment industry) (Esteves), 110
capoeira de Angola, 45–46, 48–50, 52, 67–76, 81–85, 190n48
"Capoeira de Angola" (Carneiro), 67–68
capoeiragem, 28–30, 39–40, 43, 47, 49, 59, 67
Capoeira Regional, 26, 36–47, 62–67, 76, 77–78, 101, 102–9, 110–14
capoeira regional, 6, 9, 24, 39, 92, 116–17, 120–21, 169n5, 184n146
Capoeira Regional Course (Bimba), 39–47, 44, 181n103, 182n116
Os capoeiras (Abreu), 19–20, 29
Capoeiras da Bahia (theatrical production), 135, 148, 152–61, 156, 160, 162
capoeiristas, 39–40, 53–58, 126–27, 128–29, 150–52, 157–62
La Capoera (Taquet and Ehrler), 92
Carifesta (folk festival), 147
Carneiro, Édison, 45, 48–50, 67–76, 80–83, 94–95, 102, 139–40, 143, 190n51
Cartusc, A. Gomes, 33
Carvalho, Hermínio Bello de, 147–50
Carybé (Hector Julio Páride Bernabó). See Centro de Cultural Fisica Regional
CCFR (Centro de Cultura Fisica Regional), 111

CECA. See Capoeira Angola Sports Center
Centro de Cultura Física Regional (CCFR), 111
Centro Esportivo de Capoeira Angola. See Capoeira Angola Sports Center
chamada, 90–94, 93–94, 187n187, 194nn108–109, 195n115
chapa de costas, 57, 89
chapa de frente, 89
Charley's Aunt (film), 151
choreography: and ballet aesthetic, 170n15; Biancardi's elaborated, 143–44; of Bimba, 101, 111–14; of Canjiquinha, 119; of capoeiristas, 127; elaborated, 143–44, 147–48; in *Festa Brazil*, 149–50; of folklore bearers, 141–42; and innovation, 8, 159; of Moraes, 147–48; of Pastinha, 93; use of term, 6
cintura desprezada, 43, 47, 65–66, 90, 98, 110–13
circular playing field, 25, 28, 29
The City of Women (Landes), 79–80
cocada, 29–30, 178n51
codification, 38–39, 46–47, 59, 95, 111
Coelho Netto, Henrique, 21–22, 29–30, 33, 179n82
Colmenero, J. B., 50
combat, capoeira as, 80
Comissão Nacional de Folclore (National Folklore Commission), 72–74
competitions, 25, 28, 39, 121
Conjunto Aberrê, 120–21
Conjunto Folclórico da Bahia, 136
Conjunto Folclórico Viva Bahia, 128–29, 132–48, 136, 151, 152–53, 160–62
containment, 55
contra-mestre rank, 83, 186n170
counterattacks. See attacks and defenses
Coutinho, Daniel. See Noronha, Mestre
Cunha, J. (José Antônio Cunha), 143–44
Curso de Capoeira Regional (Bimba), 110–11

Dafoe, Christopher, 150–52, 155, 157
Dance Brazil (dance company), 160
deception, 31–32, 40, 47, 54–58
dêdo nos olhos, 45, 91, 98
DeFrantz, Thomas, 6
degeneration, 34–35, 48, 71
demonstration games (escretes), 112–14,
   157–58, 165, 189n28, 199n50
Department of Education (Secretaria de
   Educação), 135–36
descaracterização. See loss of character
Desmond, Jane, 7–8
destination image, 7–8
deturpação. See disfigurement
Diário da Bahia (newspaper), 36, 66
Diario de Noticias (newspaper), 131–32
Dinâmica do folclore (Folklore's dynamics)
   (Carneiro), 73, 139–40
Diretoria Municipal de Turismo (DMT),
   100, 115
disfigurement (deturpação), 77, 144–45
disguise, 4, 55, 58, 95, 98
Dixon Gottschild, Brenda, 11–12
DMT. See Diretoria Municipal de
   Turismo
Dona Coleta (Clotildes Lopes Alves). See
   Alves, Clotildes Lopes
Dorson, Richard, 73
Downey, Greg, 10, 25–26, 28, 31, 171n31

efficacy of capoeira, 41–42, 46
efficiency, 35, 40–42, 45–47, 64–67, 80,
   83–84, 114, 120
Ehrler, Serge, 92
elaborated choreography, 143–44,
   147–48
embodied epistemology, 27, 59
embodied knowledge, 32, 41, 46, 52,
   58, 75, 83
emboscadas, 182–83n121
erudite/folk binary, 71–75, 139–40,
   143–44
Escobar, Ruth, 148, 152
escretes. See demonstration games

espada, 30
esquenta banho, 41, 120, 182n115
O Estado da Bahia (newspaper), 67–68
Esteves, Acúrsio, 110
estilizado/a (stylized), 143–44
eugenics, 21, 34–35, 47, 58–59

Fernandes, Gilson. See Lua Rasta,
   Mestre
Ferraz, Aydano do Couto, 70
Ferreira Júnior, José Serafim. See Geni,
   Mestre
Festa Brazil (theatrical production), 135,
   148, 149–52, 155, 159–61, 162
festa de arromba, 118–20, 129, 200n68
festa de largo, 120
Festas e tradições populares do Brasil (Mello
   Moraes), 29
films of capoeira, 82, 84–85, 88–90, 92,
   121–22, 124–26
floreios, 17, 159, 162, 165
folk/erudite binary, 71–75, 139–40,
   143–44
folklore, 71–76, 92–94, 103, 161–62,
   163–64
folklore bearers (portadores de folclore),
   7–8, 75, 108, 115–17, 122, 128–30,
   136–37, 140–41, 161–62
Folklore's dynamics (Dinâmica do folclore)
   (Carneiro), 73, 139–40
folkloric ensembles, 111, 120–21, 130,
   165–66. See also Conjunto Folclórico
   Viva Bahia
folkloric shows, 8, 102–8, 109–10, 115,
   127, 129, 130–48, 151, 165–67
folkloric sport, capoeira as, 39
folklorization, 25, 114
foreign borrowings, 25–26, 28, 42–47,
   49, 75, 110
formaturas. See graduation ceremonies
Foster, Susan Leigh, 6, 13
Freyre, Gilberto, 69–70, 77, 179–80n86,
   181nn107–108
Frigerio, A., 26, 169n4

galopante, 65

gangs or brotherhoods (*maltas*), 19, 29

gender norms, 118, 123–24

Geni, Mestre, 117–19, 123, 130–32, 134, 159

gente do povo, 108, 136, 161

Gia (Gil dos Prazeres Souza), 112–14, 113

ginga: Bimba's use of, 40–41, 43, 47; as foundational step, 182n111; and musical accompaniment, 95; Pastinha's use of, 35–36, 54–57; and *tapeação*, 31; as traditional movement practice, 165

The Given Word. *See O pagador de promessas* (film)

Goffman, Erving, 7

golpe de pescoço, 45, 98

golpes cinturados, 110

golpes de tapeação, 32

golpes ligados, 110, 157

Goulart, João, 103

Gracie, George, 66, 189n32

graduation ceremonies (*formaturas*), 83, 105–6, 111–13, 197n20, 199n47

Grillo, Gilda, 152–58, 160

Grupo Folclórico da Bahia, later Olodum Conjunto Folclórico, 107–8, 129–30

Grupo Folclórico do Mestre Bimba (Mestre Bimba's Folkloric Ensemble), 105, 111–14

Grupo Folclórico Olodumaré, 131

Grupo Folclórico Oxum, 130–32, 133–34, 158

guarda, 30–31

Guarda Negra (Black Guard). *See* Black Guard (Guarda Negra)

Gymnastica nacional. See National Gymnastics (Burlamaqui)

hands, use of, 79–80, 90, 95, 119, 195n112

Herskovits, Melville, 4–5, 10–11, 80, 172nn34–35

"História da capoeira e samba duro" (Acordeon), 107

"History and Tradition of Bahia" course, 106–7

Hobsbawm, Eric, 3, 169n6

humor used in capoeira, 123–24

Hurston, Zora Neal, 8

improvisation, 40–41, 59–60, 75, 87, 114, 120

innovation: and acrobatics, 158–61; and adaptability, 14–15; of Biancardi, 132, 138–39, 143–44, 152–53; of Bimba, 24–26, 40–47, 76–78; of Canjiquinha, 124–25; of capoeiristas, 127; of folklore bearers, 75–76; of Pastinha, 98; Rego on, 102–5, 108; through choreography, 8; and tradition, 3–4

Inspectorate of Music and Orpheonic Song (Inspetoria de Música e Canto Orfeônic), 135

institutional acts (*atos institucionais*), 103, 196n10

intrastyle games, 66

invented traditions, 3–4, 30, 106, 108, 116, 169n6

inversions, 9–10, 178n62

Itapoan, Mestre, 112–14, 113

João Grande, Mestre, 87, 98, 136–37, 140–41, 156–57, 156, 159–61

Jornal da Bahia (newspaper), 147–48

King, Jane, 156

Kisselgoff, Anna, 149–50

Kontik Tourism and Travel Agency, 112, 198n43

Kowal, Rebekah, 7

Kraut, Anthea, 8

Landes, Ruth, 55, 68, 79–80, 82–83, 90

legitimization of capoeira: Bimba's push for, 63, 65–67; and Burlamaqui's *National Gymnastics*, 24; and deception, 32; lent by folklore, 39; and Pastinha, 49–55, 82; and Rego, 106; through eugenicist discourse, 34; and tradition, 126

Lewis, John Lowell, 9

Lima, Cisnando, 36

Lima, Joaquim de Araújo, 62

Lomax, Alan, 172n37

Lopes, André Luiz Lacé, 177n36

loss of character (*descaracterização*), 24–25, 47, 101, 104–5, 109–10, 122–23, 158–59

Lua Rasta, Mestre, 119–20, 123, 200n73

luta regional Bahiana (Bahian regional fighting style), 65–66, 68, 182n108

Machado, Loremil (Josevaldo de Souza Machado), 154, 160

Machado, Manuel dos Reis. *See* Bimba, Mestre

maculelê, 112, 120–21, 134, 136, 140, 150, 203n23, 204n33

Maia, Carlos Vasconcelos, 103, 130, 133, 202–3n11

Maia, Cláudio Miranda, 130, 133, 202–3n11

maldade, 56–58, 187n187

Malerische Reise in Brasilien (Picturesque travels in Brazil) (Rugendas), 19

malícia (craftiness or cunning). *See* trickery

maltas. *See* gangs or brotherhoods

marmeladas. *See* rigged matches

Maynard. *See* Araújo, Alceu Maynard

media visibility, 63–64

meia-lua-de-compasso, 43

meia lua de frente, 89

Mel Howard Productions, 149

Mello Moraes Filho, Alexandre José de, 21, 29, 43–45, 90, 174n54

Mercado Modelo (Model Market). *See* Model Market

Mercês, Maria Josefa das. *See* Zefa, Mãe

mestiçagem, 191n69

Mestre Bimba's Folkloric Ensemble (Grupo Folclórico do Mestre Bimba), 105, 111–14

Model Market (Mercado Modelo), 85, 86

modernity: and Andrade, 72; of capoeira regional, 39; and folklore, 75; in folkloric shows, 143; and folkloric shows, 161–62; and folk/pop contrast, 149–50; and Pastinha, 55, 60; and primitivism, 124, 155; of twenty-first-century capoeira, 166

modernization, black, 25

Moraes, Carlos, 142–46, 162, 204n29

Morais, Antônio da Conceição. *See* Caiçara, Mestre

Morning Star (newspaper), 152, 155–56

Moura, Jair, 25, 36

movement: in Biancardi, 143–45; descriptions of in Burlamaqui, 27–31, 35; descriptions of in Penna Marinho, 35; and innovations, 75–76; patterns created by Pastinha, 87–94; patterns recycled by Bimba, 47; pedagogical method of Bimba, 39–43; in solo formats, 159; vocabulary, 13, 49, 66. *See also* attacks and defenses

mulatas, 130

mulatos, 196n4

Municipal Tourism Department. *See* Diretoria Municipal de Turismo (DMT)

music, 25–26, 39, 86–87, 88–89, 90, 95–96, 147, 150–52, 193nn100–101

muzenza, 117–18, 124

National Folklore Commission (Comissão Nacional de Folclore), 72–74

National Gymnastics (Capoeiragem) Methodized and Regulated (Burlamaqui), 26–35, 41–42

Navy Apprentice Company, 185n161

Negros bantus (Carneiro), 48–50, 69, 72, 80

The New World Negro (Herskovits), 10–11
Nina Rodrigues, Raymundo, 21, 175n13
Noronha, Mestre, 51, 62–63, 184n156, 185n162, 187–88n4
"Nosso jogo" (Our game) (Coelho Netto), 33

O.D.C., 22, 24
Odeon Center and Stadium for Physical Culture, 63–68
Odoiá Bahia (theatrical production), 135, 142–49, 145–46, 162
Olhando P'ra Lua (Looking at the Moon). *See* Lua Rasta, Mestre
Oliveira, Simone Bittencourt de, 147, 149–51
Onça Preta, 79
orixás, 142, 145
Ouest-France (newspaper), 155
"Our game" (Nosso jogo) (Coelho Netto), 33

O pagador de promessas (film), 124–26, 125–26
Panorama Brasileiro (theatrical production), 147–49
partnered throws, 43, 66, 90–92, 110–14, 157–58
passo da cegonha (lit. stork's step), 30
Pastinha, Mestre: and Capoeira Angola, 48–60, 78, 82–97; illustrations from manuscripts, 57, 93–94; leadership of, 185n162; old man image, 81–82; overview, 22–23; photo of, 89, 97; Rego on, 106; and strikes, 65; and tourism, 84–86, 96, 98–99
Pastinha, Vincente Ferreira. *See* Pastinha, Mestre
Pavão, Mestre (Eusébio Lôbo da Silva), 159
pedagogy, capoeira, 39–41, 182n116
Pé de Bode, Manuel, 134
Pelourinho, 82–84, 84, 96–97, 111, 164
peneirar. See sifting

Penna Marinho, Inezil, 35–36, 52–53, 180nn88–92
Pequeno, Mestre (João Pereira dos Santos), 90, 98, 169n2
permit system, 62–63, 187n3, 188n13
physical culture, 33–34, 36–47, 48–49, 62
physicality of capoeira, 130, 150, 153, 155, 162
physiognomy of capoeira, 46
Picturesque Travels in Brazil (Malerische Reise in Brasilien) (Rugendas), 19
Pires, Antônio Liberac Cardoso Simões, 22, 26
point system, 28–30, 38, 47, 65, 70, 180–81n97
police persecution, 20–21, 29, 70–72, 79–81
police supervision, 36, 62–63
pop and folk, 145–47, 149, 150–51, 152, 161, 163
Popó, Mestre, 120, 203n23
portadores de folclore. See folklore bearers
pricing system, Bimba's classes, 111
primitivism, 124–25, 129, 141, 144, 147–48, 153–55, 161–62
"Protection and Restoration of Popular Festivities" (Carneiro), 74
public matches, 38, 61, 62–67, 83–85, 94–95, 98, 104
puxada de rede, 120, 124, 127

queixada, 30, 37
Querido de Deus, Samuel, 65, 68, 71, 77–79, 81–83, 192n76

rabo de arraia, 29–33, 43
racial determinism, 46, 52, 70–71, 95
Ramos, Arthur, 4–5, 69–70, 190nn43–47
Ranger, Terence, 3
rasteira, 29–30, 43, 118
Rautavaara, Helinä, 83
regional capoeira, 39–40

Regionalist Movement, 181nn107–108
Rego, Waldeloir: and Bimba, 41–42;
 on Canjiquinha, 121–23; on capoeira
 songs, 201n86; description of, 196n4;
 on *muzenza*, 117–18; on Pastinha,
 176n20, 184n155; on throws, 110; on
 tourism, 102–9
Reis, Letícia, 24–25, 169n5
reproducibility of sequences (*seqüências*),
 40–41
Ribeyrolles, Charles, 186n177
rigged matches (*marmeladas*), 66–67,
 114, 181n99, 189n32
Ring of Liberation (Lewis), 9
Rio de Janeiro, 21, 72, 77, 137, 143, 151
Robato, Alexandre, 193n99
rodas, 25, 28, 62–63, 88, 159
Rozenberg, Leão, 131–32, 158
Rugendas, Johann Moritz, 19–20
rules. *See* point system

Salvador, 64, 76–77, 85, 95–96, 108,
 137, 195n1, 198n37
samango, 117–19, 124
samba de angola, 118–20, 124
samba de faca, 142
samba de roda, 112, 120–22, 144
Samba: Resistance in Motion (Browning), 10
Sampaio, Antônio, 126
Sampaio Ferraz, João Baptista, 20
Santos, João Oliveira dos. *See* João
 Grande, Mestre
Santos, Mario, 27–28, 32–33, 35, 37
Santos, Walter, 147–48
Sciência, Américo, 66
scientific racism, 5–6. *See also* eugenics
Second Afro-Brazilian Congress, 70,
 82, 108
Secretaria de Educação (Department of
 Education), 135–36
See Brazil (Veja o Brasil), 88–92, 194n106
self-defense, 41–43, 48–49, 54, 57–58,
 83, 91, 114. *See also* attacks and
 defenses

Seu Negão (Gilberto Nonato Sacra-
 mento), 136, 140–41
Shea Murphy, Jacqueline, 6
sifting (*peneirar*), 31–32, 35–36, 40, 47,
 165
Silva, Eusébio Lôbo da. *See* Pavão,
 Mestre
Silva, Paulo Santos, 51, 184–85n158,
 186n174
Silva, Washington Bruno da. *See* Canji-
 quinha, Mestre
Simões, Guilherme, 76, 115, 191n71
Sítio Caruano, 105, 111–12
Soares, Carlos Eugênio Líbano, 20–21
Sodré, Muniz, 45
Souza, Gil dos Prazeres, 112–14
Souza, Samuel de. *See* Querido de Deus,
 Samuel
Staging Tourism (Desmond), 7–8
strikes, 30–31, 37, 42, 45–47, 65, 90,
 159
stylized (*estilizado/a*), 143–44
*Subsidies for the Study of the Methodology
 for the Training of Capoeiragem* (Penna
 Marinho), 35–36, 37, 52–53, 179n67
Sunday Times (newspaper), 152–55
Superintendence of Tourism of Salvador
 (SUTURSA), 103–4, 196n11
syncretism, 4–5, 7, 58

tablado (boxing ring), 64
Tallon Karlweiss, Ninon, 148, 152
tapeação, 31–32, 35, 41, 55–58, 178–
 79nn66–67
Taquet, Bernard, 92
A Tarde (newspaper), 41–42, 46, 63, 67,
 196n11
Tatau, 134
Teatro Castro Alves (TCA), 128, 130–32,
 137
Teatro Municipal do Rio de Janeiro, 137
Terrière, Henri, 155
tesoura, 43
Thompson, Robert Farris, 11–12, 173n44

Time Out London (magazine), 153
tourism: and Canjiquinha, 115–26; and capoeira's loss of character, 100–101, 109–10; and destination image, 7–8; and folkloric shows, 135–38; and Pastinha, 84–86, 96, 98–99; promotion of, 195–96n2; Rego and, 102–9
tradition: and acrobatics, 158–59; Afro-Brazilian, 46, 85–86, 98, 148–49; Bahia's, 76–77, 103–7; Biancardi and, 136, 139–49; Canjiquinha and, 126; and Capoeira Angola, 80–85; and *chamada*, 92–93; and codification, 47; and composure, 123; and folklore, 71–76, 161–62; Frigerio on, 169n4; Grillo's altering of, 153–55; of invention, 3–4, 30; loss of, 9, 26, 36–37; and musical accompaniment, 87; onstage bearers of, 129–30; Rego on, 102–9; use of term, 10
A Tribuna da Bahia (newspaper), 143
trickery (*tapeação*), 31–32, 35, 41, 55–58, 178–79nn66–67
The Turning Wind (*Barravento*) (film), 124–25

uniforms, 104–5, 185–86n168, 197nn17–18
"A Unique Tradition Survives" (King), 155–56

Vadiação (film), 193n99
vagrancy or loitering (vadiação), 94–95
Vargas, Getúlio, 71–72
Vassallo, Simone Pondé, 189n35
Verger, Pierre, 93–94

verticality, 31
Vianna, Hildegardes, 115, 136, 138, 200n60
Victor H.U., 65, 98
Vieira, Jelon (Jelon Gomes Vieira Filho), 160
Vieira, Luiz Renato, 43–44
vigor, 81–82, 150–52, 157–58
"Vigor You Expect and Vigor You Get" (Dafoe), 150
vile metal (*vil metal*), 110
Villa-Lobos, Heitor, 71–72
violence: Bimba's use of, 45–47, 64–65; Canjiquinha's use of, 119–20; of capoeira, 19–21; Carneiro on, 80–81; and *chamada*, 90–93; choreographed, 6, 8, 114, 165; in folkloric shows, 127, 129, 153–54; Pastinha's use of, 54–58, 186n176; and police persecution, 62; and *samba de faca*, 142
virtuosity, 17, 87, 114, 118–19, 140, 142, 158, 165
Viva Bahia. *See* Conjunto Folclórico Viva Bahia
vôo do morcego, 113–14

Wesolowski, Katya, 20
whitening of capoeira, 23, 24–25, 34, 52, 109, 169nn4–5

Xaréu, Mestre, 112

Zefa, Mãe (Maria Josefa das Mercês), 130, 202n5
Zey, 65

ABOUT THE AUTHOR

....

Ana Paula Höfling is Assistant Professor of Dance in the
School of Dance at the University of North Carolina, Greensboro,
where she is also cross-appointed faculty in Women's and Gender
Studies and a Lloyd International Honors College Faculty Fellow. She
received her PhD in Culture and Performance (with an emphasis in
dance studies) from the University of California, Los Angeles, and
she was an Andrew Mellon Postdoctoral Fellow at the Center for
the Americas at Wesleyan University. She has published various
articles on capoeira and dance in Brazil; her new research
project focuses on the *bailado brasileiro* of early twentieth-
century Brazilian dancer Eros Volúsia.